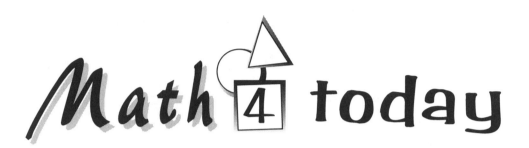

Math 4 today

10-Minute Daily Skills Practice

by Donna Pearson

Good Apple

A Division of Frank Schaffer Publications, Inc.

Contents

Senior Editors: Kristin Eclov, Mina McMullin
Copy Editor: Janet Barker
Design: Good Neighbor Press, Inc., Grand Junction, CO

Good Apple
A Division of Frank Schaffer Publications, Inc.
23740 Hawthorne Boulevard
Torrance, California 90505-5927

Introduction

What is *Math 4 Today?*

Math 4 Today is a comprehensive yet quick and easy to use supplement sequenced to complement any fourth- and fifth-grade math curriculum. Twenty-four essential math skills and concepts are reviewed in only ten minutes each day during a four-day period (presumably Monday through Thursday) with a 20-minute evaluation each fifth day (Friday).

How does it work?

Unlike many math programs. *Math 4 Today* is designed on a continuous spiral so that concepts are repeated weekly. This book supplies four problems a day for four days covering a 54-week period–based on the curricula for fourth and fifth grade. A separate ten-problem test is provided for the fifth day of each week.

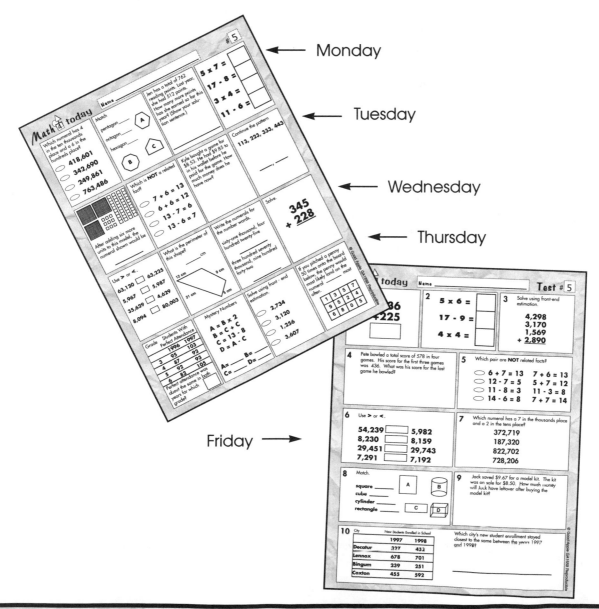

Monday

Tuesday

Wednesday

Thursday

Friday

Answer keys are provided for both daily drills and assessments (see pages 118–144). Concepts and skills are tested on an even/odd week rotation and follow a consistent format for ease of evaluation. Although the concepts and skills are individually categorized, most are interrelated so that many opportunities for practice and evaluation exist. A skills and concepts chart including objectives and a scope and sequence chart are provided.

How was it developed?

Math 4 Today was created in response to a need for ongoing practice after a skill had been addressed in the basal text. With the usual methods, a skill would be covered, and then basically abandoned until it reappeared (sometimes) in a six-week cumulative review. With the growing emphasis on standardized testing, the necessity for experience with test styles and semantics also became apparent. We began with four daily problems written on the board for students to complete while attendance was being taken. After completion, the class would briefly check and discuss the work. The problems and methods we use evolved and expanded over the years. Now, I duplicate the weekly pages for students and use overhead transparencies to check and discuss.

What are the benefits?

The daily approach of *Math 4 Today* provides risk-taking challenges, higher-level thinking exercises, problem-solving strategies, and necessary drill, emphasizing areas that frequently give students difficulty, such as subtraction with regrouping and word problems. The program targets test-taking skills by incorporating the style and syntax of standardized test such as the TAAS (Texas Assessment of Academic Skills). Because of its consistent format, *Math 4 Today* not only offers opportunities for instruction but also serves as an excellent diagnostic tool.

PLACE VALUE

- identify place values to billions and thousandths
- interpret place value charts
- identify place name and value of digits
- write numeral described by place values
- read/write numerals in expanded form
- name value of specified digit in a numeral

GEOMETRY

- distinguish between two-and three-dimensional figures
- name 2-and 3-D figures
- match congruent and similar shapes and angles
- identify lines of symmetry
- determine inclusion in overlapping shapes
- match geometric prefixes with number of sides
- find perimeter and area

WORD PROBLEMS

- solve word problems using addition, subtraction, multiplication, and division
- determine operations in multi-step problems
- exclude unnecessary information
- match solution sentences to given problem
- solve word problems using whole numbers, fractions, and decimals

COMPUTATION

- practice with basic addition, subtraction, multiplication, and division facts in a singular and mixed format
- perform 2 + digit addition, subtraction, and multiplication computations with/without regrouping

PLACE VALUE MODELS FRACTIONS

place value models

- identify place value models to thousands
- name the numeral shown by a model representation
- draw place value models to represent a given numeral
- add and subtract using models with/without regrouping

NUMBER CONCEPTS

- write/match a solution sentence to pictured operation
- recognize fact families
- use the associative, commutative and identity properties
- correlate addition and multiplication
- equalize multi-operational equations

TIME/MONEY

- solve word problems with time and money
- identify coin values
- compute (+, −, x, ÷) with money
- find the amount of change due or tax involved
- express money values using $ and ¢
- create minimal collections of coins for given amounts
- interpret charts with money

PATTERNS /PROBABILITY

- continue a given pattern of shapes or numbers
- identify the missing element(s) in a pattern sequence
- supply a specified pattern element when the sequence immediately preceding is absent

COMPARE AND ORDER NUMBERS

- identify or write numerical sets including decimals and fractions in order from least to greatest and vice versa with number values to billions and thousandths
- identify specific numerals between given numerals
- order chart information from least to greatest and vice versa

MEASUREMENT

- identify and use standard and metric units in measuring length, mass, volume, and temperature
- identify uses of measurement tools
- compare metric and standard units
- measure pictured objects within a ruled space
- measure with a nonstandard unit

NUMBER LINES/WORDS

- locate numerals or a specific group of numerals on a number line
- identify missing numbers
- identify or create a number line to match a given picture or computation
- write or identify numerals or number words for given values or places to billions

COMPUTATION

- for added practice with computational skills as in row one
- for inclusion of reasonableness, estimation, or probability

GRAPHS/TABLES

- interpret, combine, and compare chart data
- construct graphs given the chart data
- interpret and construct, tally graphs, picture graphs, bar graphs, point and line graphs, pie graphs
- combine and compare data

PROBLEM SOLVING

- use problem-solving strategies such as logical thinking, working backward, guess and check, and drawing a picture
- solve problems with multi-step and multi-informational components
- calculate missing variables by using given information

ESTIMATION REASONABLENESS

- round numerals to tens, hundreds, and thousands
- use front-end estimation or rounding to calculate sums, differences, products, and quotients
- choose a reasonable numerical value to match a given situation (time/money situations are also included here)

REPEATED PRACTICE

- for added practice with any skill/concept included on this page or in previous lessons

Note: Provisions for calculator usage in exploring patterns, number concepts, problem solving, and estimation are indicated on the scope and sequence chart.

PLACE VALUE
- compare/order digits in numerals according to place values
- determine place to which a numeral has been rounded

GEOMETRY
- label parallel, perpendicular, or intersecting lines
- count angles, vertices, faces, edges of space & solid figures
- identify: hexagon, pentagon, polygon, prism, rhombus, parallelogram, trapezoid, quadrilateral, and equilateral, isosceles, scalene triangles
- distinguish between flips, slides, and rotations

WORD PROBLEMS
- identify information needed to solve a problem
- match solution sentences to given problem
- match common clue words to operations
- use concepts of time and money to solve problems
- use calculator to assist and verify solutions

COMPUTATION
- divide 2+ digit numerals: with/without remainders; with 1+ digit divisors
- compute using zeros in all operations
- add 2+ digit columns with/without regrouping
- check subtraction with addition and vice versa
- supply missing addends, multipliers, and divisors

PLACE VALUE MODELS FRACTIONS
- use decimal representations for addition, subtraction, multiplication
<u>fractions</u>
- identify fractional parts of shaded figures and of sets
- compare/equalize/simplify fractions with/without picture representation
- add, subtract, multiply fractions and mixed numbers

NUMBER CONCEPTS
- supply missing addends
- use non-equality in equations
- identify true and non-true equations
- calculate mean, median, range, average
- apply greatest common factor, least common multiple
- perform operations with exponents

TIME/MONEY
- determine comparative money values
- compute portion when given a set group value
- identify clock face time by hour, half-hour, and minute intervals
- determine elapsed time using clocks
- determine elapsed time in word problems

PATTERNS/PROBABILITY
- describe the rule for a pattern sequence
- create a pattern using specified units
- visualize pattern to designated conclusion
- continue situational patterns
- investigate patterns with calculator

COMPARE AND ORDER NUMBERS
- use the inequality symbols < and > to compare numbers
- choose a group of numbers according to a specified order
- use odd and even numbers, skip counting, and number patterns in ordering
- compare and order units of standard and metric measurements

MEASUREMENT
- compare given measurements
- use a ruler to measure the perimeter of given shape
- estimate situational uses with the appropriate unit
- determine area, volume, perimeter with/without all dimensions
- find equivalent measurements
- use symmetry, congruence in calculating measurements
- enlarge to scale using grids

NUMBER LINES/WORDS
- match equations to number line representation
- locate representative points for fractions/decimals on a number line
- write or match words for frations/decimals

COMPUTATION

GRAPHS/TABLES
- use symbols having a value of more than 1 unit and of half a unit
- write questions regarding a graph
- determine unit of comparison in a graph
- write concise summary of graph data
- plot number pairs
- give number pair location of a symbol on a grid

PROBLEM SOLVING
- choose possible solutions given indefinite variables
- select an amount large enough to include the combined variables given
- order objects or numbers in sequence given nonsequential variables
- write questions for given solutions regarding data available

ESTIMATION REASONABLENESS
- round decimals to nearest hundredth, tenth, or whole number
- select equations for best estimate of given values
- visually estimate comparative sizes
- use calculators to verify estimations

REPEATED PRACTICE

PLACE VALUE

GEOMETRY
- select figures with specified characteristics
- classify right, acute, obtuse, corresponding angles
- name by identifying points: line, segment, ray, chord, radius, diameter, circumference

WORD PROBLEMS
- apply problem-solving strategies and concept development

COMPUTATION
- add, subtract, multiply fractions/mixed fractions
- add, subtract, multiply divide decimals to thousandths
- use calculator to verify computations

PLACE VALUE MODELS FRACTIONS
- utilize common denominators in computations
- find ratios/equivalent ratios

decimals
- identify decimal values to thousandths
- compare decimals to fractional parts
- find equivalent decimals
- add, subtract, multiply, divide decimals

NUMBER CONCEPTS
- use order of operations in multi-computational equations
- label prime/composite numbers
- complete factor trees
- decode Roman Numerals

TIME MONEY
- recognize values of standard time units
- determine equivalent measures of time
- interpret schedules
- designate a.m. or p.m.

PATTERNS PROBABILITY
probability
- choose possible outcomes or non-inclusion in a given set of conditions
- notate probability in fractional terms
- compare probability in different sets and in multi-chance situations
- compute simple odds

COMPARE AND ORDER NUMBERS

MEASUREMENT
- measure length, area, and perimeter using 1/2 units
- identify formulas for finding area, perimeter
- find area and circumference of circles

NUMBER LINES WORDS

COMPUTATION

GRAPHS TABLES
- determine number pair inclusion in overlapping shapes on grid
- interpret calendars
- plot number pairs
- give number pair location of a symbol on a grid

PROBLEM SOLVING
- solve for *n* in equations
- complete logic problems using process of elimination
- classify according to given descriptors
- write questions for given solutions regarding data available

ESTIMATION REASONABLENESS

REPEATED PRACTICE

Scope and Sequence

		1	T	2	T	3	T	4	T	5	T	6	T	7	T	8	T	9	T	10	T	11	T	12	T	13	T	14	T	15	T	16	T	17	T	18	T	19	T	20	T	21	T	22	T	23	T	24	T	25	T	26	T	27	T
1	PLACE VALUE	•	•	•	•	•	•	•	•	•	•	•	•	•	•	•	•	•	•	•	•	•	•	•	•	•	•	•	•	•	•	•	•	•	•	•	•	•	•	•	•	•	•	•	•	•	•	•	•	•	•	•	•	•	•
2	GEOMETRY	•	•	•		•	•	•		•	•	•		•	•	•		•	•	•		•	•	•		•	•	•		•	•	•		•	•	•		•	•	•	•	•	•	•		•	•	•	•	•	•	•		•	•
3	WORD PROBLEMS	•	•	•	•	•	•	•	•	•	•	•	•	•	•	•	•	•	•	•	•	•	•	•	•	•	•	•	•	•	•	•	•	•	•	•	•	•	•	•	•	•	•	•	•	•	•	•	•	•	•	•	•	•	•
4	BASIC FACTS	•	•	•	•	•	•	•	•	•	•	•	•	•	•	•	•	•	•	•	•	•	•	•	•	•	•	•	•	•	•	•	•	•	•	•	•	•																	
5	ADDITION	•	•	•	•	•	•	•	•	•	•	•	•	•	•	•	•	•	•	•		•							•	•	•	•	•	•	•	•	•	•			•									•		•	•	•	
6	SUBTRACTION	•	•	•	•	•	•	•	•	•	•	•	•	•	•	•	•	•	•	•	•	•	•	•	•	•	•	•	•	•	•	•	•	•	•			•	•	•	•					•	•			•			•	•	•
7	MULTIPLICATION									•	•	•	•	•	•	•		•	•		•	•	•	•	•	•	•	•	•	•	•	•	•	•	•	•	•	•	•	•	•	•	•	•	•	•	•	•	•	•	•	•	•	•	•
8	DIVISION																															•	•	•	•	•	•		•	•				•	•	•	•	•	•	•	•	•	•	•	•
9	PLACE VALUE	•	•	•	•	•	•	•	•	•		•	•	•	•	•		•		•		•	•	•		•																													•
10	FRACTIONS																											•		•	•	•		•	•	•		•	•	•		•	•	•		•	•	•	•	•	•	•	•	•	•
11	DECIMALS																																																						
12	NUMBER CONCEPTS	•	•	•		•	•	•		•	•	•	•	•	•	•		•	•	•		•	•	•		•	•	•		•	•	•		•	•	•		•	•	•		•	•	•		•	•	•		•	•	•		•	•
13	TIME													•	•	•		•	•					•	•	•	•					•	•	•	•			•	•	•		•	•			•	•	•	•			•	•	•	•
14	MONEY	•	•	•		•	•	•		•	•	•	•							•		•	•					•	•	•	•					•	•	•						•						•	•				
15	PATTERNS	•		•	•	•		•	•	•		•	•	•		•		•		•	•	•		•	•	•		•		•		•	•	•		•	•	•		•	•	•		•		•		•		•		•		•	
16	COMPARE/ORDER #'S	•	•	•		•	•	•		•	•	•		•	•	•		•	•	•		•	•	•		•	•	•		•	•	•		•	•	•		•	•	•		•	•	•	•	•	•	•		•	•	•		•	•
17	MEASUREMENT	•		•	•	•		•	•	•		•		•		•	•	•		•	•	•		•	•	•		•	•	•		•	•	•		•	•	•	•	•		•		•	•	•		•	•	•		•	•	•	
18	NUMBER LINES	•		•	•	•		•	•					•		•	•	•		•	•					•	•	•	•					•		•	•							•	•					•					
19	NUMBER WORDS									•		•	•									•		•	•					•		•	•	•	•	•	•	•	•	•	•	•				•		•	•			•	•	•	
20	GRAPHS/TABLES	•		•	•	•		•	•	•	•	•	•	•		•	•	•	•	•	•	•		•	•	•		•		•	•	•	•	•		•	•	•		•	•	•		•	•	•	•	•	•	•	•	•	•	•	•
21	PROBLEM SOLVING	•		•	•	•		•	•	•		•		•		•	•	•		•	•	•		•		•		•		•		•		•		•		•		•	•	•		•	•	•		•		•		•		•	
22	ESTIMATION											•		•	•	•	•	•	•	•								•	•	•	•	•	•	•	•	•	•	•	•	•	•	•	•	•	•	•	•	•	•	•	•	•	•	•	•
23	REASONABLENESS	•	•	•		•	•	•												•		•		•	•	•	•																												
24	PROBABILITY	•		•		•		•		•		•										•	•	•	•	•		•	•	•										•		•		•	•	•		•	•	•		•	•	•	
25	REPEATED PRACTICE/ CALCULATOR OPPORTUNITY					•										•						•				•						•		•		•		•												•				•	

T = WEEKLY TEST · INDICATES SKILL OR CONCEPT INCLUDED and/or TESTED

Scope and Sequence

Columns (left to right): 28 T 29 T 30 T 31 T 32 T 33 T 34 T 35 T 36 T 37 T 38 T 39 T 40 T 41 T 42 T 43 T 44 T 45 T 46 T 47 T 48 T 49 T 50 T 51 T 52 T 53 T 54 T

Skill rows:

1	PLACE VALUE
2	GEOMETRY
3	WORD PROBLEMS
4	BASIC FACTS
5	ADDITION
6	SUBTRACTION
7	MULTIPLICATION
8	DIVISION
9	PLACE VALUE
10	FRACTIONS
11	DECIMALS
12	NUMBER CONCEPTS
13	TIME
14	MONEY
15	PATTERNS
16	COMPARE/ORDER #'S
17	MEASUREMENT
18	NUMBER LINES
19	NUMBER WORDS
20	GRAPHS/TABLES
21	PROBLEM SOLVING
22	ESTIMATION
23	REASONABLENESS
24	PROBABILITY
25	REPEATED PRACTICE/ CALCULATOR OPPORTUNITY

T = WEEKLY TEST   • INDICATES SKILL OR CONCEPT INCLUDED and/or TESTED

9

Math 4 today

Name ____________________

#1

Which numeral has a **3** in the hundreds place?

- ⬭ **231**
- ⬭ **390**
- ⬭ **803**
- ⬭ **730**

Which shape is a triangle?

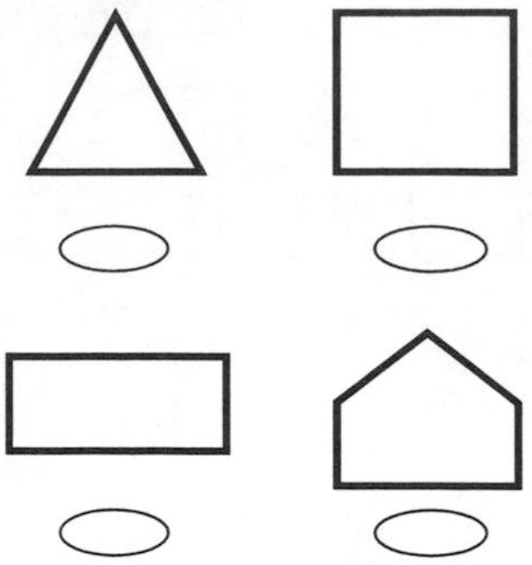

One of the largest jigsaw puzzles was built in Oklahoma and measured 48 feet long. Compared to an average jigsaw puzzle which measures about 2 feet long, how much longer was the Oklahoma puzzle?

____

4 + 7 = ☐

2 + 9 = ☐

8 + 5 = ☐

7 + 7 = ☐

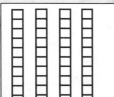

What numeral is shown by the base ten models?

____

Write the family of facts for **8, 6, 14**

Show how to find the value of five dimes, and four pennies.

Continue the pattern.

8, 10, 12, 14

____ ____ ____

Write these numerals in order from least to greatest.

89 ____________

72 ____________

105 ____________

68 ____________

94 ____________

About how many inches tall is the music note?

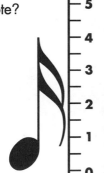

5
4
3
2
1
0

________ inches

0 1 2 3 4 5

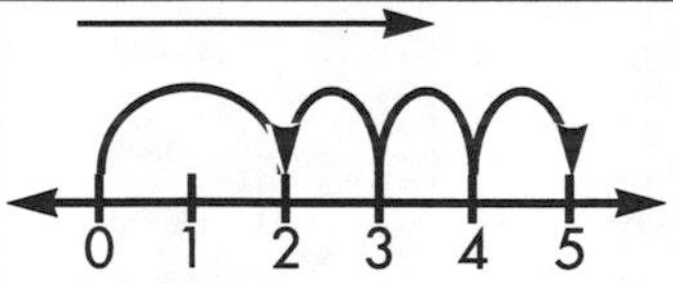

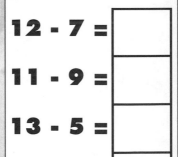

This number line shows:

- ⬭ **8 - 7 = 1**
- ⬭ **5 + 8 = 13**
- ⬭ **2 + 3 = 5**
- ⬭ **5 - 5 = 0**

12 - 7 = ☐

11 - 9 = ☐

13 - 5 = ☐

16 - 8 = ☐

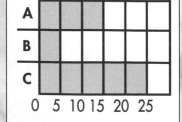

A
B
C
0 5 10 15 20 25

This graph shows:

A =________ B = ________

C = ________

In a roll of candy, the grape is before the cherry. There are two candies between cherry and lime. The orange is next to the lime, and the lemon is last. Color the candies in their order.

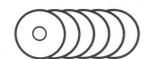

About how many television programs are on one channel between 6:00 and 10:00 at night?

- ⬭ **8**
- ⬭ **80**
- ⬭ **800**
- ⬭ **8,000**

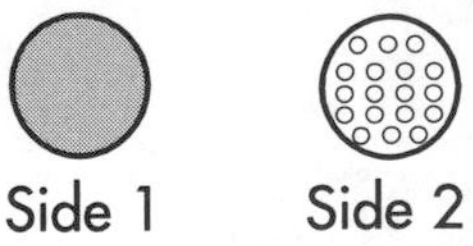

Side 1
Side 2

If you tossed the above chip 1 time, which would NOT be a possible way for it to land?

1

8 + 5 =

9 + 2 =

6 + 7 =

2

15 - 8 =

14 - 5 =

17 - 9 =

3 About how many pieces of mail would 1 family receive in a day?

◯ 6000

◯ 600

◯ 60

◯ 6

4 One of the largest beds was built in 1430 in Belgium. The bed was 19 feet long. Today, an average bed is about 6 feet long. How much longer was the bed built in 1430?

5 Write the family of facts for **3, 6,** and **9.**

_____

_____

_____

_____

6 Write these numerals in order from least to greatest.

50 _____

65 _____

89 _____

85 _____

79 _____

7 Which numeral has a 2 in the tens place?

◯ 921

◯ 192

◯ 2

◯ 209

8 Which shape is a triangle?

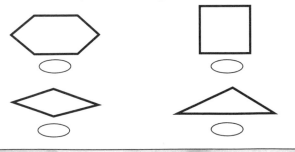

◯   ◯

◯   ◯

9 Show how to find the value of six dimes and eight pennies.

10 What numerals are shown by the base ten models?

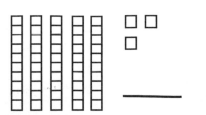   _____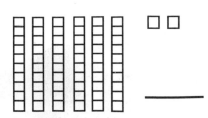

© Good Apple GA1659 Reproducible

In **673**

the _____ is in the tens place.

the _____ is in the hundreds place.

the _____ is in the ones place.

Which shape best represents a cube?

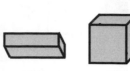

Rashana had 16 children's picture books. She gave 9 of them to her younger cousin. How many picture books does Rashana now have? (Show your solution sentence.)

---

6 + 6 =

7 + 7 =

8 + 8 =

9 + 9 =

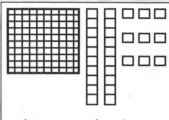

What numeral is shown by the base ten models?

_____

Write the fact family for
6, 4, 10

_____

_____

_____

What is the value of

4 dimes, and 2 nickels?

_____ ¢

Continue the pattern.

55, 60, 65, 70

_____ , _____ , _____

Write these numerals in order from greatest to least.

120 _____
920 _____
617 _____
912 _____
198 _____

About how many inches long is this arrow?

_____
inches

—11
—10
—9
—8
—7
—6
—5
—4
—3
—2
—1
—0

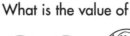

This number line shows:

○ **14 - 4 = 10**

○ **13 + 1 = 14**

○ **13 - 9 = 4**

○ **13 - 5 = 8**

---

14 - 9 =

15 - 9 =

16 - 9 =

17 - 9 =

Spelling Test Grades

Jana
Karen
Amy

Which two girls have spelling test grades that are about the same?

_____ _____

? **Mystery Number** ?
? ? ? ?

I am a number between 10 and 20. You can add 2 to me and get the number that is the sum of 7 and 9.
  What number am I?

_____

About how many M & M™ candies come in a small package?

○ **3**

○ **30**

○ **300**

○ **3,000**

These cubes are in a box. If you drew one out without looking, you would probably draw a

○

○

Math 4 today

1

$5 + 5 =$

$9 + 9 =$

$7 + 7 =$

2

$11 - 9 =$

$13 - 4 =$

$15 - 9 =$

3 Continue the pattern.

35, 40, 45, 50

_____ , _____ , _____

4

This number line shows:

◯ $9 + 9 = 18$ ◯ $17 - 8 = 9$

◯ $8 + 5 = 13$ ◯ $17 - 10 = 7$

5 Nina bought 17 peppermints. She shared 8 of them with her friend. How many peppermints does Nina now have?

6 Fourth Grade's Favorite Pets

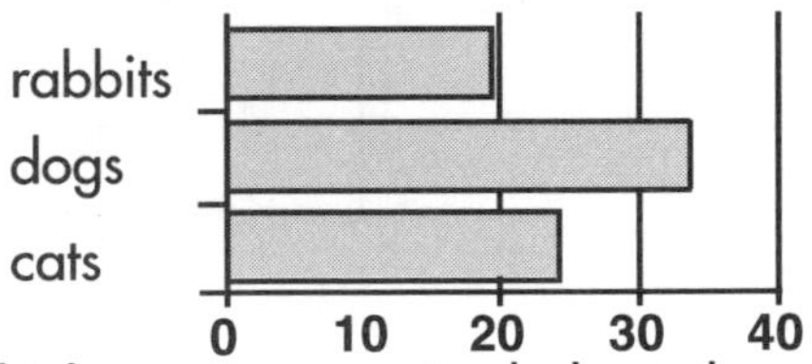

Which two pets received about the same number of votes? _____ _____

7 **Mystery Number** ?

? ? ? ? ?

I am an even number between 10 and 30. You can add 4 to me and get the sum of 10 and 10. What number am I?

_____

8 About how many inches long is the line?

about _____ inches long

9

In **842**

The _____ is in the ones place.

The _____ is in the hundreds place.

The _____ is in the tens place.

10

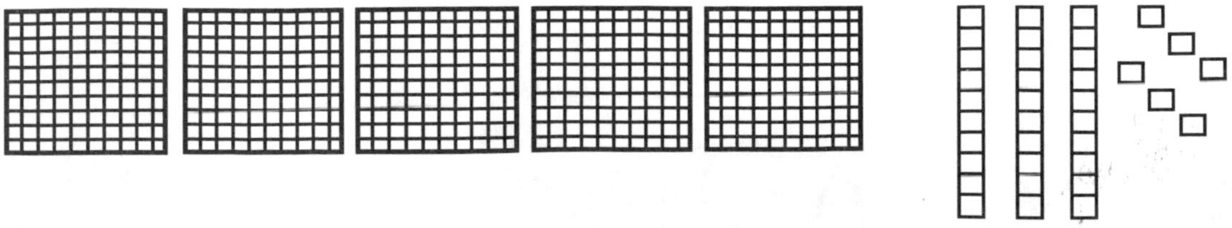

What numeral is shown by the base ten models?

Math 4 today

Name _____

3

Which numeral has a 6 in the hundreds place?

◯ **46,201**

◯ **62,490**

◯ **93,601**

◯ **93,716**

Which shape is a rectangle?

Fran has 459 stamps in her collection. Erica has 969 stamps in her collection. Show how many more stamps Erica has than Fran.

---

8 + 7 =

12 - 4 =

9 + 5 =

13 - 7 =

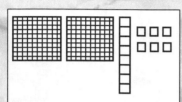

What numeral is shown by the base ten models?

_____

Write the family of facts for **5, 9,** and **14.**

_____

_____

_____

Show how to find the value of two quarters, three dimes, and four nickels.

Continue the pattern.

4, 7, 10, 13

____ , ____ , ____

Write these numerals in order from least to greatest.

620 _____

696 _____

602 _____

599 _____

679 _____

About how many inches tall is the paintbrush?

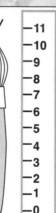

_____
inches

This number line shows:

◯ **14 - 7 = 7**

◯ **8 + 8 = 16**

◯ **14 - 8 = 6**

◯ **8 + 6 = 14**

Solve.

235
+ 524

Shade in the graph to show
A = 60 B = 20
C = A + B

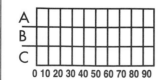

Jack, Sam, and Ed live on the same road. Sam lives 7 miles from Jack. Ed lives 13 miles from Jack. How far does Ed live from Sam?

_____ miles

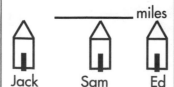

About how many pages are in your spelling book?

◯ **50**

◯ **500**

◯ **5**

◯ **150**

The numerals 1, 2, 3, 4, 5, 6 are on a dice. If you rolled the dice two times, which would **NOT** be a possible combination?

◯ **2, 3**

◯ **5, 5**

◯ **6, 7**

◯ **1, 6**

1

$$736$$
$$+ 253$$

2

$$15 - 8 =$$

$$14 - 5 =$$

$$6 + 7 =$$

3 About how many pages are in a child's picture book?

- ⬭ 3000
- ⬭ 30
- ⬭ 300
- ⬭ 3

4 Ben has 562 baseball cards. Al has 783 baseball cards. Show how to find how many more baseball cards Al has.

5 Write the family of facts for

8, 9, and **17.**

_____

_____

_____

_____

6 Write these numerals in order from least to greatest.

850 _____
865 _____
895 _____
856 _____
799 _____

7 Which numeral has a 9 in the tens place?

- ⬭ 907
- ⬭ 192
- ⬭ 9,517
- ⬭ 829

8 Which shape is a rectangle?

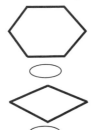

9 Show how to find the value of seven dimes, 3 quarters, and six nickels.

10

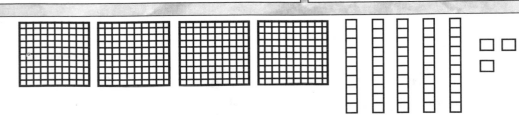

What numeral is shown by the base ten models?

Which numeral has 8 in the ten thousands place?

- ◯ **48,201**
- ◯ **82,490**
- ◯ **93,801**
- ◯ **73,786**

Which shape is a square?

Bill had 562 shells. He gave 130 to his friend Mark. How many shells does Bill now have? (Show your solution sentence.)

_____

---

4 + 7 =

13 - 4 =

8 + 5 =

15 - 6 =

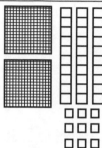

What numeral is shown by the base ten models?

_____

Write the 3 other related facts for

5 + 6 = 11

_____

_____

_____

What is the value of 3 quarters, 3 dimes, and 2 nickels?

_____

Continue the pattern.

32, 27, 22, 17

___ , ___ , ___

Write these numerals in order from greatest to least.

6,120 _____

6,967 _____

5,629 _____

6,994 _____

5,792 _____

About how many inches long is this line?

_____ inches

This number line shows:

- ◯ **14 - 4 + 10**
- ◯ **7 + 4 = 11**
- ◯ **11 - 5 = 6**
- ◯ **8 + 3 = 11**

Solve.

835
- 321

Mark the true statements.

- ◯ **A** is 3 less than **C**.
- ◯ **B** is 20 less than **A**.
- ◯ **A + B** = 100
- ◯ **B** is more than **A**.

The church, library, school, and museum are all on Maple Street. The church is 7 miles east of the library, and the museum is 8 miles to the west. The school is 4 miles to the west of the museum. How far is it from the church to the school?

_____ miles

About how many birthday hats come in a package?

- ◯ **20**
- ◯ **200**
- ◯ **2**
- ◯ **200**

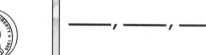

These tiles are in a box. If you drew out two without looking, you could possibly draw...

Math 4 today

1

736
- 420

2

11 - 7 =

13 - 5 =

9 + 6 =

3 Continue the pattern.

37, 31, 25, 19

_____ , _____ , _____

4

This number line shows:

○ 9 + 9 = 18   ○ 16 - 9 = 7

○ 8 + 5 = 13   ○ 9 + 7 = 16

5 Amber built a domino train with 378 dominoes. When she pushed the first domino 237 dominoes fell. How many dominoes were left standing?

6 Which statement is true for this graph?

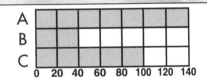

A
B
C

0 20 40 60 80 100 120 140

○ B = 2
○ C is 60 more than B
○ C is 100 less than A

7 Coleytown is 10 miles to the east of Midtown and 7 miles to the west of Oakview. Cape City is 4 miles to the west of Midtown. What is the distance in miles from Cape City to Oakview?

_____

8 About how many inches long is this line?

_____

○ 1 inch
○ 7 inches
○ 2 inches
○ 4 inches

9 Which numeral has a 4 in the thousands place?

○ 143,122
○ 412,720
○ 234,876
○ 211,453

10

What numeral is shown by the base ten models?

Math 4 today

Which numeral has 4 in the ten thousands place and 6 in the hundreds place?

- ⬭ **418,601**
- ⬭ **342,690**
- ⬭ **249,861**
- ⬭ **763,486**

Match.

pentagon _____

octagon _____

hexagon _____

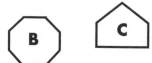

Jen has a total of 762 reading points. Last year, she had 512 points. How many more points has she earned so far this year? (Show your solution sentence.)

_____

---

5 x 7 =

17 - 8 =

3 x 4 =

11 - 6 =

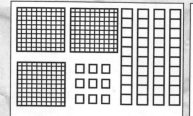

After adding six more units to this model, the numeral shown would be

_____

Which is **NOT** a related fact?

- ⬭ **7 + 6 = 13**
- ⬭ **6 + 6 = 12**
- ⬭ **13 - 7 = 6**
- ⬭ **13 - 6 = 7**

Kyle bought a game for $8.53. He had $9.85 to in his wallet before he paid for the game. How much money does he have now?

Continue the pattern.

113, 223, 333, 443

_____, _____

Use **>** or **<**.

63,120 ☐ 63,225

5,967 ☐ 5,987

35,629 ☐ 4,629

8,094 ☐ 80,003

What is the perimeter of this shape?

_____ cm

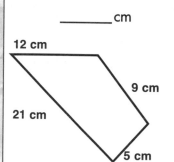

12 cm
9 cm
21 cm
5 cm

Write the numerals for the number words.

sixty-one thousand, four hundred twenty-five

_____

three hundred seventy thousand, nine hundred forty-two

_____

Solve.

345
+ 228

Students With Perfect Attendance		
Grade	1996	1997
3	95	103
4	87	92
5	92	93
6	82	105

Perfect attendance was about the same in both years for which grade? ☐

? Mystery Numbers ?
? ? ? ?

A = B x 2
B = C + C
C = 13 - 8
D = A - C

A= _____   B= _____
C= _____   D= _____

Solve using front-end estimation.

2,734

3,120

1,256

3,607

If you pitched a penny 50 times onto the board below, the penny would most likely land on the numeral _____ most often.

1	3	5	7
9	5	2	4
6	8	0	5

18

1 Solve.

736
+225

2

5 x 6 = ☐

17 - 9 = ☐

4 x 4 = ☐

3 Solve using front-end estimation.

4,298
3,170
1,569
+ 2,890

4 Pete bowled a total score of 578 in four games. His score for the first three games was 436. What was his score for the last game he bowled?

5 Which pair are **NOT** related facts?

◯ 6 + 7 = 13   7 + 6 = 13
◯ 12 - 7 = 5   5 + 7 = 12
◯ 11 - 8 = 3   11 - 3 = 8
◯ 14 - 6 = 8   7 + 7 = 14

6 Use **>** or **<**.

54,239 ☐ 5,982
8,230 ☐ 8,159
29,451 ☐ 29,743
7,291 ☐ 7,192

7 Which numeral has a 7 in the thousands place and a 2 in the tens place?

◯ 372,719
◯ 187,320
◯ 822,702
◯ 728,206

8 Match.

square _____
cube _____
cylinder _____
rectangle _____

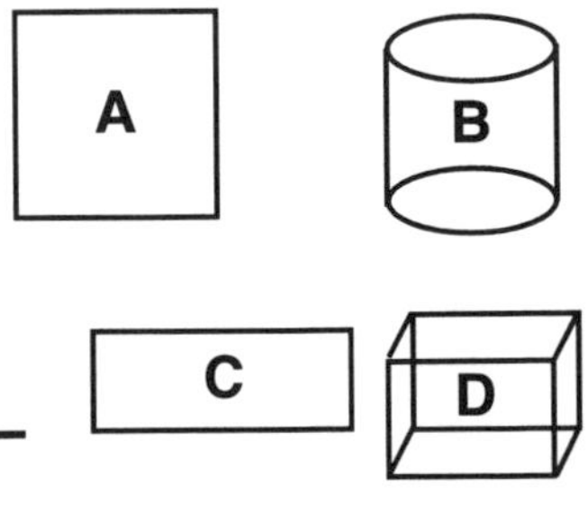

A   B   C   D

9 Jack saved $9.67 for a model kit. The kit was on sale for $8.50. How much money will Jack have leftover after buying the model kit?

10

City	New Students Enrolled in School	
	1997	1998
Decatur	327	452
Lennox	678	701
Bingum	239	251
Coxton	455	592

Which city's new student enrollment stayed closest to the same between the years 1997 and 1998?

_____

Math 4 today

Name _____

6

In the numeral **872,391**

the **7** is in the ____ place

_____

the **3** is in the ____ place

_____

the **8** is in the ____ place

_____

Circle the shape that best represents a rectangular prism.

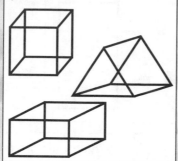

The student council sold 32 cupcakes and 25 brownies at the bake sale. They also sold 12 pies. How many baked goods did the student council sell? (Show your solution sentence.)

_____

---

4 x 2 =

11 - 8 =

3 x 3 =

15 - 6 =

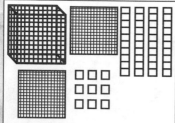

After adding 7 more tens to this model, the numeral shown would be:

_____ .

Which is **NOT** a related fact?

◯ **9 + 3 = 12**

◯ **3 + 9 = 12**

◯ **12 - 7 = 5**

◯ **12 - 9 = 3**

Jim spent $4.13 on a kite and 2 quarters to play a video game. Show how to find the amount of money Jim spent.

Continue the pattern.

220, 215, 210, 205

____, ____, ____

Use **>** or **<**.

23,534 ☐ 23,530

9,967 ☐ 3,987

75,629 ☐ 104,629

894 ☐ 8,004

What is the perimeter of this shape?

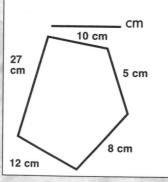

_____ cm

10 cm

27 cm

5 cm

8 cm

12 cm

Write the numeral for the number words.

two hundred five thousand, one hundred nineteen

_____

nine hundred thousand, six hundred five

_____

Solve.

2,757
+ 6,229

GRADE	Number of boys	girls
3	115	103
4	98	92
5	125	112
6	107	111

Which grade has 10 more boys than grade 3?

☐

?₂ Mystery Numbers ₂?

A = C - D

B = D - 2

C = B + B

D = the difference between 24 and 14.

A= ____   B= ____

C= ____   D= ____

Solve using front-end estimation.

23,734

42,120

12,256

15,607

If you pitched a penny 20 times onto the board below, the penny would most likely land on the numbers _____ and _____ the least often.

7	3	5	7
7	5	2	7
5	2	1	5

© Good Apple GA1659 Reproducible

Math 4 today

1

$$4,609 + 3,285$$

2

2 x 6 =

11 - 3 =

3 x 5 =

3 Continue the pattern.

206, 203, 200, 197

_____, _____, _____

4 Write the numeral for the number words.

two hundred seventy-one thousand, four hundred nine _____

one hundred four thousand, three hundred six _____

5 Which pair are **NOT** related facts?

- 2 + 7 = 9   9 - 6 = 3
- 12 - 9 = 3   3 + 9 = 12
- 9 - 8 = 1   9 - 1 = 8
- 10 - 6 = 4   6 + 4 = 10

6

Team Scores in Weekly Bowling Tournament

Day Team:	Stars	Jets
Saturday	327	152
Sunday	478	599
Wednesday	432	557
Friday	455	422

On which day did the Jets have 125 more points than the Stars? _____

7 Hannah spent $1.25 on popcorn and 6 dimes on candy at the movies. Show how to find the amount of money she spent.

8 What is the perimeter of this shape?

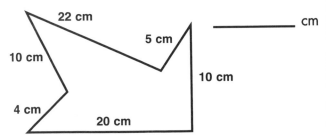

22 cm
5 cm
10 cm
10 cm
4 cm
20 cm

_____ cm

9 In the numeral **568,120**

The **8** is in the_____place.

The **2** is in the_____place.

The **5** is in the_____place.

10 After adding 8 more tens to this model, the numeral shown would be _____.

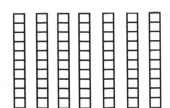

Math 4 today

For each numeral below, write the digit that is in the ten thousands place and the digit that is in ten millions place.

234,459,880 _____

_____

54,182,635 _____

_____

Which letter is in the triangle and circle but not in the square?

_____

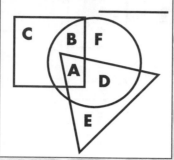

Lane did thirty-seven math problems on Monday. He worked forty-eight more problems on Tuesday. How many math problems did Lane work on these two days?

_____

---

14 - ☐ = 7

11 - ☐ = 8

3 + ☐ = 12

6 + ☐ = 15

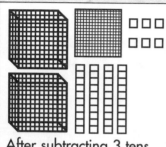

After subtracting 3 tens from this model, the numeral shown would be

_____ .

Check the other names for **21**?

_____ **9 + 10**

_____ **3 x 7**

_____ **1 ten, 2 ones**

_____ **2 tens, 1 one**

_____ **10 + 11**

_____ **6 + 6 + 6 + 3**

_____ **25 - 5**

What time is shown on this clock?

_____

Draw the tenth pattern.

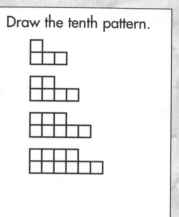

Which group of numerals is in order from least to greatest?

◯ **254, 165, 138, 97**

◯ **889, 976, 981, 872**

◯ **567, 475, 330, 290**

◯ **654, 678, 732, 751**

About how tall is the candle?

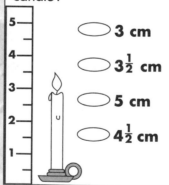

◯ **3 cm**

◯ **3½ cm**

◯ **5 cm**

◯ **4½ cm**

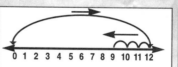

This number line shows:

◯ **12 + 3 = 15**

◯ **12 - 3 = 9**

◯ **12 - 9 = 3**

Solve.

752
+ 289

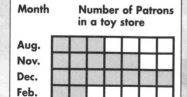

Month | **Number of Patrons in a toy store**

Aug.
Nov.
Dec.
Feb.

0 50 100 150 200 250 300 350

In which month did more than 300 patrons visit the store? _____

Bill is 2 inches taller than Sam. Sam is shorter than Joe. Roy is 4 inches taller Tyler. What information do you need to find out Roy's height?

◯ **Sam's height**

◯ **Joe's height**

◯ **Tyler's height**

Round each number to the nearest ten.

23 ⟶ _____

42 ⟶ _____

18 ⟶ _____

87 ⟶ _____

Which shows the **most accurate** way to estimate the sum of 3,452 and 5,321?

◯ **5,321 - 3,452**

◯ **3,400 + 5,300**

◯ **3,000 + 5,000**

Math 4 today

1

$$667$$
$$+ 285$$

2

$12 - \boxed{} = 3$

$7 + \boxed{} = 15$

$15 - \boxed{} = 9$

3 Round to the nearest ten.

26 ⟶ _____

83 ⟶ _____

92 ⟶ _____

4 Ben collected eighty-nine aluminum cans on Saturday. He collected eighteen more cans on Sunday. How many cans did Ben collect on Saturday and Sunday?

5 Which are other names for 35?

○ 3 + 5

○ 3 tens, 5 ones

○ 5 x 7

○ 50 - 3

6 Which group of numbers is in order from least to greatest?

○ 534, 567, 572

○ 743, 778, 723

○ 248, 238, 223

7 For each numeral below, write the digit that is in the one millions place and the digit that is in the thousands place.

245,329,017 _____
_____

520,291,386 _____
_____

8 Which letter is in the square and rectangle but not in the circle? _____

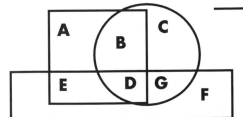

9 What time is shown on this clock? _____

10 After subtracting 6 tens from this model, the numeral shown would be _____ .

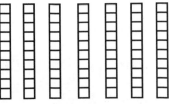

Math 4 today

For each numeral below, write the digit in the ten thousands place and the digit in the hundred millions place.

831,459,620 _____

_____

954,182,635 _____

_____

Which letter is in the triangle, circle, and rectangle but not in the square?

_____

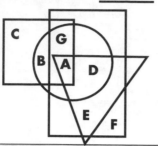

Marty's kite flew 254 decimeters high. Andy's kite flew 876 decimeters high. How much higher did Andy's kite fly?

_____

Solve.

752
524
+ 236

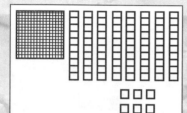

Use the model to show how to subtract 9 ones. What numeral is left?

_____

Use **>**, **<**, or **=** .

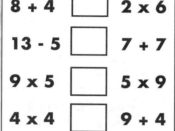

8 + 4 ☐ 2 x 6

13 - 5 ☐ 7 + 7

9 x 5 ☐ 5 x 9

4 x 4 ☐ 9 + 4

What time is shown on this clock?

_____

Draw the sixth pattern in the empty box.

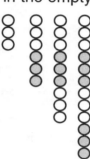

City Streets	Length
Bok Ave.	52,400 m
Syl Street	23,452 m
Lyd Blvd.	47,220 m
Nox Street	59,198 m

Name the streets in order from greatest to least.

_____

_____

_____

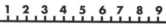

About how long is the leaf?

- ⬭ **9 cm**
- ⬭ **5 ½ cm**
- ⬭ **6 cm**
- ⬭ **7 ½ cm**

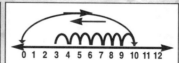

This number line shows:

- ⬭ **3 + 7 = 10**
- ⬭ **10 - 3 = 7**
- ⬭ **10 - 7 = 3**

Solve.

392
- 269

Child	Allowance
Tim	○ ○ ○ ○ ○ ○
Beth	○ ○
Sal	○ ○ ○ ○ ○
Jake	○ ○ ○ ○

Each ○ = 10¢

Who earned 20¢ more than Beth?

_____

Don ate 4 slices of pizza. Greg ate less pizza than Stan. Tom ate 2 more slices than Greg. To find out how much pizza was eaten by Tom, you need to know the number of slices eaten by.

Stan **Greg** **Don**
⬭   ⬭   ⬭

Round each number to the nearest hundred.

253 ⟶ _____

412 ⟶ _____

183 ⟶ _____

87 ⟶ _____

Which shows the **most accurate** way to estimate the difference between **412** and **521**?

- ⬭ **500 - 400**
- ⬭ **412 + 521**
- ⬭ **520 - 410**

1

$$\begin{array}{r} 365 \\ 121 \\ + 557 \\ \hline \end{array}$$

2

$$\begin{array}{r} 962 \\ - 124 \\ \hline \end{array}$$

3 What is the **most accurate** estimate of the difference between 747 and 862?

- ⬭ 747 + 862
- ⬭ 800 - 700
- ⬭ 860 - 750
- ⬭ 900 - 700

4

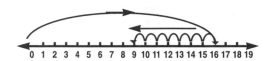

Write the number sentence shown by this number line.

5 The bookshelves in Mrs. Kim's class are 671 centimeters tall. Mr. Hym's shelves are 832 centimeters tall. How much taller are the shelves in Mr. Hym's classroom?

6 Which graph shows that Mary planted 10 more flowers than Sue? graph_____

Beth	✿✿
Jill	✿✿✿✿✿✿
Mary	✿✿✿✿✿
Sue	✿✿✿

✿ = 5

graph A

Beth	✿
Jill	✿✿✿
Mary	✿✿✿✿✿
Sue	✿✿✿

✿ = 2

graph B

7 Kelly earned $5.00. Annie earned $2.00 more than Liz. Gina earned less than Liz. To find out how much money Annie earned, you need to know the amount of money earned by

Liz   **Gina**   **Kelly**
⬭   ⬭   ⬭

8 How many centimeters long is the bead pattern?

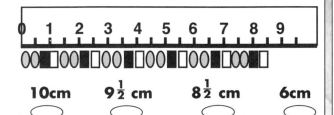

| 10cm | 9½ cm | 8½ cm | 6cm |
| ⬭ | ⬭ | ⬭ | ⬭ |

9 For each numeral, write the digit that is in the millions place and the digit that is in the hundred thousands place.

254,307,199 _____ _____

589,620,413 _____ _____

10 Round each number to the nearest hundred.

197 ⟶ _____   231 ⟶ _____   552 ⟶ _____

Name _____

Write each numeral in expanded form

259,341

_____

_____

182,635

_____

_____

Which pair of figures is congruent? _____

(same size, same shape)

A ☐ ☐

B ⬭ ○

C ◺ ◿

D △ △

Ms. Silva's class collected 347 pounds of trash on clean up day.
Mr. Garcia's class collected 412 pounds of trash. How many more pounds of trash were collected by Mr. Garcia's class?

_____

Solve.

$$\begin{array}{r} 853 \\ 227 \\ 412 \\ +\ 337 \end{array}$$

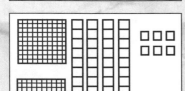

Use the model to show how to subtract 8 tens. What numeral is left?

_____

Use **>**, **<**, or **=** .

8 x 3 ☐ 3 x 6

11 - 5 ☐ 3 x 2

8 x 5 ☐ 4 x 9

15 - 7 ☐ 11 - 8

What time is shown on this clock?

_____

Draw the eighth pattern in the empty box.

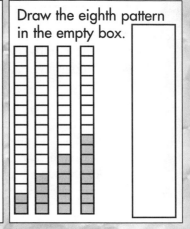

Library	Number of Books
University	82,437
Children's	8,932
Archives	801,920
Historical	89,478

List the library names in order from the least to greatest number of books.

_____

_____

_____

_____

9 10 11 12 13 14 15

About how long is the tack?

◯ **15 cm**

◯ **9 cm**

◯ **5 cm**

◯ **14 cm**

← **222 224 226 228** →

What does this number line show?

◯ The odd numbers between 200 and 230.

◯ The even numbers between 200 and 210.

◯ The even numbers between 220 and 230.

Solve.

743
- 569

Child	Allowance
Tim	○ ○ ○ ○ ○ ○
Beth	○ ○ ○
Sal	○ ○ ○ ○ ○
Jake	○ ○ ○ ○

Each ○ **= 10¢**

How much money was earned by all the children?

_____

Elm Street is 5 blocks longer than Oak Street. Hickory Street is 3 blocks shorter than Pine Street. May Street is as long as Elm. To find out how long Hickory Street is you need to know the length of which street?

Pine   **Oak**   **May**

◯   ◯   ◯

Round each number to the nearest thousand.

8,153 → _____

2,512 → _____

983 → _____

6,710 → _____

Which shows the **most accurate** way to estimate the difference between 387 and 951?

◯ **380 + 950**

◯ **1,000 - 400**

◯ **950 - 390**

26

Math 4 today

1

```
  125
  332
  797
+ 455
```

2

```
  531
- 184
```

3 Round each numeral to the nearest thousand.

5,672 ⟶ _____

881 ⟶ _____

7,199 ⟶ _____

4 Mr. Ortez's class read 538 books. Mr. Mile's class read 731 books. How many more books were read by Mr. Mile's class?

(Show your solution sentence.)

5 Use **>**, **<**, or = .

7 x 4 ☐ 7 x 6

13 - 5 ☐ 4 x 2

8 x 4 ☐ 5 x 6

6

CD-ROM Program Name	Number of Graphics
Art Plus	56,120
Paintbrush	6,789
Colorific	65,882
Designs	556,022

List the CD-ROM names in order from the least number of graphics to the greatest number.

_____
_____
_____
_____

7 Write each numeral in expanded form.

572,486 = _____

_____

325,147 = _____

_____

8 Which pair of figures is congruent? _____

A

B

C

D

9 What time is shown on the clock?

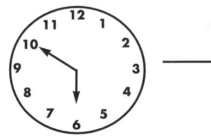

_____

10

Children	Number of Flowers Planted	❀ = 5
Jenny	❀ ❀ ❀ ❀ ❀	
Sarah	❀ ❀ ❀ ❀ ❀ ❀ ❀	
Keira	❀ ❀	
Billy	❀ ❀ ❀ ❀ ❀ ❀ ❀	

What is the total number of flowers planted by the children?

_____ flowers

300,000 + 40,000 + 6,000 + 100 + 50 + 2 =

○ 34,652
○ 436,125
○ 346,152
○ 3,462

Which pair of figures is **NOT** congruent? _____

(same size, same shape)

A
B
C
D

Deb's math book has 421 pages. Her spelling book has 276, and her science book has 352 pages. Her math book has how many more pages than her science book?

_____

Solve.

8,850
- 2,472
_____

Use the model to show how to subtract 6 tens. What numeral is left?

_____

---

4 x 3 = ☐ x 6

25 - 5 = ☐ x 4

6 x 5 = 26 + ☐

To make **$3.47** you would need:

(Answers will vary.)

_____ dollar bills
_____ quarters
_____ dimes
_____ nickels
_____ pennies

Continue the pattern.

25, 27, 30, 32, 35, 37, 40

_____, _____, _____

Which is an even number that is less than 5,620 but more than 4,996?

○ 5,644
○ 5,328
○ 4,986
○ 6,248

What is the perimeter of a square that measures 8 inches on one side?

← 531 533 535 537 →

This number line shows

○ the odd numbers between 530 and 539.

○ the even numbers between 530 and 540.

○ the odd numbers between 527 and 540.

Solve.

2,640
- 1,569
_____

Hen   Eggs laid

Goldy ○○○○
Red ○○○○○○○
Sal ○○○○
Lulu ○○○

Each ○ = 20 eggs

Add symbols to the graph to show that Goldy laid 80 more eggs than Lulu.

In a horse race, Champ is 4 lengths ahead of Prince. Prince is 6 lengths behind Jetta. Star is 3 lengths ahead of Jetta. How many lengths is Champ behind Star?

What might be reasonable dimensions for the size of a kitchen?

○ 20 in. x 30 in.
○ 10 ft. x 14 ft.
○ 10 miles x 14 miles

Which shows the **most accurate** way to estimate the sum of 231 and 482?

○ 380 + 500
○ 400 + 300
○ 230 + 480

1

$$3,310$$
$$- 1,084$$

2

$$9,760$$
$$- 8,299$$

3 Continue the pattern.

69, 74, 78, 83, 87, 92

_____, _____, _____

4

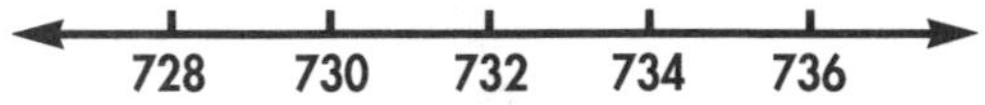

728　730　732　734　736

This number line shows

◯ the even numbers between 730 and 740.

◯ the even numbers between 726 and 738.

◯ the odd numbers between 725 and 739.

5 Steve collected 741 stamps. Steve's grandfather collected 672 stamps. Steve's father collected 523 stamps. How many more stamps did Steve collect than his father? (Show your solution sentence.)

6

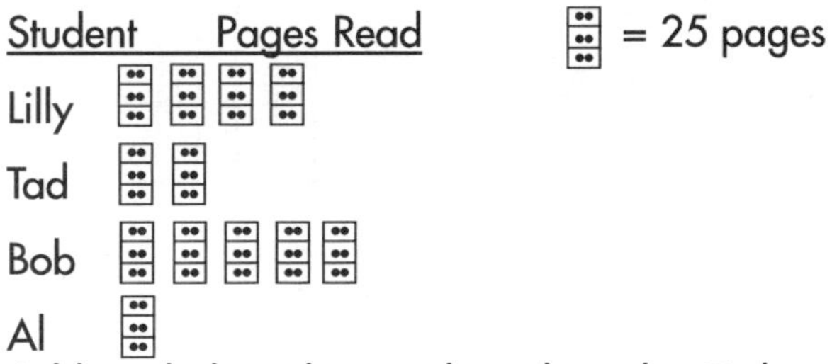

Student   Pages Read   ⊞ = 25 pages

Lilly   ⊞ ⊞ ⊞ ⊞

Tad   ⊞ ⊞

Bob   ⊞ ⊞ ⊞ ⊞ ⊞

Al   ⊞

Add symbols to the graph to show that Tad read 75 more pages than Al.

7 In a marathon race, Ben was 5 meters ahead of John. Frank was 12 meters ahead of Ben, and Sam was 4 meters behind Frank. Use the chart to find out how many meters ahead of John was Sam?

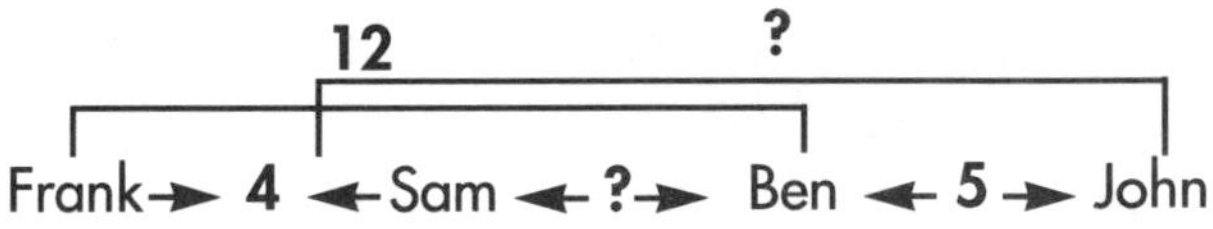

12   ?

Frank→ 4 ←Sam ←?→ Ben ← 5 → John

8 What is the perimeter of a square that measures 12 centimeters on one side?

9 900,000 + 50,000 + 3,000 + 700 + 20 + 6 =

◯ 95,372

◯ 9,326

◯ 935,726

◯ 953,726

10 What might be reasonable dimensions for a bedroom?

15 inches x 20 inches   15 miles x 20 miles   15 feet x 20 feet

◯   ◯   ◯

What is the value of the 5 in each numeral?
Example: 35,622 **5,000**

34,652 _____

436,125 _____

356,102 _____

3,562 _____

Match.

A 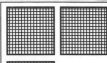 _____ pentagon

B  _____ quadrilateral

C _____ octogon

D _____ hexagon

Joe scored 1,243 points on a video game. Matt's score was 1,458 and David's score was 985. Show how to find the difference between David's score and Joe's score.

Solve.

4,706
- 3,438
_____

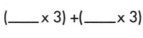

Use the model to show how to subtract 8 ones. What numeral is left?

_____

8x3 =

(___ x 3) +(___ x 3)

7x4 =

(___ x 4) +(___ x 4)

9x6 =

(___ x 6) +(___ x 6)

To make **$2.83** you would need: (Answers will vary.)

_____ dollar bills

_____ quarters

_____ dimes

_____ nickels

_____ pennies

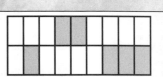

Continue the pattern by shading in the figure below.

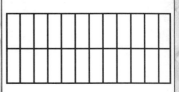

Which is an odd number that is more than 7,821 but less than 10,000?

◯ **9,340**

◯ **10,351**

◯ **1,975**

◯ **8,243**

What is the perimeter of a rectangle that measures 27 inches on one side and 56 inches on the other side?

_____

97,435 is read

◯ ninety thousand, four hundred three five

◯ ninety-seven thousand, four hundred thirty-five

◯ ninety-seven thousand, three hundred five

Solve.

9,901
- 2,569
_____

Favorite Pizza
Each △ = 2 votes

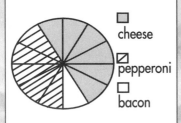

☐ cheese
▨ pepperoni
☐ bacon

How many votes for:
pepperoni pizza _____
cheese pizza _____

A phone company wants to create some new area codes. Each new area code will have 3 numbers. Using the digits 1, 5, and 7 only once in each code, how many new codes can the phone company create?
(Show your work on the back.)

_____ new area codes

About how many gallons of gasoline can a car hold?

◯ **2 gallons**

◯ **20 gallons**

◯ **200 gallons**

◯ **2,000 gallons**

4	7	3	4	2

These cards are shuffled and placed face down after each turn. You draw 1 card, look at it, and return it to the deck. After drawing 10 times, you would probably draw a ☐ the most often.

1

$$9,402 - 1,027$$

2

$$5,705 - 2,299$$

3 About how many gallons of water would it take to fill the kitchen sink?

- ◯ 3
- ◯ 30
- ◯ 300
- ◯ 3,000

4 Rob, Sid, and Mark read 3 books each. The total number of pages Rob read was 2,134. Mark's total was 1,087 and Sid read a total of 876 pages. Show how to find the difference between the number of pages Sid read and the number of pages Rob read.

5

$5 \times 7 =$
(____ × 7) + (____ × 7)

$9 \times 4 =$
(____ × 4) + (____ × 4)

6 Which is an even number that is more than **8,234** but less than **9,933**?

- ◯ 8,328
- ◯ 9,641
- ◯ 9,944

7 What is the value of the 8 in each numeral?

85,231 _____

12,890 _____

8,725,231 _____

8 Match.

hexagon _____

pentagon _____

quadrilateral _____

octagon _____

A   B

C   D

9 To make $4.94, you would need:

(Answers will vary.)

_____ dollar bills
_____ quarters
_____ dimes
_____ nickels
_____ pennies

10 Use the model to show how to subtract 5 ones. What number is left? _____

© Good Apple GA1659 Reproducible

Name_____

What is the value of the 2 in each numeral?
Example: **35,620** ___20___

234,651 _____

436,102 _____

2,356,109 _____

23,562 _____

By definition, which shape could be considered a:

A  **pentagon** ____

B **quadrilateral** ____

C **octagon** ____

D **hexagon** ____

Ms. Baker weighed 174 pounds before she went on a diet. She lost 4 pounds a week for 12 weeks for a total of 48 pounds lost on the diet. How much does Ms. Baker now weigh?

_____

Solve.

94,020
- 13,438
_____

Draw a base ten model to show this numeral:
2, 485

---

7 x 5 =

(____ x 5) + (____ x 5)

6 x 7 =

(____ x 7) + (____ x 7)

12 x 8 =

(____ x 6) + (____ x 6)

What time will this clock show in fifteen minutes?

_____

Continue the pattern by shading in the figure below.

Which numeral would go in the empty box?

342, 344, [   ], 348

⬭ 351

⬭ 340

⬭ 345

⬭ 346

What is the perimeter of an octagon that measures 4 inches on each sides?

_____

2,597,401 is read

⬭ two million, five hundred ninety-seven thousand, four hundred one

⬭ twenty-five thousand, five hundred nine, four hundred one

⬭ two hundred fifty thousand ninety-seven, four hundred one

---

7 x 4 = _____

8 x 5 = _____

6 x 6 = _____

3 x 9 = _____

4 x 8 = _____

Favorite Colors
Each △ = 3 votes

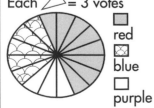

🟦 red
🔲 blue
⬜ purple

How many more votes for: Red than...
Purple? _____
Blue? _____

Using a red, blue, green, and yellow block only once in each row, how many 4 block patterns can you make that have a red block in the first position?
(Show your work on the back.)

_____ block patterns

** Bonus: How many patterns can be made in all?

About how long does it take to listen to a song?

⬭ **3 seconds**

⬭ **3 minutes**

⬭ **30 minutes**

⬭ **3 hours**

Shade in the spinner which would give you the best chance of landing on the number 3?

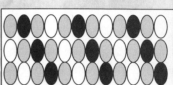

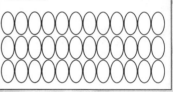

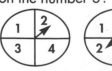

1

$$52,020$$
$$- 11,627$$

2

5 x 8 = _____

9 x 3 = _____

8 x 4 = _____

4 x 7 = _____

3 Continue the pattern by shading in the blank grid.

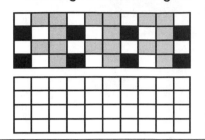

4   **3,457,198** is read

○ thirty-four thousand, four hundred ninety-eight thousand

○ three hundred fifty-seven million, one hundred ninety-eight

○ three million, four hundred fifty-seven thousand, one hundred ninety-eight

5 For the first 6 months of this year, Marcie watched 321 hours of television. For the last 6 months, she watched 1 hour of TV a night for a total of 183 hours. How many more hours of television did she watch during the first 6 months of the year?

(Show your solution sentence.)

6 Which graph shows football having 20 more votes than basketball? _____

☐ basketball
▦ football
▨ baseball

Each △ = 5 votes

A   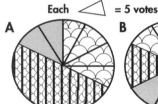   B   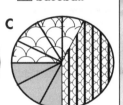   C

7 What time will the clock show in fifteen minutes?

_____

8 What is the perimeter of a pentagon if each side measures 9 centimeters?

(Show how to solve.)

9 What is the value of the **3** in each numeral?

83,467,109 _____

92,637,001 _____

157,472,139 _____

10 About how long does it take to brush your teeth?

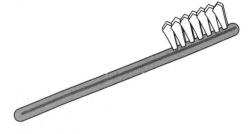

○ **5 seconds**

○ **180 seconds**

○ **25 minutes**

○ **3 hours**

Name_____

Which numeral has a digit of greater value in the tens place than in the thousands place?

- ⬭ 67,169
- ⬭ 82,505
- ⬭ 13,681
- ⬭ 21,910

Match.

A   cylinder _____

B   rectangular prism _____

C   cube _____

    triangular prism _____

D

Cindy was making floral arrangements for the Christmas banquet. She put 7 red carnations in each of 5 vases. Show how to find the number of carnations she used?

_____

Subtract, then check by adding.

$$9,010 - 8,623$$

Draw the missing pieces to make this base ten model show **3,476**.
(Show your work on the back.)

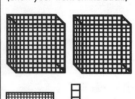

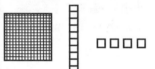

$2 \times (3 + 4) =$

$(2 \times 3) + (\underline{\quad} \times \underline{\quad})$

$5 \times (7 + 8) =$

$(5 \times 7) + (\underline{\quad} \times \underline{\quad})$

$4 \times (8 + 3) =$

$(4 \times 3) + (\underline{\quad} \times \underline{\quad})$

What time was shown on this clock twenty minutes ago?

_____

Study the pattern on the cards below. What will the **tenth** pattern look like?

1	2	3	4
3	6	9	12

tenth pattern

Which numeral would go in the empty box?

210, 200, ☐ , 180

- ⬭ 220
- ⬭ 190
- ⬭ 100
- ⬭ 205

What is the area of the figure below?

_____ square units

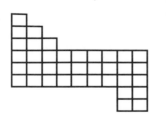

0 1 2 3 4 5 6 7 8 9 10 11 12 13

This number line shows:

- ⬭ **12 - 12 = 0**
- ⬭ **4 x 3 = 12**
- ⬭ **7 + 5 = 12**
- ⬭ **12 ÷ 2 = 6**

---

7 x 3 = _____

6 x 5 = _____

8 x 2 = _____

9 x 4 = _____

4 x 7 = _____

Good Citizenship Reports

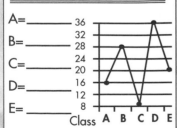

A=_____
B=_____
C=_____
D=_____
E=_____

How many good citizenship reports were received by each class?

Marvin bought 8 party bags for his birthday guests. What information is needed in order to find out how much Marvin spent?

- ☐ Marvin's age
- ☐ the number of guests he invited
- ☐ the cost of each party bag
- ☐ the date of his birth

About how tall is a street delivery mailbox?

- ⬭ **3 kilometers**
- ⬭ **3 meters**
- ⬭ **3 centimeters**
- ⬭ **3 kilograms**

Shade in the spinner that would give you the best chance of landing on the number 1.

1

$$6,020 - 5,928$$

2

5 x 6 = _____

4 x 9 = _____

2 x 8 = _____

3 x 7 = _____

3 About how long is a school bus?

◯ **10 millimeters**

◯ **10 centimeters**

◯ **10 meters**

◯ **10 kilometers**

4 Jenna made 9 autumn collages. She used 4 leaves in each collage. How many leaves did Jenna use to make all her collages?

5

5 x (8 + 2) = (5 x 8) + (_____ x _____)

2 x (6 + 4) = (2 x 4) + (_____ x _____)

8 x (9 + 7) = (8 x 7) + (_____ x _____)

6 Which numeral goes in the empty box?

308, 304, 300, [   ] , 292

◯ **302**

◯ **290**

◯ **310**

◯ **296**

7 Which numeral has a digit of greater value in the ten thousands place than in the millions place?

◯ **25,431,207**

◯ **147,358,110**

◯ **4,129,782**

◯ **43,847,208**

8 Match.

A   B   C   D

_____ rectangular prism   _____ cube

_____ cylinder _____ triangular prism

9

What time was shown on this clock twenty-five minutes ago?

_____

10 This number line shows:

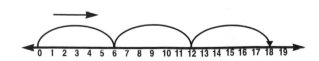

◯ **6 x 3 = 18**

◯ **18 ÷ 2 = 9**

◯ **6 + 6 = 12**

◯ **18 - 12 = 6**

Which numeral has a digit of lesser value in the ten thousands place than in the ten millions place?

○ 11,427,169

○ 891,250,505

○ 138,681,456

○ 201,910,872

Which shape has a line of symmetry?

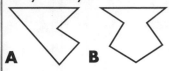

A   B

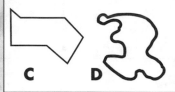

C   D

Ray ordered pizza for 9 of his friends. In order for each of his friends to have four pieces of pizza, how many pieces of pizza did Ray need to order?

_____

Subtract. Check by adding.

5,000
- 2,716
_____

Write the fraction for the shaded part of each shape.

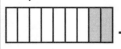 _____

  _____

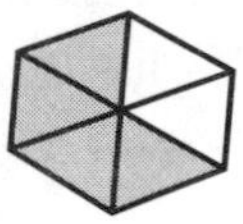

---

8 x (5 + 2) =

(_____ x _____) +

(_____ x _____)

= ☐ or

8 x _____ = ☐

Using a minimal collection of coins (the least amount possible), show how to make **$1.17**.

Study the pattern on the cards below. What will the tenth pattern look like?

1	2	3	4
7	14	21	28

tenth → ☐
pattern

Which numeral is 100 less than **2,458**?

○ 2,258

○ 2,558

○ 1,458

○ 2,358

What is the area of the figure below?

_____ sq. cm

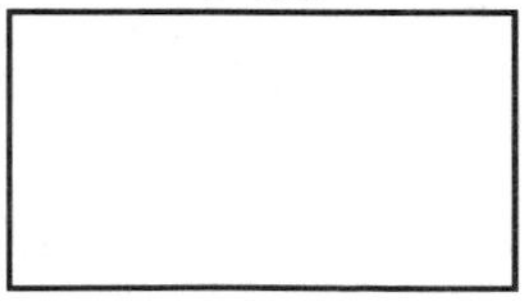

8 cm

6 cm ▭

0 1 2 3 4 5 6 7 8 9 10 11 12 13 14 15

This number line shows:

○ **3 x 5 = 15**

○ **4 x 3 = 12**

○ **7 + 8 = 15**

○ **10 ÷ 2 = 5**

---

7 x 6 = _____

9 x 5 = _____

8 x 8 = _____

6 x 3 = _____

7 x 7 = _____

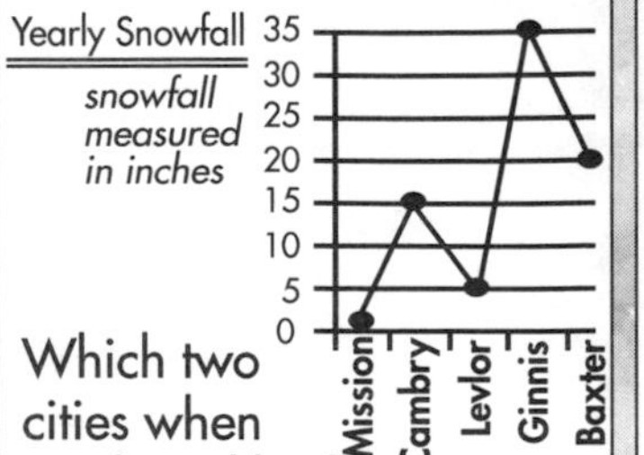

Yearly Snowfall

snowfall measured in inches

35 30 25 20 15 10 5 0

Mission Cambry Levlor Ginnis Baxter

Which two cities when combined had a total snowfall equal to the town of Ginnis? _____

Todd swam 7 laps a day last summer. Phil swam 5 laps every three days. What information do you need to find out the total number of laps that Todd swam last summer?

☐ the distance Todd swam

☐ the number of days Phil swam

☐ the number of days Todd swam

Estimate the sum by rounding to the hundreds place.

587
217
620
188

The marbles above are in a sack. With one draw, the chances are 1 out of 7 that you could draw a ⬤ . What would be the probability of drawing a ⬤ ?

_____ out of _____

1 Subtract. Check by adding.

$$8,000$$
$$- 2,817$$

2

$3 \times 6 = $ _____

$5 \times 9 = $ _____

$8 \times 8 = $ _____

$6 \times 7 = $ _____

3

If the above tiles are placed in a box, what are the chances of drawing a ☐ in the first draw?

_____ out of _____

4

This number line shows:

⬭ $20 - 20 = 0$ ⬭ $20 \div 4 = 5$

⬭ $11 + 9 = 20$ ⬭ $4 \times 5 = 20$

5 Amy bought gifts for her seven cousins. Each gift cost four dollars. How much money did Amy spend for all the gifts?

(Show your solution sentence.)

6 Class President Election

Number of votes: 70 60 50 40 30 20 10 0

Student: Ali Meg Joe Sly Pam

Which two students' combined votes equal the same number of votes Pam received?

_____

_____

7 Using a minimal collection of coins (the least amount possible), show how to make **$1.38**.

8 Find the area.

_____ square cm

9 cm

4 cm

9 Which numeral has a digit of lesser value in the hundred millions place than in the thousands place?

⬭ **457,126,990**

⬭ **825,992,132**

⬭ **175,071,976**

⬭ **239,190,843**

10 Estimate the sum by rounding to the hundreds place.

781
411
652
293

© Good Apple GA1659 Reproducible

How many digits are needed to create a numeral in the

hundred millions
_____

ten thousands
_____

hundreds
_____

Which shape has two lines of symmetry?_____

 A

 B

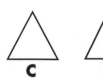 **C**   **D**

Hannah completed 4 pages of homework everyday for 7 days. How many pages of homework did she complete in all?

_____

Subtract. Check by adding.

3,000
- 2,971
_____

Write the fraction for the shaded parts of each shape.

    _____

    _____

---

5 x (8 + 2) =

(5 x 8) + (5 x ☐)

= ☐

3 x (7 + 1) =

(3 x 7) + (3 x ☐)

= ☐

Using a minimal collection of the coins below (the least amount possible), show how to make **$1.74**.

____quarters ____dimes

____nickels____pennies

31, 28, 25, 22

The formula for the above pattern is

◯ add 3

◯ subtract 3

◯ count by 5's

◯ subtract 2

Which numeral is 1,000 more than **9,235?**

◯ **9,335**

◯ **8,235**

◯ **10,235**

◯ **11,235**

What is the perimeter of the figure below?
_____ units
the area?
_____ square units

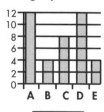

Write the number word for:
2,000,405 _____
_____
_____

610,240 _____
_____

9x8= _____

8x7= _____

7x6= _____

9x7= _____

8x4= _____

Use >, <, = to describe this graph.

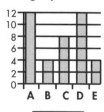

A [ ] D

E [ ] C

D [ ] B

Mystery Numbers
A = B x 3
B = D - 10
C = The sum of 7 and 3.
D = C + C

A =____ B = ____
C =____ D = ____

Estimate the sum by rounding to the tens place.

2,832
1,179
6,208
4,385

●▲▲▲▲▲■■

The above shapes are in a sack. With one draw, the chances of drawing a ▲ would be:

_____ out of _____

Math 4 today

1 Subtract. Check by adding.

$$7,000$$
$$- 6,294$$

2

6 x 7= _____

8 x 9= _____

4 x 8= _____

7 x 8= _____

3 Estimate the sum by rounding to the tens place.

4,352
4,174
3,238
5,155

4 Nate was at summer camp for 9 days. He went fishing each day. If he caught 6 fish every time he went fishing, how many fish did he catch while he was at camp? (Show your solution sentence.)

5

6 x (4 + 5) = (6 x 4) + (6 x ☐) = ☐

5 x (2 + 7) = (5 x 2) + (5 x ☐) = ☐

6 Which numeral is 1,000 less than **10,247**?

◯ **9,247**

◯ **11,237**

◯ **10,357**

◯ **9,147**

7 How many digits are needed to create a numeral in the

hundred thousands _____

ten millions _____

thousands _____

8 Which figure has two lines of symmetry? figure _____

A   **B**   **C**

9 Using a minimal collection of the coins below, show how to make **$2.49**.

_____   _____   _____   _____
quarters   dimes   nickels   pennies

10 Write the fraction for the shaded part of each figure.

  _____   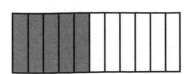 _____   _____

Math 4 today

Name_____

Write the numbers.

eight ten thousands, five hundreds, two tens, seven ones

_____

six hundred millions, two hundred thousands, one thousand, nine tens, four ones

_____

Shade the figures that have dotted lines showing the lines of symmetry.

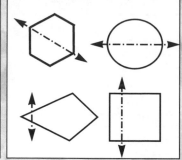

Mr. Knox has 24 students in his science class. He would like to have 4 students at each table. How many tables will he need for his class?

_____

---

9 x 9 = _____

8 x 8 = _____

7 x 7 = _____

6 x 6 = _____

5 x 5 = _____

Write the fractions.

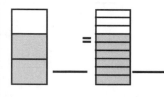

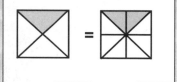

_____ _____

Write the fact family for **7, 8,** and **56.**

_____

_____

_____

_____

Kim began her piano practice at 4:20. She practiced for 35 minutes. At what time, did she stop practicing?

_____

1	2	3	4
1	4	9	16

Which equation describes the pattern?

◯ **n + n**

◯ **n x n**

◯ **n - n**

◯ **n + 2**

Which numeral is less than **11,437** and more than **10,992**?

◯ **10,990**

◯ **11,531**

◯ **10,005**

◯ **11,235**

What is the perimeter of the figure below?

_____ cm

the area?

_____ square cm

8 cm

[rectangle]

6 cm

Write each number word.

15,320,100 _____

_____

_____

350,205,500 _____

_____

_____

---

16 ÷ 2 = _____

25 ÷ 5 = _____

8 ÷ 4 = _____

12 ÷ 3 = _____

15 ÷ 3 = _____

Gymnastic Meet Total Scores	
Christy	35
Alicia	40
Leyla	25
Kalyn	50

On the back, draw a bar graph to describe the data in the chart with **1 bar = 5.** Write 3 summary statements.

Mystery Numbers

A = B x 7
B = 12 ÷ 3
C = D - A
D = A + B

A = _____ B = _____

C = _____ D = _____

Dennis bought a game for $27.50, a book for $6.25, a model kit for $14.95, and a shirt for $22.99. About how much money did he spend?

◯ **$71.00**

◯ **$85.00**

◯ **$100.00**

◯ **$92.00**

Match.

_____ 10 centimeters

_____ 100 centimeters

_____ 10 decimeters

_____ 1,000 meters

A. kilometer
B. meter
C. decimeter

Name _____

1

16 ÷ 8 = _____

18 ÷ 2 = _____

25 ÷ 5 = _____

15 ÷ 3 = _____

2

6 x 6 = _____

8 x 8 = _____

4 x 4 = _____

9 x 9 = _____

3

20	18	16	14
10	9	8	7

The equation for this pattern is:

◯ even $n + 5$

◯ even $n - 4$

◯ even $n \div 2$

4 Write each number word.

251,718,400 _____

_____

62,502,194 _____

_____

5 Kala has 35 stickers to give to each of her 5 friends. How many stickers will she give each friend if each one gets the same number of stickers?

6

100's on Spelling Tests

Which statements are true for this graph?

◯ 1 bar = 3

◯ Bob > Meg

◯ Hal > Sam

◯ Meg = Ann

◯ Sam = 9

◯ Ann+Meg+Hal=Bob

7 Margo and Patsy went to see a play. The play began at 3:20 and lasted for 45 minutes. At what time did the play end?

8 What is the perimeter of the figure? the area?

_____ cm.

_____ sq. cm

7 cm

4 cm

9 Write each numeral.

six hundred thousands, eight-thousands, nine hundreds, zero tens, seven ones

_____

eighty millions, four hundred thousands, two hundreds, nine tens, five ones

_____

10 Heidi was doing chores to earn money. She earned $7.54 during the first week of November. She earned $32.99 during the second week, $12.50 the third week, and $24.95 the last week of the month. About how much money did Heidi earn during November?

◯ **$100.00**

◯ **$85.00**

◯ **$66.00**

◯ **$79.00**

Fill in the missing digits.

seven hundred sixty-two million, nine hundred, forty-five thousand, two hundred fifty eight.

7___ 2,___ ___ 5,___ ___ 8

Match.

line *X Y* _____

line segment *X Y*_____

ray *X Y* _____

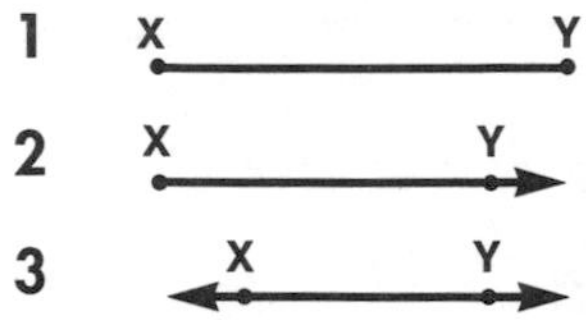

1   X_____Y

2   X_____→Y

3   ←X_____Y→

Ms. Rye has 12 roses, 18 daisies, and 3 vases. She wants an equal number of roses and an equal number of daisies in each vase. Show how to find the number of roses and daisies she will put in each vase.

---

9 x 6 = _____

8 x 5 = _____

9 x 8 = _____

8 x 7 = _____

9 x 4 = _____

Shade in the second figure and complete the equivalent fractions.

  $\frac{1}{2}$ = _____ _____

 = _____ _____

  = _____ _____

Which pair are **NOT** related facts?

◯ 8 x 9 = 72   72 ÷ 9 = 8

◯ 6 x 6 = 36   6 - 6 = 0

◯ 8 x 4 = 32   4 x 8 = 32

◯ 7 x 5 = 35   35 ÷ 5 = 7

The Hampton family arrived at their grandparents' home at 6:40 Sunday evening. The drive had taken 1 hour and 10 minutes. At what time, did the Hamptons leave home?

1, 6, 4, 9, 7, 12, 10, 15, 13, 18, 16, 21

What is the rule for the above pattern?

_____

_____

Which numeral is more than **125,437** but less than **220,151**?

◯ **110,790**

◯ **251,031**

◯ **100,005**

◯ **211,835**

What is the perimeter of the figure below?

_____ units.

the area?

_____ square units

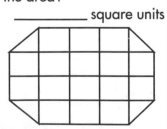

0 1 2 3 4 5 6 7 8 9 10 11 12 13 14 15

This number line shows:

◯ **14 - 9 = 5**

◯ **7 + 8 = 15**

◯ **14 ÷ 7 = 2**

◯ **7 x 7 = 49**

---

18 ÷ 3 = _____

24 ÷ 6 = _____

27 ÷ 9 = _____

36 ÷ 6 = _____

20 ÷ 4 = _____

Student	Spelling Stars
Kira	★★★★★
Mike	★★★
Lance	★★★★★★
Deb	★

Each ★ = 6 A+ spelling tests

What is the total number of A+ spelling tests shown on this graph? _____

Max is older than Ivan. Hal is younger than Ivan but older than Greg.

Which statements could be true?

◯ Max is older than Hal.

◯ Ivan is younger than Greg.

◯ Hal is the youngest.

◯ Greg is younger than Max.

Quaid picked 82 bushels of apples on Monday and 91 bushels on Tuesday. Carmen picked 52 bushels on Wednesday and 75 bushels on Thursday. About how many more bushels of apples did Quaid pick?

◯ **70**   ◯ **20**

◯ **40**   ◯ **100**

---

10 centimeters = 1 decimeter

It takes 8 decimeters of shipping paper to wrap a large package for mailing. How many centimeters of paper would be needed?

_____

1

$20 \div 5 =$ _____

$18 \div 6 =$ _____

$24 \div 4 =$ _____

$27 \div 3 =$ _____

2

$4 \times 9 =$ _____

$7 \times 8 =$ _____

$8 \times 9 =$ _____

$6 \times 9 =$ _____

3 Eva read 22 pages on Monday and 91 pages on Tuesday. Mario read 89 pages on Monday and 63 pages on Tuesday. About how many more pages did Mario read?

⬭ 20   ⬭ 50

⬭ 40   ⬭ 90

4 Juan has 48 stamps and 36 stickers. He wants to glue the same number of stamps and the same number of stickers onto 6 pages in his collector's album. Show how to find the total number of stamps and stickers he will put on each page?

5 Which pair are **NOT** related facts?

⬭ $8 \times 8 = 64$ $64 \div 8 = 8$

⬭ $8 + 8 = 16$ $8 - 8 = 0$

⬭ $4 \times 6 = 24$ $6 \times 4 = 24$

⬭ $5 \times 9 = 45$ $45 \div 9 = 5$

6 Which numerals are more than **347,129** but less than **412,076**?

⬭ 418,000   ⬭ 398,899

⬭ 409,778   ⬭ 362,901

⬭ 447,202   ⬭ 332,388

⬭ 4,001,033   ⬭ 34,100

7 Fill in the missing digits for each number.

nine hundred eighty-six thousand, four hundred thirty-five

9_____ _____ , _____ 3 _____

seven hundred twenty-one thousand, two hundred ninety-eight

_____ _____ 1, _____ _____ 8

8 Match.

_____ line AB

_____ ray AB

_____ line segment AB

_____ ray YX

_____ line segment XY

1   X •———————• Y

2   ←—•——•—→ A B

3   ←—•———————• X Y

4   A •——•——→ B

5   A •———————• B

9 A new play is opening in the city. It begins at 8:00. It takes Carol's family 1 hour and 25 minutes to drive to the city. At what time should Carol's family leave home in order to arrive at the play on time?

10 Shade in the second figures to complete the equivalent fractions.

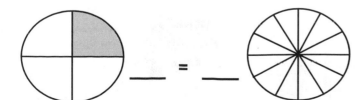

____ = ____   ____ = ____

Write in expanded form.

sixty-two thousand, four hundred twenty-five

_____

_____

two hundred ninety-one thousand, eight hundred fifteen

_____

_____

Match.
A. ray   B. line
C. line segment

_____ a straight figure with two end points.

_____ a straight figure with no end points that extends forever in both directions.

_____ a straight figure with one end point extending forever in one direction.

Holly displays her 54 music boxes on 6 shelves in her room. She also keeps 12 dolls on the shelves. If she arranges the music boxes and the dolls equally, how many items are on each shelf?

```
34        43
x 2       x 3


51        52
x 5       x 4
```

Shade in the second figures to complete the equivalent fractions.

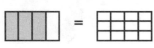

_____ = _____

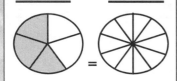

=

_____

A common factor of 4 and 8 is 2 because 2 x 2 = 4 and 2 x 4 = 8.

Other than 1, what is a common factor for these number pairs.

10 and 15 _____
12 and 21 _____
7 and 14 _____

Name the coins and amount needed for change.

Cost: **Amount given**
$.79   **$1.00**
change?_____

_____

$.37   **$.50**
change?_____

_____

2, 4, 7, 14, 17, 34, 37, 74, 77, 154

What is the rule for the above pattern?

_____

_____

Mountain	Feet in Height
Annapurna	26,504
Kilimanjaro	19,340
Dapsang	28,250
Everest	29,028
Cho Oyu	26,750

List the mountains in order of height from least to greatest.

_____
_____
_____
_____
_____

What is the perimeter of the figure below?

_____ units

the area?

_____ square units

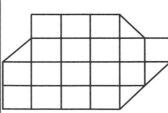

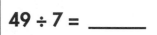

This number line shows

◯   15 ÷ 3= 5

◯   7 + 8 =15

◯   5 ÷ 5 =1

◯   5 x 5 = 25

---

49 ÷ 7 = _____

54 ÷ 6 = _____

63 ÷ 9 = _____

72 ÷ 8 = _____

81 ÷ 9 = _____

Hours of TV Watched Per Month By The 4th Grade

Room 401   D D
Room 402   D D D D
Room 403   D D D D D

Each D = 25 hours
How many more hours of TV were watched by Room 403 than Room 401?

_____

Ann read fewer books than Susan. Linda read more books than Ann, but fewer than Tammy. Which statements could be true?

◯   Ann read the least number of books.

◯   Tammy read the most.

◯   Linda read more books than Tammy. last summer.

The chart shows the money Todd earned doing odd jobs last summer.

June	$57.98
July	$92.33
August	$66.88

About how much money did Todd earn last summer?

◯ $220   ◯ $250
◯ $300   ◯ $120

---

10 decimeters = 1 meter
Sam measured 8 meters to make a pen for his pet rabbits. At the store, the fencing he wanted for the pen was sold only in decimeters. How many decimeters of fencing would he need to buy?

_____

Name _____ Test #18

1

$63 \div 7 =$ _____

$72 \div 9 =$ _____

$54 \div 9 =$ _____

$49 \div 7 =$ _____

2

43	12	63
x 2	x 4	x 3

3 What is the rule for this pattern?

1, 3, 2, 6, 5, 15, 14, 42, 41

_____

4

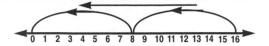

This number line shows:

⬭ $8 + 8 = 16$ ⬭ $16 \div 8 = 2$

⬭ $8 \times 8 = 64$ ⬭ $8 - 8 = 0$

5 Marcus is setting the table for his party. He has invited 8 guests. For party favors, he bought 24 balloons and 16 candy bars. How many party favors will he set at each place if each guest gets an equal number of balloons and candy bars?

6 Students Wearing Glasses in Hanston Elementary Schools. Each b = 30 students

GRADE	A	GRADE	B
Third bbbb		Third bbb	
Fourth bbb		Fourth bbbbb	
Fifth bbbbb		Fifth bbbbbb	
Sixth bbbb		Sixth b	

Which graph shows that 90 more students in fifth grade wear glasses than the students in fourth grade?   graph _____

7 Name the coins and amounts needed for change.

Cost **$ 5.49**   Amount Given **$6. 00**

_____

_____

Cost **$ 3.22**   Amount Given **$4.12**

_____

_____

8 What is the perimeter and the area of the figure below?

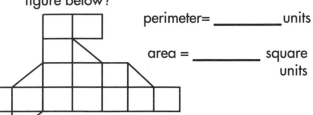

perimeter= _____ units

area = _____ square units

9 Write each number in expanded form.

fifty-seven thousand, three hundred eighty-one

_____

_____

seven hundred ninety-two thousand, six hundred five _____

_____

10 The chart shows the number of long distance calls made by the School Computer Supply Company for the fall months of 1997.

Month	Number of Calls
September	297
October	341
November	196

About how many calls were made by the company during these months?

⬭ **700**   ⬭ **900**

⬭ **600**   ⬭ **800**

Name _____

400,000+90,000 +3,000+500 +7 =

◯ forty-nine thousand, three hundred fifty-seven

◯ four hundred nine thousand, three thousand seven

◯ four hundred ninety-three thousand, five hundred seven

Which show right angles?

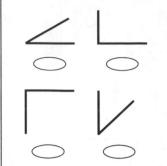

James is making collages for his 4 aunts. For decoration, he wants to put 6 leaves, 4 shells, and 3 flowers on each collage. How many decorations will he need to make all the collages?

```
 44      13
x 5     x 7

 58      29
x 5     x 4
```

Shade in $\frac{1}{3}$ of each set.

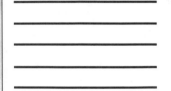

```
777777
777777
```

```
LLLLLL
LLLLLL
LLLLLL
```

A common factor of 4 and 8 is 2 because 2 x 2 = 4 and 2 x 4 = 8

Other than 1, what is a common FACTOR for these number pairs.

27 and 18 _____

30 and 40 _____

35 and 21 _____

Name the bills, coins and amount needed for change.

Cost	Amount given
$3.81	$5.00

change?_____
_____

$7.17	$10.00

change?_____
_____

Continue the pattern.

45	42	39	36
15	14	13	12

33			
11			

Write the odd numbers between **3,497** and **3,511**.

_____
_____
_____
_____
_____

Mrs. Thomas drove from Dallas, Texas to Ft. Worth, Texas. She traveled about

◯ 55 kilograms

◯ 55 liters

◯ 55 kilometers

◯ 55 decimeters

Write **a.m.** or **p.m.**

Julio's party begins at 3:00 _____

The school tardy bell rings at 8:15 _____

The toy store opens at 9:30 _____

The evening news comes on at 6:00 _____

9x ___ =72

3x ___ =27

___ x 4=32

___ x 7=63

City Science Fair

School	Solar System Projects
Dayton	★★★★⭑
Ryan	★★★
Adly	★★★★★⭑
Marcus	★⭑

Each ★ = 4

How many solar system projects were entered in the science fair?

_____

Tyesha and Eric together have 29 posters. Eric has 7 more posters than Tyesha. How many posters does each child have?

Estimate the differences by rounding to the hundreds place.

```
2,359    7,944
1,231    5,679
```

1,000 meters = 1 kilometer

Tam and Issac walked 2 and $\frac{1}{2}$ kilometers along a hiking trail. How many meters did they walk?

Math 4 today

Name _____

1

$9 \times \underline{\quad\quad} = 63$

$8 \times \underline{\quad\quad} = 32$

$\underline{\quad\quad} \times 9 = 27$

$\underline{\quad\quad} \times 9 = 72$

2

29	38	69
$\times\ 2$	$\times\ 4$	$\times\ 3$

3 Estimate the difference by rounding to the hundreds place.

8,712
4,189

4 Mrs. Wong is making centerpieces for 7 tables. She wants to put 8 daisies, 7 carnations, and 5 roses in each centerpiece. How many flowers will she need?

5 What is a common factor for each pair of numbers.

45 and 10 _____

81 and 72 _____

36 and 30 _____

6 Write the even numbers between **5,996** and **6,010**.

_____

_____

_____

_____

_____

7 600,000 + 70,000 + 2,000 + 10 + 4 =

◯ six hundred seventy-two thousand fourteen

◯ six hundred seven thousand, two hundred fourteen

◯ sixty-seven million, two thousand, one hundred four

8 Lilly's family left home from Dallas, Texas for a ski trip to Denver, Colorado. About how far did they travel?

◯ **1,200 grams**

◯ **1,200 centimeters**

◯ **1,200 kilometers**

◯ **1,200 meters**

9 Write a.m. or p.m.
Raul's parents went to a late movie. They returned home at 11:30_____ .
Cindy had a piano lesson after school. Her lesson started at 4:30 _____.
Gerad's Dad took an early flight. His plane left at 7:30 _____.

10 Shade in $\frac{1}{5}$ of each set.

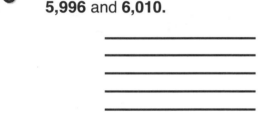

47

Name_____

What is the value of the 5 in each numeral?

3,458,201 _____

152,670,400 _____

61,250 _____

Which show acute angles?
(less than a right angle)

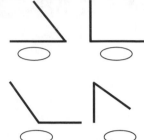

At Midland Elementary, there are 22 students in each of seven fourth-grade classes. How many students are in fourth-grade at Midland?

---

17 x 10	23 x 10
84 x 10	33 x 10

Shade in $\frac{2}{6}$ of each set.

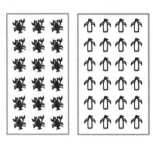

Other than 1, what are the common factors for these number pairs?

24 and 12 _____ ,
_____ , _____ ,
_____ , _____

10 and 30 _____ ,
_____ , _____

What time will the clock show in 2 hours and 15 minutes?

_____

What figure would come next in this pattern?

145,298 ☐ ☐ 167,109

Which two numerals could go in the empty boxes?

- ⬭ 168,231 169,345
- ⬭ 142,789 234,188
- ⬭ 14,388   15,632
- ⬭ 156,954 162,599

Mr. Valdez was loading stones to put into wheelbarrow. The wheelbarrow can carry the weight of about

- ⬭ 80 grams
- ⬭ 80 kilograms
- ⬭ 80 kilometers
- ⬭ 80 centimeters

Write the numeral for seven hundred eighty-six million, four hundred two thousand, five hundred ninety-one

_____

six billion, two hundred one million, nine hundred forty-seven thousand, eight hundred thirteen

_____

---

100 x 15	100 x 46
100 x 72	100 x 93

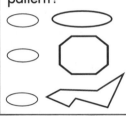

Volleyball Tournament Points

What is the difference between the number of points scored by Mark and the number of points scored by Hank?

_____

Judy and Ramey together have 42 stuffed animals. Judy has 12 fewer animals than Ramey. How many stuffed animals does each girl have?

Lynn's Reading Chart

Monday	36 pages
Tuesday	42 pages
Wednesday	39 pages
Thursday	0 pages

How could you estimate the total number of pages Lynn read?

- ⬭ 42 ÷ 4
- ⬭ 42 - 39
- ⬭ 40 x 3
- ⬭ 20 x 4

In a deck of 52 cards there are 2 jokers and 4 each of the number cards 1–10. The probability of picking a joker is 2 out of 52 or 2/52. Write as a fraction, the probability of drawing a number 7 card.

Math 4 today

1

$$85 \times 10 \qquad 79 \times 10$$

2

$$100 \times 51 \qquad 100 \times 62$$

3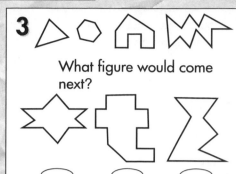

What figure would come next?

4 Write each numeral.
seventy-nine million, three hundred twenty-nine thousand, five hundred forty

_____

four hundred ten million, three thousand, one hundred eighty-two

_____

5 There are 9 photographs on each page of a travel book. The book has 67 pages. How many photographs are in the book?

6 What is the difference between the pounds of paper recycled by Max and the pounds of paper recycled by Lou?

(bar graph: values 0–32; labeled Tom, Bet, Lou, Jen, Max)

_____

7 In art class, Kaly and Nate together painted 33 pictures during the year. Kaly painted 9 less pictures than Nate. How many pictures did each child paint?

8 Label each angle.
RA = right angle   **AA** = acute angle

___ ___ ___ ___ ___

9 What is the value of the **3** in each numeral?

321,890,267 _____

889,0**3**2,901 _____

3,290,177,200 _____

10

Basketball Goals For the Season	
Ty	17
Jamal	23
Pete	24
Kito	2
Nino	21

How could you estimate the number of goals made by all the boys?

- ⬭ **23 + 24 + 17**
- ⬭ **4 x 20**
- ⬭ **5 x 20**
- ⬭ **5 x 25**
- ⬭ **25 - 5**

© Good Apple GA1659 Reproducible

What is the value of the **2** in each numeral?

9,468,**2**01

_____

752,610,400

_____

21,390

_____

Which show obtuse angles?
(more than a right angle)

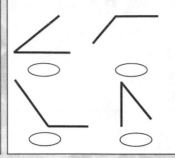

If there are 365 days in one year, how many days are in 7 years?

$$\begin{array}{r} 37 \\ \times\ \underline{30} \end{array}$$

$$\begin{array}{r} 54 \\ \times\ \underline{40} \end{array}$$

$\frac{1}{6}$ of 48 = _____

$\frac{1}{8}$ of 40 = _____

$\frac{1}{2}$ of 10 = _____

List the common factors for these number pairs. Circle the greatest common factor for each pair.

40 and 8 ___ , ___ ,
___ , ___ ,

36 and 24 ___ ,
___ , ___ , ___ ,
___ ,

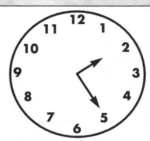

What time did the clock show 2 hours and 20 minutes before?

_____

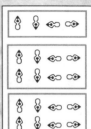

Draw the sixth box in this pattern.

100,051 ☐☐ 99,109

Which two numerals could go in the empty boxes?

◯ 105,231   109,345
◯ 906,789   902,188
◯ 99,838   99,632
◯ 98,054   93,107

Sandy made a jug of lemonade to serve five friends. About how much lemonade did she make?

◯ 3 meters

◯ 3 grams

◯ 3 liters

◯ 3 mililiters

Write each numeral.

six million, twenty-two thousand, four hundred eighty-seven

_____

twenty-five million, three hundred seventeen thousand, fifty-nine

_____

$$\begin{array}{r} 357 \\ \times\ \underline{8} \end{array}\qquad \begin{array}{r} 652 \\ \times\ \underline{7} \end{array}$$

$$\begin{array}{r} 229 \\ \times\ \underline{5} \end{array}\qquad \begin{array}{r} 934 \\ \times\ \underline{3} \end{array}$$

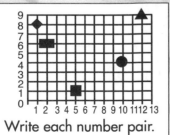

Write each number pair.

■ _____   ● _____

◆ _____   ● _____

▬ _____

Mother needs to buy paper cups for 42 people. Which two packages could she buy to have enough paper cups without too many left over?

_____ and _____

10	15	20	25
A	B	C	D

---

472 people bought concert tickets for $21.05 each. Which would be a way to estimate how much money was paid for the tickets?

◯ 400 x $20.00 = $8,000
◯ 500 x $20.00 = $10,000
◯ 470 + $20.00 = $4970.
◯ 500 − $25.00 = $475,

●● ◯◯◯◯◯

If these marbles are placed in a bag and one is drawn out, what is the probability that it will be white? (Write as a fraction.)

_____

black? _____

Math 4 today

1

$$\begin{array}{r} 95 \\ \times\ 50 \\ \hline \end{array} \qquad \begin{array}{r} 62 \\ \times\ 80 \\ \hline \end{array}$$

2

$$\begin{array}{r} 498 \\ \times\ 7 \\ \hline \end{array} \qquad \begin{array}{r} 873 \\ \times\ 7 \\ \hline \end{array}$$

3 While on vacation, the Carter family drove 337 miles a day for 16 days. How could you estimate the number of miles they drove?

- ⬭ 300 x 20 = 6,000
- ⬭ 400 x 20 = 8,000
- ⬭ 337 - 16 = 321
- ⬭ 300 + 20 = 320

4 There are 168 hours in one week. How many hours are in 9 weeks?

5 List the common factors for these number pairs. Circle the greatest common factor.

64 and 16 _____ , _____ ,
_____ , _____ ,

40 and 8 _____ , _____ ,
_____

6 Which two numerals could go in the empty boxes?

103,032 [ ][ ] 100,091

- ⬭ 101,997   99,090
- ⬭ 104,234   100,459
- ⬭ 99,821   98,305
- ⬭ 100,621   100,243

7 What is the value of the **9** in each numeral?

391,820,267 _____

889,032,501 _____

3,270,179,200 _____

8 Label the angles. **RA** = right angle; **AA** = acute angle; **OA** = obtuse angle

___ ___ ___ ___ ___

9

What time did the clock show 4 hours and 20 minutes ago?

10

$\frac{1}{7}$ of 49 = _____ $\frac{1}{4}$ of 20 = _____ $\frac{1}{9}$ of 36 = _____

Math 4 today

Which numeral shows 7 thousands, 4 hundreds, 6 tens, and 18 ones?

◯ 76,418

◯ 74,618

◯ 7,478

Which figures are polygons?

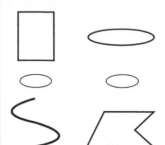

Marly's Country Store has 20 gum drops in each of 6 candy jars. Which method could be used to find the total number of gum drops?

◯ **Add 20 and 6**
◯ **Multiply 20 by 6**
◯ **Subtract 6 from 20**
◯ **Divide 20 by 6**

500
X 28

300
X 56

$\frac{1}{5}$ of 25 = _____

$\frac{1}{3}$ of 33 = _____

$\frac{1}{7}$ of 56 = _____

A. sum   B. difference
C. quotient D. product

_____ the answer to a division problem

_____ the answer to an addition problem

_____ the answer to a subtraction problem

_____ the answer to a multiplication problem

Kyle bought six new model kits. Each kit cost $8.79. How much money did Kyle spend on model kits?

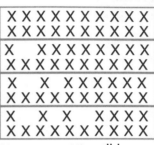

How many X's will be in the tenth box?

_____ X's

President	Term Served
Harry Truman	1945–1953
James Monroe	1817–1825
John Tyler	1841–1845
Herbert Hoover	1929–1933
John Adams	1797–1801

List the presidents in order beginning with the earliest term to the most recent.

_____
_____
_____
_____

A. 9 Kilograms
B. 3 meters   C. 2 grams
D. 300 liters
E. 20 mililiters
F. 1,500 kilograms
G. 80 kilograms
Which is the best estimate of mass for a
car _____
sack of groceries _____
pencil _____
television _____

Which number line shows the whole numbers that are great than 4 and less than 10?

_____

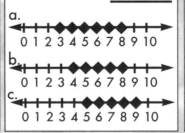

★★★★★★
★★★★
★★★★

3)‾14‾

★★★★
★★★★ 5)‾19‾
★★★★
★★★★
★★★

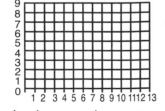

Plot these number pairs.

(11, 9)   (3, 0)

(13, 4)   (1, 8)

To decorate 6 dozen cupcakes with red hot candies, Nan needs about 550 red hots. Which two sacks of candy would be the best buy? _____

_____

353 177 255 379

---

937 people are seated at 28 tables for a banquet. How could you find the best estimate of the number of people at each table?

◯ **900 ÷ 30 = 30**

◯ **900 x 20 = 18,000**

◯ **1,000 - 28 = 972**

◯ **1,000 ÷ 20 = 50**

If these marbles are placed in a bag and one is drawn out, what is the probability that it will be white or black?
(Write as a fraction.)

Math 4 today

Name _____

1

$$900 \times 13 \qquad 600 \times 72$$

2

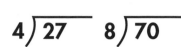

$$4\overline{)27} \qquad 8\overline{)70}$$

3

□ □ □ ○ ○ ○ ◆

If these shapes are in a bag, what is the probability (expressed as a fraction) of drawing out a ◆ or a □ ?

4 Which number line shows the numerals that are less than 12 and more than 5? ☐

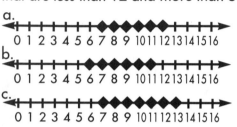

a.
0 1 2 3 4 5 6 7 8 9 10 11 12 13 14 15 16

b.
0 1 2 3 4 5 6 7 8 9 10 11 12 13 14 15 16

c.
0 1 2 3 4 5 6 7 8 9 10 11 12 13 14 15 16

5 Zeke packs 45 cans in each box. Today, he packed 35 boxes. What method could be used to find the number of cans Zeke packed today?

○ Add 45 and 35.

○ Multiply 45 by 35.

○ Subtract 35 from 45.

6 Graph the number pairs.

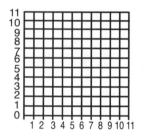

(9,11)

(3,6)

(0,10)

(7,5)

7 Ms. Silva needs to buy napkins for her company's picnic. She needs 715 napkins. Which 2 packages would be the best buy? _____ and _____

256   395   125   500

8 What is the best estimate of mass for.

a pumpkin _____   a bus _____
a football _____   a spoon _____

A. 2,000 kilograms   B. 2,000 kilometers
C. 10 grams   D. 10 liters
E. 15 meters   F. 15 kilograms
G. 2 mililiters   H. 2 kilograms

9 Which numeral shows 56 thousands, 2 hundreds, 37 tens, 8 ones?

○ 562,378

○ 56,378

○ 56,578

○ 56,478

10 815 new compact disks arrived at the music store. The disks are put on display racks in groups of 52. How could you find the best estimate of the number of display racks needed for the compact disks?

○ 800 x 50 = 40,000

○ 900 x 60 = 54,000

○ 800 + 50 = 850

○ 800 ÷ 50 = 16

Which numeral shows 8 thousands, 4 hundreds, 11 tens, and 6 ones?

◯ **8,411**

◯ **8,516**

◯ **9,116**

Which letter is inside the square and circle, but not inside the rectangle?

_____

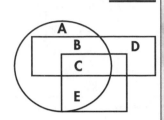

Hannah was baking a cherry pie for 8 of her friends. She had a carton of 241 cherries. When she finished the pie, Hannah had 17 cherries left. How many cherries did she use in the pie?

200
x 41

400
x 12

Write each fraction in its simplest form.

$\frac{2}{4}$ = _____

$\frac{3}{9}$ = _____

$\frac{5}{15}$ = _____

Multiples are numbers made by multiplying a number by another number. For example multiples of 5 are 5, 10, 15, 20, 25... List 3 multiples for each number.

3 _____, _____, _____

7 _____, _____, _____

9 _____, _____, _____

This clock shows about:
◯ **5:55** ◯ **11:35**
◯ **11:20** ◯ **11:27**

```
0000000000000
0000000000000
000000000000
000000000000
00000000000
00000000000
```

How many 0's will be in the sixth box?

_____ 0's

Use **>** or **<**.

$\frac{1}{8}$ ☐ $\frac{1}{3}$

$\frac{1}{2}$ ☐ $\frac{1}{10}$

$\frac{1}{4}$ ☐ $\frac{1}{12}$

Which is the best estimate for the length of a

paper clip _____
dining table _____
pencil _____
bandage _____
railroad route _____
scissors _____

A. centimeter B. decimeter
C. meter   D. kilometer

Write each number word.

$\frac{2}{8}$ _____

$\frac{5}{7}$ _____

$\frac{1}{2}$ _____

```
***** **
*****
*****
```
$5\overline{)17}$

```
XXX X
XXX
XXX
XXX
XXX
XXX
```
$3\overline{)19}$

January					
1	2	3	4	5	6
7	8	9	10	11	12	13
14	15	16	17	18	19	20
21	22	23	24	25	26	27
28	29	30	31			

Which weeks have the greatest number of **odd** numbers? _____
The greatest number of **even** numbers? _____

Favorite Numbers
Eve's number is greater than 15. Dan's number is not evenly divisible by 2. Meg's number is more than Eve's. Ken's number is a prime number.

	15	16	17	18
Eve				
Dan				
Meg				
Ken				

---

621 people bought tickets to the Community Theater's production of Pinnochio. The tickets cost $4 each. Which is the best estimate of the ticket sales?

◯ **$ 1,400**

◯ **$ 2,400**

◯ **$ 3,400**

A

B

If these shapes are placed in a box and one is drawn out, which box, A or B, would give the best chance of drawing a ◯ ? _____

1

100   300
x 43   x 15

2

5)18   4)17

+++++   ● ● ● ●
+++++   ● ● ● ●
+++++   ● ● ● ●
+++   ● ● ● ●
          ●

3 479 people attended the Brigham School's Winter Festival. Each person paid $8 for a ticket. About how much did the school make from ticket sales?

⬭ $4,000 ⬭ $5,000
⬭ $6,000 ⬭ $7,000

4 At a sleepover, Karen and 12 of her friends toasted marshmallows in the fireplace. There were 161 marshmallows in two bags. When the girls finished, there were 39 marshmallows leftover. How many marshmallows did they toast?

5 Multiples are numbers made by multiplying a number by another number. For example multiples of 5 are 5, 10, 15, 20, 25... List 3 multiples for each number.

8 _____ , _____ , _____

2 _____ , _____ , _____

6 Use > or <.

$\frac{1}{10}$ ☐ $\frac{1}{8}$ $\frac{1}{4}$ ☐ $\frac{1}{2}$

$\frac{1}{5}$ ☐ $\frac{1}{12}$ $\frac{1}{16}$ ☐ $\frac{1}{2}$

7 Which numeral shows 3 thousands, 9 hundreds, 17 tens, and 2 ones?

⬭ **4,072**
⬭ **3,979**
⬭ **4,172**
⬭ **5,721**

8 Which letter is inside the square and rectangle but not inside the circle? _____

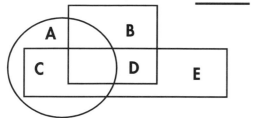

9 This clock shows about:

⬭ **2:00**
⬭ **2:30**
⬭ **2:45**
⬭ **2:53**

10

	February				
	1	2	3	4	5
6	7	8	9	10	11	12
13	14	15	16	17	18	19
20	21	22	23	24	25	26
27	28	29	30	31		

Which week(s) have the greatest number of even numbers? _____ and _____ weeks.

The greatest number of odd numbers? _____ weeks.

Math 4 today

Name _____

Which numeral shows 17 hundreds, 3 tens, and 9 ones?

○ 170,039

○ 1,739

○ 10,739

Which letter is inside the square and triangle, but not inside the rectangle or circle? _____

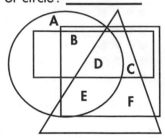

Mickey bought 3 packages of blank cassette tapes to record 17 of his favorite CDs. Each package contained 8 tapes. How many tapes did Mickey buy?

900
x 55

600
x 44

Write each fraction in its simplest form.

$\frac{5}{10}$ = _____

$\frac{6}{9}$ = _____

$\frac{12}{16}$ = _____

Least Common Multiple (LCM) List 6 multiples for:

3 ____, ____, ____,
____, ____, ____,

4 ____, ____, ____,
____, ____, ____,

6 ____, ____, ____,
____, ____, ____,

Circle the least numeral that is the same for all three.

_____ is the LCM for 3,4,6.

This clock shows about:
○ 12:07   ○ 1:00
○ 12:55   ○ 2:10

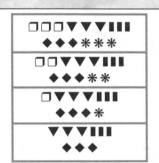

Draw the 7th box.

Use > or <.

$\frac{1}{12}$ ☐ $\frac{1}{20}$

$\frac{1}{42}$ ☐ $\frac{1}{5}$

$\frac{1}{7}$ ☐ $\frac{1}{50}$

Which is the best estimate for the length of a

fever thermometer _____
needle _____
interstate highway _____
fingernail _____
river _____
tree trunk _____

A. centimeter B. decimeter
C. meter   D. kilometer

Write each number word.

$5\frac{3}{9}$ _____

$6\frac{7}{10}$ _____

$9\frac{1}{5}$ _____

✳✳✳✳✳✳✳✳
✳✳✳✳✳✳✳✳
✳✳✳✳✳✳✳✳
✳✳✳✳✳   8)29

XXXXXXX
XXXXXXX   7)18
XXXX

S	M	T	W	Th	F	S

Fill in the dates. The third Thursday is the 13th. Mark the 22nd and the 7th. On what day of the week does this month begin? _____

Favorite Numbers

Joe's number is greater than 25. Lil's number is a multiple of 5. Hal's number is less than Joe's. Ray's number is divisible by 8.

	20	23	35	40
Joe				
Lil				
Hal				
Ray				

Seventy-eight dollars was spent to buy new trees for the city park. 12 people paid for the trees. About how much did each person spend?

○ 2 dollars

○ 8 dollars

○ 12 dollars

If these bunnies are in a magician's hat and one is drawn out, it will most likely be a

_____ bunny.

1

200   400
x 61   x 22

2

9)23   6)22

+++
+++
+++
+++
+++
++++
++++

● ● ● ● ● ●
● ● ● ● ● ●
● ● ● ● ● ●
● ● ● ●

3

▲ ▲ ▲ ▲
▲ ▮ ■ ○

If these shapes were in a sack and you drew one out without looking, circle the shape you would most likely draw   ▲ ▮ ■ ○ .

4 Write each number word.

$7\frac{5}{8}$ _____
_____

$10\frac{2}{6}$ _____
_____

5 Maria was making a quilt for her 4 cousins. She used 9 material squares for each row. So far, she has sewn 6 rows. How many squares has she used?

6 Fill in these calendar dates.

S	M	T	W	Th	F	S

The 15th is on the third Monday. Label the 4th and the 27th. On what day of the week does this month begin?

_____

7 This clock shows about

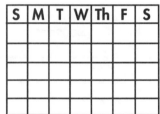

○ 6:00

○ 5:30

○ 6:34

○ 7:30

8 Which is the best estimate for the length of a
A. centimeters   B. decimeters
C. meters   D. kilometers

ladies handbag _____
the Hoover Dam _____
a toothpick _____
a sidewalk to the front door _____

9 Which numeral has 19 hundreds and 8 tens?

○ 1,908

○ 1,980

○ 190,008

○ 190,080

10 91 children in a youth group divided into 14 teams to go on a scavenger hunt. What is the best estimate of the number of children on each team?

○ 9

○ 19

○ 90

○ 190

Which numeral shows 3 thousands, 2 hundreds, 15 tens, and 0 ones?

◯ 30,215

◯ 3,350

◯ 3,215

Which figures are polygons?

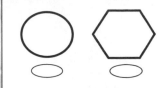
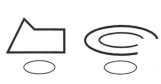

Ms. Lucas ordered 4 dozen glazed donuts and 10 chocolate donuts. Which method could be used to find the total number of donuts she ordered?

◯ Add 4 and 10.
◯ Multiply 4 x 12 and add 10.
◯ Subtract 4 from 10 and add 12.
◯ Divide 12 by 4 and subtract 10.

700
x 35

900
x 42

Add.

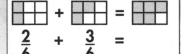

$\frac{2}{6} + \frac{3}{6} =$ _____

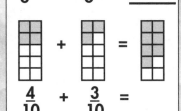

$\frac{4}{10} + \frac{3}{10} =$ _____

A. add   B. multiply
C. divide   D. subtract

_____ to find the quotient

_____ to find the sum

_____ to find the product

_____ to find the difference

Craig bought 9 folders for $.67 each. How much money did Craig spend on folders?

| ff |
| ffff |
| ffffff |
| ffffffff |

How many f's will be in the ninth box?

_____ f's

$\frac{1}{8}, \frac{1}{2}, \frac{1}{4}, \frac{1}{12}, \frac{1}{3}$

Write the above fractions in order from greatest to least.

_____
_____
_____
_____
_____

A. grams   B. meters
C. liters   D. centimeters
E. mililiters F. kilograms
G. kilometers

To measure...

mass_____, _____,

distance _____, _____,

_____

volume_____, _____,

Which number line shows the whole numbers that are greater than 43 and less than 49?_____

A
42 43 44 45 46 47 48 49 50

B
42 43 44 45 46 47 48 49 50

C
42 43 44 45 46 47 48 49 50

★★★★★★★★★
★★★★★★★★★
★★★★

8)20

★★★★★
★★★★★
★★★★★
★★★★★
★★★★★

9)25

Refreshments Sold at the Festival

30
25
20
15
10
5
0
   Wed Th. Fri. Sat.

■ lemonade   ▨ fruit punch

On which day was more lemonade than fruit punch sold?_____

Joey lives ten blocks to the west of Ned. Ned lives two blocks to the east of Sue. Fran lives seven blocks to the east of Sue. How many blocks is it from Fran's to Joey's house?_____
From Fran's to Ned's house? _____

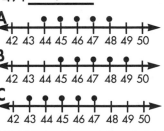
Joey Sue Ned Fran

21,899 people attended a football game. It began raining and 2,688 people left. About how many people remained at the game?

◯ 10,000
◯ 19,000
◯ 20,000
◯ 23,000

A ■ ■ ☐ ☐ ☐ ☐
B ■ ■ ☐ ☐ ☐ ☐ ☐ ☐

If these tiles are placed in a box and one is drawn out, which box, A or B, would give the best chance of drawing a black tile?_____

1

$$400 \times 83 \qquad 200 \times 79$$

2

$$5\overline{)34} \qquad 7\overline{)53}$$

3 33,589 people booked flights in December. 5,102 people canceled their flights because of snowstorms. About how many people kept their flights?

◯ 28,000 ◯ 30,000
◯ 38,000 ◯ 20,000

4 For a bake sale, Ms. Murphy baked 7 dozen cookies and 5 cakes. Which method could be used to find the number of baked goods Ms. Murphy prepared?

◯ Add 7 and 5.   ◯ Subtract 5 from 84.
◯ Divide 12 by 5 and add 7.   ◯ Multiply 7 by 12 and add 5.

5 Match.

A. multiplication   ____ sum
B. division   ____ difference
C. addition   ____ product
D. subtraction   ____ quotient

6 Write these fractions in order from least to greatest.

$$\frac{1}{10} \qquad \frac{1}{8} \qquad \frac{1}{25} \qquad \frac{1}{3} \qquad \frac{1}{16}$$

____ , ____ , ____ , ____ , ____

7 Which numeral shows 6 thousands, 7 hundreds, 12 tens, and 9 ones?

◯ 67,129
◯ 6,829
◯ 6,709
◯ 76,129

8 Which figures represent polygons?

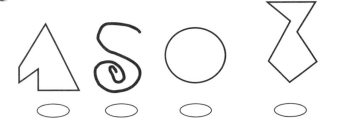

◯   ◯   ◯   ◯

9 Lynn sold 8 games at a garage sale. She charged $.95 for each game. How much money did she make by selling her games at the garage sale?

10

girls ☐   boys ■

The graph shows the points made by the boys' team and the girls' team in a volleyball tournament. In which game did the boys and girls score the same number of points?

game _____

Which numeral shows 22 thousands, 13 hundreds, and 9 ones?

◯ 22,139

◯ 22,309

◯ 23,309

How many faces does this figure have?

_____ faces

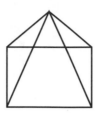

Jamie had 25 sand art packages. She gave 10 to her little sister. Then she bought 8 more. Which equation could be used to find the number of sand art packages Jamie has now?

◯ (25 + 10) + 8

◯ (25 + 10) - 8

◯ (25 - 10) + 8

852
x 5

437
x 6

Subtract.

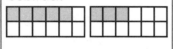

$$\frac{5}{12} - \frac{3}{12} = \frac{2}{12}$$

$$\frac{4}{5} - \frac{2}{5} = \frac{2}{5}$$

Underline the true equations:

(4 x 5) + 3 = 4 x (5 + 3)

(5 x 2) x 2 = 5 x (2 x 2)

(9 x 1) - 1 = 9 x (1 - 1)

(4 x 4) ÷ 1 = 4 x (4 ÷ 1)

Carlos practices his clarinet for one half hour each time he practices. What is the total number of **hours** Carlos practices in five days?

How many v's will be in the 20th box?

_____ v's

vvvvv

vvvvv
vvvvv

vvvvv
vvvvv
vvvvv

vvvvv
vvvvv
vvvvv
vvvvv

$$\frac{2}{15} \quad \frac{2}{12} \quad \frac{2}{9} \quad \frac{2}{42} \quad \frac{2}{5}$$

Write the above fractions in order from greatest to least.

_____

_____

_____

_____

Circle the best unit for measuring:

the distance across Africa.
centimeters   decimeters
meters   kilometers

the height of a swingset.
centimeters   decimeters
meters   kilometers

Write each numeral.

four-fifths _____

two-thirds _____

seven-eighths _____

Solve.

7)$\overline{54}$

6)$\overline{23}$

Pounds of Recyclables Collected

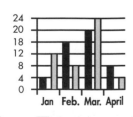

■ paper   ▨ glass

Comparing totals, the pounds of paper recycled is (>, <, =) to the pounds of recycled glass.

These are klinkers.

These are NOT klinkers.

Which of these are klinkers?

◯   ◯   ◯

There were 1,460 paintings and 3,977 drawings entered in a children's art festival. There were also 315 collages and 89 clay sculptures entered. About how many total entries were there?

❑ between 5,000 and 6,000

❑ between 6,000 and 7,000

❑ between 4,000 and 5,000

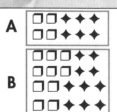

The chances of drawing a ❑ are ...

◯ greater with box A

◯ greater with box B

◯ equal with box A or B

Math 4 today

Name _____

1

$$436 \times 4 \qquad 925 \times 9$$

2

$$8\overline{)77} \qquad 6\overline{)53}$$

3

A | wwwaaa aa | B | wwwaa a |

The chances of drawing a **w** are
(greater, less, or equal)
with box B.

4 Write each numeral.

seven-ninths _____

four-fifths _____

one-third _____

5 Michael had 72 baseball cards. He traded 20 to his friend for a yo-yo. The next week, Michael got 13 more baseball cards for his birthday. Which equation could be used to find out how many baseball cards Michael has now?

○ (72 - 20) +13   ○ (72 + 20) +13

○ 72 - (20 - 13)   ○ 72 + 13

6

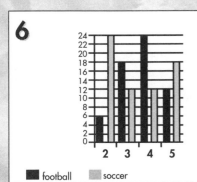

football ■   soccer ▨

A. The total number of votes for football was...
(>, <, =)
the votes for soccer.

B. Which grades had the same number of votes for soccer?
grades _____ and _____

7 It takes Maria 15 minutes to walk home from school each day. In two weeks, how many hours does she spend walking home from school?

8 Circle the best unit for measuring

the height of a house.
centimeters   decimeters
meters   kilometers

the distance of a trolley ride around town.
centimeters   decimeters
meters   kilometers

9 Which numeral shows 34 thousands, 17 hundreds, and 6 tens?

○ 34,176

○ 35,760

○ 37,460

○ 34,706

10 In a statewide science fair, there were 2,398 projects exhibited on recycling and 1,598 projects on solar energy. The fair also had 79 ecology projects and 221 electricity projects. About how many projects were exhibited at the science fair?

○ between 2,000 and 3,000

○ between 3,000 and 4,000

○ between 4,000 and 5,000

○ between 5,000 and 6,000

Which numeral shows 10 thousands, 22 hundreds, and 4 tens?

- ⬭ 12,240
- ⬭ 10,224
- ⬭ 22,104

How many faces does this figure have?

_____ faces

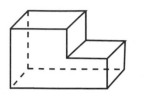

Xavier shared a package of 37 pizza bites with 4 of his friends. If all the boys ate the same number of pizza bites, how many were left over?

705
x 6

$\frac{5}{9} + \frac{2}{9} =$ _____

$\frac{3}{12} + \frac{7}{12} =$ _____

Write each fraction as a whole number or mixed number in its simplest form.

$\frac{24}{3} =$ _____

$\frac{30}{7} =$ _____

Underline the true equations:

$(9 + 8) + 7 = 9 + (8 + 7)$

$(8 \times 4) \times 0 = 8 \times (4 \times 0)$

$(12 - 3) - 2 = 12 - (3 - 2)$

$(6 \times 6) \div 1 = 6 \times (6 \div 1)$

Computer Lab Schedule
Minutes of Time Used Per Week

Grade	M	T	W	Th	F
3	15		15		
4		30		45	
5	15		60		15

For the week shown, how many minutes was the computer lab used?

_____ minutes =

_____ hours _____ minutes

384

192

96

48

What numeral will be in the 7th box?

$\frac{30}{3}$ $\frac{4}{2}$ $\frac{16}{2}$ $\frac{20}{5}$

Write the above fractions in order from least to greatest.

_____

_____

_____

_____

What is the area of the figure shown on the grid?

_____ square units

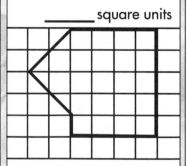

Write each numeral.

six and seven-tenths

_____

ten and four-fifths

_____

fifteen and eight-twentieths

_____

Solve.

4)84

$\frac{7}{16} - \frac{4}{16} =$ _____

$\frac{4}{5} - \frac{3}{5} =$ _____

Temperatures for the School Week

The greatest difference in temperature occured between which two days?

_____ and _____

These are gloopies.

These are **NOT** gloopies.

Which of these are gloopies?

2,378 people came on the opening day of the county fair. 1,932 people came the next day. On the third day, 781 people came, and on the last day, 1,032 people came. About how many people came to the fair?

- ❑ between 4,000 and 5,000
- ❑ between 5,000 and 6,000
- ❑ between 6,000 and 7,000

The chances of drawing a ▲ are

- ⬭ greater than drawing a ✚
- ⬭ less than drawing a ✚
- ⬭ equal to drawing a ✚

Math 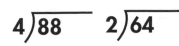 today

Name _____

Test # 27

1

$$903 \quad 201$$
$$\times 7 \quad \times 8$$

2

$$4\overline{)88} \quad 2\overline{)64}$$

3

7,802 visitors attended the museum's African exhibit. 2,107 visitors attended the Eqyptian exhibit, and 5,890 visitors saw the Japanese exhibit. About how many visitors attended these exhibits?

◯ between 14,000 and 15,000
◯ between 15,000 and 16,000
◯ between 16,000 and 17,000

4

Natasha bought a package of cookies to share with her six friends. The package contained 45 cookies. If Natasha and her friends each get the same number of cookies, how many cookies will be leftover?

_____

5

Which equations are true?

◯ $(12 + 5) - 4 \quad = \quad 12 + (5 - 4)$

◯ $(6 \times 5) \times 0 \quad = \quad 6 \times (5 \times 0)$

◯ $(9 \times 8) \div 1 \quad = \quad 9 \times (8 \div 1)$

◯ $(14 - 5) - 2 \quad = \quad 14 - (5 - 2)$

6

$$\frac{25}{5} \quad \frac{21}{7} \quad \frac{30}{5} \quad \frac{18}{9} \quad \frac{54}{6}$$

Write the above fractions in order from greatest to least.

_____ _____ _____ _____ _____

7

Which numeral shows 50 thousands, 35 hundreds, and 4 tens?

◯ 50,354
◯ 55,304
◯ 53,540
◯ 5,354

8

How many faces does this figure have?

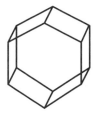

_____ faces

9

Science Lab Schedule Minutes of Time Used Per Week					
Grade	Mon.	Tues.	Wed.	Thurs.	Fri.
2	30		30		30
3	45			45	
4	20	20	20		30

For the week shown on the chart, how many minutes was the science lab in use?

_____ minutes = _____ hours _____ minutes

10

Average Temperature for February

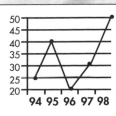

The graph shows the average temperature for the month of February during the years 1994–1998.

During which two years was the difference in the average temperature the greatest? _____ and _____

the least? _____ and _____

Chama flipped through the dictionary. The page he landed on had a 4 in the ones place, a 5 in the thousands place, and a 2 in the tens place. What was Chama's page number?

_____

How many corners does this figure have?

_____ corners

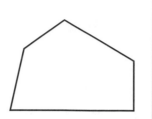

Mrs. Hernandez made coffee for the 7 members of her bridge club. Her coffee maker makes 30 cups. If she and her club members drink an equal number of cups, how many cups of coffee will still be in the coffee maker when her guests leave?

$$\begin{array}{r} 22 \\ \times\ 13 \end{array}\Big\}$$

$$\begin{array}{r} 20+2 \\ \times\ 3 \end{array}$$

$$\begin{array}{r} 20+2 \\ \times\ 10 \end{array}$$

$$\begin{array}{r} 34 \\ \times\ 32 \end{array}$$

Write each fraction as a whole number or mixed number in its simplest form.

$\frac{31}{3}$ = _____

$\frac{45}{7}$ = _____

Which equation does **NOT** belong?

○   7 x 8 = 56

○   8 x 7 = 56

○   56 ÷ 8 = 7

○   7 + 8 = 15

What time will the clock show in 2 hours and 45 minutes?

_____

| 9 |
| 18 |
| 27 |
| 36 |

What numeral will be in the 10th box?

[ ]

Use **>**, **<**, or **=**.

$\frac{4}{2}$ [ ] $1\frac{1}{5}$

$2\frac{3}{8}$ [ ] $\frac{20}{4}$

$5\frac{2}{8}$ [ ] $\frac{42}{8}$

What is the area of the figure shown on the grid?

_____ square units

the perimeter?

_____ units

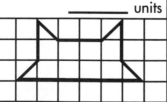

```
 ←─┼──┼──┼──┼──┼──┼─→
   12  13  14  15  16
```
(A marked above between 15 and 16)

Which numeral belongs where you see the letter A?

○ $15\frac{1}{32}$

○ $15\frac{1}{2}$

○ $15\frac{7}{8}$

Solve.

$7\overline{)490}$

$9\overline{)1,800}$

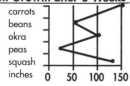

Plant Growth after 3 Weeks

Circle the best estimate of the growth difference between the squash and peas.

100 in.   **150** in.   **50** in.

Use the graph to the left.

Together the peas and the _____ grew about the same as the squash. Shade the chart that matches the graph?

carrots	150		carrots	150
beans	50		beans	50
okra	100		okra	100
peas	25		peas	50
squash	125		squash	100

3,593 people were seated on 9 rows of stadium bleachers. About how many people were sitting on each row?

○   **200**

○   **300**

○   **400**

○   **500**

Tymo wants to mount his 6 miniature puzzles in one frame. What information does Tymo need before buying the frame?

○ the number of pieces in each puzzle

○ the combined areas of the puzzles

○ the cost of the puzzles

Math 4 today

Name _____

1

$$31 \times 12 \qquad 13 \times 23$$

2

$$6\overline{)360} \qquad 8\overline{)5,600}$$

3

12
24
36
48

What numeral will be in the 8th box? ☐

4

A number line labeled 24, 25, 26, 27, 28, 29, 30 with A between 27 and 28.

Which numeral belongs where you see the letter A?

○ $26\frac{1}{2}$ ○ $27\frac{1}{8}$ ○ $27\frac{11}{12}$ ○ $27\frac{1}{2}$

5

Jeff's mother made pizzas for his birthday. She sliced the pizzas into 59 slices. She served Jeff and his 7 guests the same number of slices, and she ate the rest. How many pieces of pizza did Jeff's mother eat?

6

Complete the chart.

Number of Students Ordering Lunch Items

(graph with items: chili, pizza, hot dogs, tuna; x-axis 0, 25, 50, 75, 100, 125)

Item	Number Ordered
tuna	_____
_____	15
_____	55
pizza	_____

7

What time will the clock show in 4 hours and 15 minutes?

_____

8

What is the area of the figure shown on the grid? _____ square units

(figure on grid)

The perimeter is _____ units.

9

Heather wrote a number with a 6 in the ones place, a 2 in the thousands place, and a 9 in the tens place. What number did Heather write?

_____

---

10 5,521 illustrations are included in a 6 volume set of children's dictionaries. About how many illustrations are in each volume?

○ 600

○ 700

○ 800

○ 900

Name_____

Leslie was writing the populations of several cities. The population of Nawton had a 9 in the thousands place, a 5 in the ones place, and a 6 in the ten thousands place. What number did Leslie write for Nawton's population?

_____

How many corners does this figure have?

_____corners

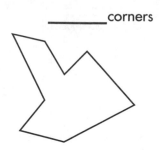

Adam is studying for an end-of-semester spelling test. There are 6 word lists that have 15 words each. Adam studies for his spelling test by writing the words three times. How many words will Adam write?

$$\begin{array}{r} 45 \\ \times\ 25 \end{array}\Big\}$$

$$\begin{array}{r} 40+5 \\ \times\ 5 \end{array}$$

$$\begin{array}{r} 40+5 \\ \times\ 20 \end{array}$$

$$\begin{array}{r} 62 \\ \times\ 43 \end{array}$$

Add or subtract. Simplify if needed.

$$\frac{5}{8} + \frac{2}{8} = \underline{\hspace{1cm}}$$

$$\frac{2}{10} + \frac{1}{10} = \underline{\hspace{1cm}}$$

$$\frac{4}{6} - \frac{2}{6} = \underline{\hspace{1cm}}$$

To find the average of a group of numbers, add the numbers together. Then divide the total by the number of addends.
Example:
5, 7, 9, 3
5 + 7 + 9 + 3 = 24
24 ÷ 4 = 6
6 is the average for this group of numbers.
Find the average for:
8, 7, 2, 3, 15

Robert saved $52.00 so he could attend a concert. He paid $23.50 for the tickets. At the concert, he bought a program for $7.25 and a t-shirt for $15.00. How much money did Robert have after the concert?

88, 81, 74, 67, 60

What is the rule for the above pattern?

_____

_____

Use >, <, or =.

$$\frac{9}{3} \ \square\ 3\frac{1}{3}$$

$$7\frac{1}{4} \ \square\ \frac{30}{4}$$

$$2\frac{1}{16} \ \square\ \frac{20}{4}$$

Use >, <, or =.

3 inches $\square$ 3 yards

6 feet $\square$ 2 yards

12 inches $\square$ 1 foot

8 feet $\square$ 1 yard

12 ——|——|——A——13

Which numeral belongs where you see the letter A?

◯ $13\frac{1}{2}$

◯ $12\frac{1}{2}$

◯ $12\frac{3}{4}$

Solve.

$$3\overline{)9,360}$$

$$4\overline{)8,048}$$

James 🌳🌳🌳🌳🌳

Kevin 🌳🌳🌳🌳🌳

Steve 🌳🌳🌳🌳🌳

each tree = 8

Shade in the graph to show Kevin trimmed 36 trees. Steve trimmed 44 trees. James trimmed 20 trees.

Use the graph to the **left**. How many trees were trimmed by all the boys?

_____ trees

One half a tree shaded =

_____ trees

Steve trimmed about_____ times the number of trees trimmed by James.

1,593 people were waiting to board 8 planes. About how many passengers will get on each plane?

◯ **100**

◯ **200**

◯ **300**

◯ **400**

Mrs. Jordan needs to make lemonade for the school's field day. A can of lemonade serves 30 people. What information does Mrs. Jordan need before she makes the lemonade?

◯ The cost of the lemonade per can.

◯ How many cans it takes to make a gallon

◯ The number of people who will drink lemonade

Math 4 today

Name _____

1

$$67 \times 26 \qquad 39 \times 47$$

2

$$7\overline{)4,200} \qquad 8\overline{)5,600}$$

3 During 1 week, 5,598 people booked tours. The tour line has 7 buses. About how many people did each bus carry during the week?

- ⬭ 600
- ⬭ 700
- ⬭ 800
- ⬭ 900

---

4 During 25 days at summer camp, Lisbet swam three times a day. She swam 20 meters each time. How many meters did Lisbet swim during summer camp?

5 Find the average for this group of numbers.
17, 3, 12, 8, 5

---

6 Use **>**, **<** or **=**.

$$4 \quad \Box \quad \frac{12}{3}$$

$$2\frac{4}{5} \quad \Box \quad 2\frac{6}{5}$$

$$5\frac{7}{3} \quad \Box \quad 7\frac{1}{3}$$

7 Weston used his computer's word count on a report he was writing. The computer counted the words in his report and displayed a 9 in the hundreds place, a 2 in the tens place, and a 1 in the thousands place. How many words were in Weston's report?

---

8 How many corners does the figure below have?

_____ corners

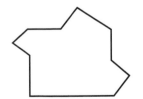

9 Javier saved $72.30 to buy some new compact disks for his CD-ROM. He bought Rocket Race for $21.77 and Pro Ball for $19.85. The tax on the two CDs was $5.75. How much did Javier have after buying the CDs?

_____

---

10 Add or subtract. Write the answer in simplest form.

$$\frac{3}{7} + \frac{1}{7} = \underline{\qquad} \qquad \frac{6}{16} - \frac{2}{16} = \underline{\qquad} \qquad \frac{7}{9} - \frac{5}{9} = \underline{\qquad}$$

Math 4 today

30,000 + 7,000 + 200 + 3 =

- ⬭ 37,230
- ⬭ 372,003
- ⬭ 30,702,003
- ⬭ 37,203

Write **C** if the pair of figures is congruent. Write **S** if the pair is similar.

_____ ▫ ◇

_____ △ ◁

_____ ▱ ▱

Neva bought 3 packages of gum. Each package has twelve pieces. How can Neva share the gum with 8 of her friends so that she and her friends each get the same number of pieces?

```
   15
 x 75
```

```
  6,247
+ 4,788
```

Add or subtract. Simplify.

$\frac{5}{12} + \frac{4}{12} =$ _____

$\frac{8}{13} - \frac{5}{13} =$ _____

$\frac{12}{32} + \frac{12}{32} =$ _____

The **range** of a group of numbers is the difference between the least and the greatest number in the group.

The **median** of a group of numbers is the middle number when the group is arranged from least to greatest. Example:
5, 12, 15, 21, 25
range = 25-5=20; median = 15

For **8, 5, 3, 20, 2**
the range = _____
the median = _____

Janette bought nail polish for $3.89, 2 tubes of lip gloss for $2.49 each and perfume for $9.22. The total after tax was added was $19.54. How much tax did Janette pay on the items she bought?

2, 9, 23, 51, 107

What is the rule for the above pattern?

_____

_____

Some of the largest Earth Filled Dams measured in cubic yards

Tarbela	186,000,000
Oahe	92,000,000
Cornelia	274,026,000
Pati	261,590
Atatürk	110,522

List the names of the dams in order of size from least to greatest. (Show your answers on the back of this sheet.)

Use **>**, **<**, or **=**.

24 inches ☐ 3 feet

9 feet ☐ 3 yards

36 inches ☐ 1 yard

10 feet ☐ 2 yards

Which numeral is read **two hundred seventy-five million, nine hundred thousand, forty-six?**

- ⬭ 275, 900,046
- ⬭ 275,946
- ⬭ 200,759,460

Solve.

$5\overline{)4,525}$

$9\overline{)7,245}$

Margie's Gift Wrapping

Sept. ☐☐☐☐▯
Oct. ☐☐☐
Nov. ☐☐☐☐☐☐▯
Dec. ☐☐☐☐☐☐☐☐▯
each ☐ = 50 gifts wrapped
How many gifts were wrapped in October? _____

How many gifts were wrapped in September? _____

Use the graph to the **left**.

How many gifts were wrapped during all four months? _____
How many more gifts were wrapped in November and December than were wrapped in September?

How many more ☐ would be needed to show 250 gifts wrapped in October? _____

What is 675,789 rounded to the nearest thousand?

- ⬭ 700,000
- ⬭ 676,000
- ⬭ 680,000
- ⬭ 674,000

Shane spent $25.00 on vacation souvenirs. His mother spent $40.00, and his dad spent $30.00. Judy, Shane's sister, spent more than Shane and Dad but less than Mother. Which could be true?

- ⬭ Judy spent $45.00
- ⬭ Judy spent $32.00
- ⬭ Judy spent $29.00

1

$$\begin{array}{r} 69 \\ \times\ 47 \end{array} \qquad \begin{array}{r} 3,987 \\ +\ 4,776 \end{array}$$

2

$$4\overline{)3,624} \qquad 3\overline{)1,512}$$

3

6, 21, 66, 201

What is the rule for the above pattern?

_____

_____

4 Match.
1. three hundred ninety-five million, two hundred six thousand, four hundred one ☐
2. three million, ninety-five thousand, two hundred sixty-one ☐
3. thirty-nine thousand, two hundred sixty-four ☐

A. 395,206,401   B. 39,264   C. 3,095, 261

5 Ron bought 3 boxes of juice drinks for his track team. Each box contains 6 drinks. If Ron and his 8 team members each have the same number of juice drinks, how many will each person receive?

6 Operator Assisted Phone Calls From Hotel Farrington 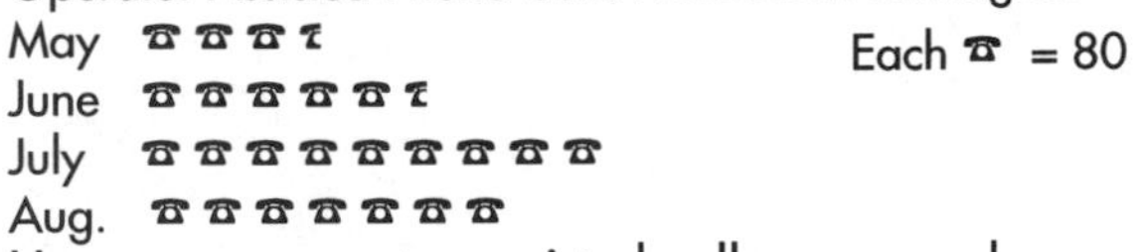
May ☎ ☎ ☎ ☎   Each ☎ = 80
June ☎ ☎ ☎ ☎ ☎ ☎
July ☎ ☎ ☎ ☎ ☎ ☎ ☎ ☎
Aug. ☎ ☎ ☎ ☎ ☎ ☎
How many operator assisted calls were made
in June?_____in August? _____
in May _____
How many more calls were made in August than
in May?_____
In all, how many calls were made? _____

7 Emil earned $57.00 doing odd jobs. Mark earned more than Emil, but less than Jake. Jake earned $72.00. Which could be true?

◯ **Mark earned $55.00**
◯ **Mark earned $75.00**
◯ **Mark earned $67.00**

8 Use **>**, **<**, or **=**.

36 inches	☐	2 feet
3 yards	☐	9 feet
24 inches	☐	1 foot
1 yard	☐	24 inches

9

$60,000 + 3,000 + 500 + 4 =$

_____

$500,000 + 80,000 + 2,000 + 1 =$

_____

$20,000 + 300 + 90 + 7 =$

_____

10 What is 782,432 rounded to the nearest thousand?

◯ **780,000**
◯ **790,000**
◯ **781,400**
◯ **782,000**

What is 816,710 rounded to the nearest thousand?

◯ **810,000**
◯ **817,000**
◯ **822,400**
◯ **825,000**

500,000 + 30,000 + 400 + 20 + 7 =

○ 530,427

○ 500,003,427

○ 53,427

○ 534,270

Write **C** if the pair of figures is congruent. Write **S** if the pair is similar.

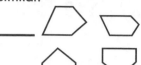

Mrs. Barker picked 22 red flowers, 40 yellow flowers, 58 miniature daisies, and 24 white flower buds from her garden. She places the same number of plants in each of 4 baskets. How many plants are in each basket?

315
x 7

7,938
+ 2,677

Add or subtract the fractions. Simplify.

$9\frac{5}{7} - 4\frac{4}{7} =$ _____

$3\frac{1}{12} + 7\frac{5}{12} =$ _____

$16\frac{8}{24} - 5\frac{5}{24} =$ _____

Find the median, range, and average for

13, 57, 23, 42, 15

median = _____

range = _____

average = _____

What time will the clock show in 2 hours and 25 minutes?

_____

| 1,1 | 2,4 | 3,9 |
| 4,16 | 5,25 | |

What would the 8th box look like?

Some Famous Volcanoes Height in Feet

Aconcagua	22,831
Lassen	10,457
Mauna Loa	13,677
Cotopaxi	19,347
Mt. Etna	11,122

List the names of the volcanoes in order of height from greatest to least. (Show your answers on the back of this sheet.)

The temperature on this thermometer shows about

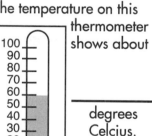

_____ degrees Celcius.

Which numeral is read: **three million, nine hundred sixty-two thousand, four hundred twenty-one**

○ 396, 241

○ 3,962,421

○ 300,962,421

8,247
- 5,872

5,104
- 2,652

Average Temperature

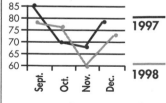

In 1997, the month of _____ had about the same temperature as the month of _____ in 1998.

| 2 | 12 | 5 | 7 |
| 9 | 11 | 3 | 6 |

If 3 bean bags were tossed onto the above board so that no number was repeated, what could be a possible score?

○ 50
○ 8
○ 32
○ 100

Round these numerals to the nearest ten thousand.

775,320 _____

621,990 _____

482,589 _____

907,125 _____

Using only the above beads, what is a possible arrangement?

○

○

○

1

$$209 \times 8 \qquad 8{,}356 + 3{,}784$$

2

$$6{,}159 - 4{,}882$$

3 Round these numerals to the nearest ten thousand.

884,298 _____

466,132 _____

525,017 _____

4 Andy bought 55 gum drops, 82 peppermints, 50 sour balls, and 35 lemon drops to fill six candy jars for the nursing home. How many pieces of candy will he put in each jar?

5 Find the median, range, and average for this group of numbers:

13, 12, 5, 26, 11, 8, 9

median _____

range _____

average _____

6 List the months in order from greatest to least amount of water used for lawn care.

Gallons of Water Used for Lawn Care in Reskin, Illinois	
May	89,129
June	92,456
July	89,752
August	92,488

_____

_____

_____

_____

7

$$900{,}000 + 80{,}000 + 2{,}000 + 400 + 80 =$$

_____

$$70{,}000 + 1{,}000 + 50 + 1 =$$

_____

$$200{,}000 + 3{,}000 + 600 + 70 + 8 =$$

_____

8 Write **C** if the pair of figures is congruent. Write **S** if the pair is similar.

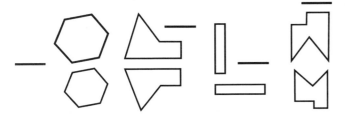

9 What time will the clock show in 2 hours and 35 minutes?

10

Alan ———

Martin ———

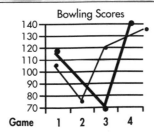

Bowling Scores

During which game did Alan and Martin score about the same? Game _____

During which game was the difference in their scores the greatest? Game _____

Write in expanded form:
43,209

_____

_____

_____

_____

Label: **S** = slide;   **F**=flip

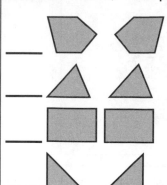

____

____

____

____

____

Angie had 408 stickers on 8 pages of her sticker album. If each page has the same number of stickers, which equation could be used to show the number of stickers on each page?

○ 408 + 8 = 416
○ 408 - 8 = 400
○ 408 x 8 = 3,264
○ 408 ÷ 8 = 51

942
x 8

9,527
+ 4,658

Simplify.

$3 \frac{16}{12} = $ _____

$9 \frac{24}{8} = $ _____

$7 \frac{32}{6} = $ _____

Find the median, range, and average for

2, 16, 32, 15, 3, 9, 7

median = _____

range = _____

average = _____

Tristan arrives at school at 8:15. He has 4 hours and 20 minutes of classes until lunch time. At what time does Tristan eat lunch?

_____

1,4	2, 5	3, 6

4, 7	5, 8

What would the 21st box look like?

Which group of numbers is in order from greatest to least?

○ 7,234; 7,432; 7,243

○ 8,021; 8,012; 8,003

○ 5,921; 5,812; 5,993

○ 2,005; 2,415; 2,501

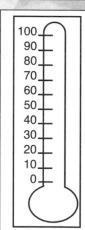

Shade in this thermometer to show about 75 degrees Celcius.

---

300 305 310 315 320

This number line shows:

○ multiples of 5 between 305 and 345

○ multiples of 10 between 300 and 330

○ multiples of 5 between 295 and 325

5,040
- 3,217

9,200
- 7,643

Money earned doing odd jobs

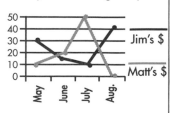

Jim's $

Matt's $

During which month did Jim and Matt earn about the same amount of money? _____

If 3 darts burst three of the above balloons, what could be a possible score?

○ **50**
○ **45**
○ **15**
○ **38**

A reasonable estimate of the number of hours a fourth grade student might spend doing homework during the week would be about:

○ **100 hours**
○ **45 hours**
○ **5 hours**
○ **1 hour**

Mighty Marvels Video Game

PLAYER	SCORE
Jason	2,450
Roger	3,100
Alex	4,200

The answer is 1,750. Using the chart, write a question for this answer.

1

934   6,107
x 7   + 7,999

2

8,020
- 2,731

3

| 10,9 | 20, 19 |
| 30, 29 | 40, 39 |

What would the 12th box look like?

4

196 200 204 208 212 216 220 224 228

This number line shows:

○ multiples of 2 between 194 and 230

○ multiples of 4 between 192 and 232

○ multiples of 5 between 195 and 230

5 Kyle has 105 models on 5 shelves. If each shelf has the same number of models, which equation could be used to find the number of models on each shelf?

○ 105 ÷ 5= 21   ○ 105 x 5 = 525

○ 105 - 5 = 100   ○ 105 + 5 = 110

6 Pages read by Kay and Gina

Kay = _____
Gina = _____

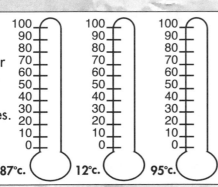

On which day was the difference in pages read the greatest? _____

the least? _____

On which day did both girls read more than 35 pages?

_____

7 Summer school classes begin at 8:45 and last for 4 and a half hours. At what time do summer school classes end?

8 Shade in each thermometer to show the given temperatures.

87°c.   12°c.   95°c.

9 Write the expanded forms.

27,170 _____

_____

50,936 _____

_____

10 A reasonable estimate of the number of hours a student might spend watching television during the school week would be about:

○ 1 hour

○ 10 hours

○ 100 hours

○ 1,000 hours

Math 4 today

Name_____

33

Write in expanded form:
390,682

_____

_____

_____

_____

_____

Label: **S** = slide; **F** = flip

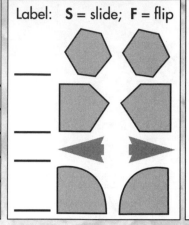

___

___

___

Luis is reading a novel for a book report due on Friday. His novel has 150 pages. He read 27 pages on Monday, 42 pages on Tuesday, and 59 pages on Wednesday. How many more pages must he read to finish the book?

$$42 \times 20$$

$$93 \times 30$$

Add or Subtract. Simplify.

$2\frac{1}{3} + 8\frac{2}{3} =$ _____

$4\frac{3}{12} + 7\frac{10}{12} =$ _____

$9\frac{1}{4} + 5\frac{3}{4} =$ _____

Bowling League Finals

Team	Points Scored
A	767
B	906
C	760
D	851
E	593

Which teams scored an odd number of points?

_____

Sheila saw these ads in the newspaper.

Maxi's Essentials	Sav-Co
💡 ✂	☎ 💡
$19.95 $2.98	$21.98 $15.25
☎	✂
$25.00	$2.50

How much money can Sheila save by buying the three items at Sav-Co?

		35	42
49	56	63	

What numbers go in the three empty boxes?

_____

_____

_____

Which group of numbers is in order from least to greatest?

◯ 6,434; 6,532; 6,943

◯ 5,021; 5,012; 5,003

◯ 9,921; 8,812; 8,983

◯ 1,005; 1,015; 1,001

The keys weigh:

grams

◯ 1 gram

◯ more than 1 gram

◯ less than 1 gram

◯ 100 grams

This number line shows:

0 6 12 18 24 30 36

◯ 24 - 6 = 18

◯ 24 ÷ 2 = 12

◯ 4 x 6 = 24

◯ 6 + 6 + 6 + 6 = 24

$$9{,}010 - 8{,}736$$

$$6\overline{)636}$$

Bicycle Color Choices

RED
BLUE
PINK
BLACK

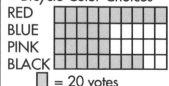

☐ = 20 votes

Circle the true statements.
1. The number of people who chose red was twice the number who chose blue.
2. Blue received the least number of votes.

(Use the graph to the **left**)
3. Pink received 60 votes.
4. Black received 20 less votes than red.
5. Blue received 100 votes.
6. The difference between the number of votes received by black and blue is 60.
7. The number of votes received by pink is one half those received by black.

If you use one sheet of notebook paper for each of four different subjects everyday, about how many sheets of notebook paper will you use in two weeks?

◯ 200 sheets

◯ 100 sheets

◯ 50 sheets

◯ 5 sheets

Greg ate 3 slices of pizza. Joey ate 3 times as many as Greg, but 4 less than Mark. Mario ate two more slices than Greg. On the back, write a question for each answer given below:

1.) 5 slices

2.) 13 slices

3.) 30 slices

Math 4 today

Name _____ **Test #33**

1

$$64 \times 20 \qquad 4,070 - 2,398$$

2

$$8\overline{)648}$$

---

3 Billy reads an average of 7 pages a night during the **school week.** About how many pages will he read in 3 weeks?

- ◯ 35
- ◯ 50
- ◯ 100
- ◯ 135

---

4 Jay's baseball team set a goal of getting 5 more runs this season than in the last 3 seasons combined. In 1996, the team had 23 runs, in 1997 the team had 19 runs, and in 1998, they had 14 runs. So far this year, they have 17 runs. How many more runs does Jay's team need in order to meet their goal?

---

5 Number of Babysitting Jobs Last Year

Milly	72
Jean	24
Susan	63
Andrea	41
Carla	58

Which girls had an even number of babysitting jobs last year?

_____

_____

---

6 Which group of numbers is in order from least to greatest?

- ◯ 7,892; 7,880; 7,782
- ◯ 5,208; 5,590; 5,579
- ◯ 6,890; 6,895; 6,080
- ◯ 3,207; 3,227; 3,303

---

7 Write the expanded forms.

801,267 _____

_____

420,198 _____

_____

---

8 Label: **S** = slide   **F** = flip

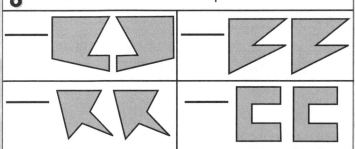

---

9 Mrs. Amyx usually buys burgers at Dot's Drive In, but this week Busy B's is having a sale. How much will Mrs. Amyx save by buying 4 burgers, 4 fries, and 4 frosties at Busy B's?

Dot's Drive In	
4 burgers	$14.45
4 fries	$ 8.75
4 frosties	$ 8.80

Busy B's	
4 burgers	$12.25
4 fries	$ 7.50
4 frosties	$ 8.00

How much will Mrs. Amyx save by buying 4 burgers, 4 fries, and 4 frosties at Busy B's?

---

10 Add or Subtract. Simplify the fractions

$$15\tfrac{3}{7} - 7\tfrac{5}{7} = \underline{\quad} \qquad 6\tfrac{9}{18} + 8\tfrac{11}{18} = \underline{\quad} \qquad 5\tfrac{5}{20} + 9\tfrac{15}{20} = \underline{\quad}$$

Which numeral shows
7 hundred thousands,
12 ten thousands,
4 hundreds, 2 tens?

◯ **701,242**

◯ **712,042**

◯ **820,420**

◯ **802,452**

Name the vertex of each angle.

B   A
C

_____

L   N
M

_____

X
Y   Z

_____

Before dieting, Debra weighed 132 pounds. She lost an average of 2 pounds a month last year. Which equation shows how to find Debra's current weight?

◯   132 - 2 = 130

◯   132 - (2 x 12) = 108

◯   132 ÷ (2 x 6) = 11

267
x 300

578
x 600

Write the fraction and the decimal shown by each model.

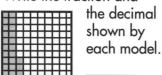

_____

_____

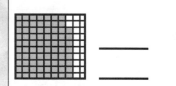

_____

_____

Which numeral could be a remainder when dividing by 6?

◯   4

◯   7

◯   9

when dividing by 10?

◯   15

◯   25

◯   8

FOOD TOWN
1 pound coffee	$ 3.50
2 pound bag sugar	$ 2.00
10 pack paper plates	$ 2.25

MINI MARKET
2 pounds coffee	$ 7.50
3 pound bag sugar	$ 2.50
5 pack paper plates	$ 1.00

Ms. Wan needs 2 pounds of coffee, 6 pounds of sugar, and 20 paper plates. Which store will save her money on these items?

			57
63	69	75	81

What numbers go in the three empty boxes?

_____

_____

_____

Dictionary	Number of Entry Words
Meridim's	467,897
Collegiate	674,987
Duke Press	460,809
Gorktles	669,989

List the dictionaries in order from the least number of entry words to the greatest number.

_____

_____

_____

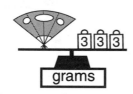
grams

The paper fan weighs:

◯   3 grams

◯   more than 9 grams

◯   less than 9 grams

◯   9 grams

Write the number word for:

45, 206 _____

_____

_____

631, 520 _____

_____

2,000
-1,218

4)929

Garden	Flowers Blooming
Mrs. Willis	24
Ms. Jones	36
Mr. Bates	44
Miss Sax	52

Draw a picture graph on the back to show the chart data above.
Each ✿ = 8

Mystery Numbers

A = C ÷ 7
B = a multiple of 5 less than 20
C = B + 6
D = A x C

A =_____ B =_____

C =_____ D =_____

Round each number to the nearest 10.

467,125 _____

235,942 _____

551,932 _____

348,701 _____

Box A   [◆ ☐ ■]
Box B   [◆ ◆ ◆ ☐ ☐ ■]

The chances of drawing a ◆ are:

◯ Equal between box A and B

◯ 3 times greater with box B

◯ 2 times greater with box B

Name _____

Test # 34

1

$$398 \times 600$$

$$5{,}000 - 4{,}231$$

2

$$5\overline{)288}$$

3

			65
74	83	92	101

What numbers go in the three empty boxes?

_____ _____ _____

4 Write the number word for:

503,291 _____

_____

48,603 _____

_____

5 Eight months ago Tad weighed 98 pounds. He has gained an average of 3 pounds a month. Which equation could be used to find Tad's current weight?

◯ 98 - 8=   ◯ 98 - (3 x 8)=

◯ 98 x 3 =   ◯ 98 + (3 x 8) =

6 Snow Cones Sold   💡 = 6

Blueberry Ice   33   Coconut Freeze   27
Mocha Cream   18   Cherry Blizzard   42

Shade the graph to match the chart data.

Blueberry Ice   🍦🍦🍦🍦🍦🍦🍦

Coconut Freeze 🍦🍦🍦🍦🍦🍦🍦

Mocha Cream   🍦🍦🍦🍦🍦🍦🍦

Cherry Blizzard 🍦🍦🍦🍦🍦🍦🍦

7

Apple School Supply	
10 pencils	$5.00
Notebook	$12.50
Writing Tablets	
	3 for $3.75

ABC School Supply	
5 pencils	$2.00
2 Notebook	$26.00
Writing Tablets	
	2 for $3.50

Raul needs to buy 10 pencils, 2 notebooks, and 6 writing tablets for school. Which store will save him the most money on these items?

8

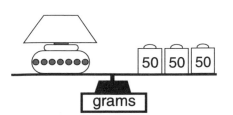

The plastic lamp weighs about _____ grams.

9 Which numeral shows 9 hundred thousands, 25 ten thousands, 7 tens?

◯ 1,150,070

◯ 900,250, 070

◯ 9, 257

◯ 902,507

10 Round each number to the nearest 100,000.

872,559 _____   430,925 _____   289,601 _____

© Good Apple GA1659 Reproducible

Which numeral shows 2 million, 17 hundred thousands, 8 ten thousands, 4 tens, 3 ones? ⬭ **3,780,043** ⬭ **2,170,843** ⬭ **3,878,403** ⬭ **2,170,800,443**	How many vertices are in the figures below? _____ _____ 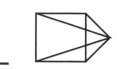	Luigi sold a total of 1,321 raffle tickets in three weeks. He sold 467 tickets the first week and 299 tickets the second week. How many tickets did Luigi sell in the third week?	**52** **x 33** **28** **x 56**
Write the fraction and the decimal shown by each model. 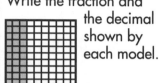 _____ _____  _____ _____	Which numeral could be a remainder when dividing by 9? ⬭ 12 ⬭ 7 ⬭ 9 when dividing by 3? ⬭ 10 ⬭ 5 ⬭ 1	Floyd and Kyle have 17 Super NES video games, 13 Nintendo video games, and 20 Sega video games. If they played each game for thirty minutes, could they play all the games in one day? _____	○ ○ ✳ ✳ ✳ ✗ ✗ ★ ✔ ★ ✔ ○ ○ ✳ Which series below would continue the pattern? _____ 1. ✳ ✳ ✳ ✗ ★ ✔ 2. ✗ ✗ ★ ✔ ★ ✔ 3. ✳ ✳ ✗ ✗ ★ ✔
Write the numeral that is 100 more than: 234, 967 _____ 529, 920 _____ 862, 425 _____ 999, 901 _____	1 cup = 8 ounces 1 pint = 2 cups 1 quart = 2 pints 1 gallon = 4 quarts 3 gallons = _____ quarts 5 pints = _____ cups 8 quarts = _____ pints 1 quart = _____ ounces	Write the number word for: 2,450, 137 _____ _____ 5,320, 664 _____ _____	6)727 4)838
RED = 36 GREEN = 48 BLUE = 24 BLACK = 12 To correctly color the pie graph so that it matches the above data, each section must stand for the same number. Determine **that** number, then color the graph. Each part =_____	Mystery Numbers A = 18 - (D x D) B = C ÷ 4 C = D + A D = the remainder of 47÷9 A =_____ B =_____ C =_____ D =_____	On Tuesday, Jet Air sold 45,951 airline tickets. Concourse Flights sold 31,764 tickets, and Miami Intrastate sold 18,752 tickets. What is the best estimate of the number of tickets sold by all 3 airlines? ⬭ **100,000 tickets** ⬭ **125,000 tickets** ⬭ **150,000 tickets**	Box A L L B B B Box B L L L L B The chances of drawing an L are: ⬭ Equal between box A and B ⬭ Less with box B ⬭ 2 times greater with box B

Math 4 today

1

$$98 \times 52 \qquad 44 \times 61$$

2

$$9 \overline{)748}$$

3 CompuCom made 55,210 computer chips in March, 71,560 chips in April and 66,102 chips in May. What is the best estimate of the number of computer chips made in all three months?

- ◯ 250,000
- ◯ 200,000
- ◯ 150,000
- ◯ 100,000

4 Megan's Girl Scout troop collected 1,072 pounds of aluminum cans last summer. In June, they collected 397 pounds and in July they collected 289 pounds. How many pounds of aluminum cans did they collect in August?

5 Which numeral could be a remainder when dividing by 4?

- ◯ 7   ◯ 2
- ◯ 8   ◯ 10

when dividing by 8?

- ◯ 7   ◯ 16
- ◯ 9   ◯ 10

6 Write the numeral that is 100 less than:

782,945 _____

541,099 _____

610,056 _____

7 Which numeral shows 6 million, 29 hundred thousands, 6 ten thousands, 1 ten, 5 ones?

- ◯ 6,296,150
- ◯ 8,960,015
- ◯ 6, 290,615
- ◯ 82,900,105

8 How many vertices are in the space figures below?

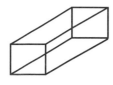   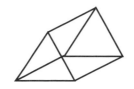

_____   _____

9 Elliot has a playoff game on Saturday at 4:00. This week, he has offered to do 3 chores for his grandmother, 5 chores for his mom, and 2 chores for his dad. Each chore takes about thirty minutes. Will he have time to do all the chores and still make it to the game on time if he gets up at 10:00?

10 Write the fraction and the decimal for each model.

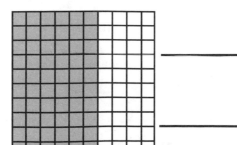   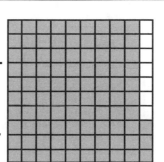

© Good Apple GA1659 Reproducible

Math today

Name _____

#36

Which numeral has a larger digit in the hundreds place than in the ten thousands place?

◯ 3,928,743

◯ 5,190,812

◯ 6,278,421

◯ 2,593,928

A square has 4 lines of symmetry.

How many lines of symmetry does a hexagon have?

_____

Kalyn is baking 7 batches of cookies for the church social. Each batch uses the same amount of sugar. If she uses a total of 28 cups of sugar, which equation would tell the cups of sugar needed for each batch?

◯ 7 x 28 = ❑

◯ 28 ÷ 7 = ❑

◯ 28 + 7 = ❑

◯ 28 - 7 = ❑

Solve.

```
  8,679
  4,527
+ 6,382
```

```
  622
x  52
```

Write the decimal shown by each model.

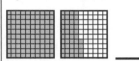 _____

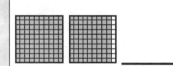 _____

Which equation below best expresses the quotient for a number fact that equals 5?

◯ 1 + 4 = 5

◯ 25 - 20 = 5

◯ 5 x 1 = 5

◯ 25 ÷ 5 = 5

Mrs. Ganzer spends an hour doing laundry, 45 minutes vacuuming, a half hour dusting, and 25 minutes mopping when she cleans house. How long does it take her to complete her housework?

... ✄ ✿ ✦ ✦ ✌ ✦ ✪
✿ ★ ✦ ✄ ✌ ✦ ✌
✌ ✌ ✪ ✌ ...
Which series continues the pattern? _____

1. ✄ ✿ ✌ ✪ ★ ✄
2. ★ ✌ ✄ ✪ ✿ ✪
3. ✄ ★ ★ ✿ ✦ ✌

(Can you draw the series that begins this pattern?)

Continue counting.

739,995
739,996
739,997

_____

_____

_____

_____

Find the volume for each solid figure below:

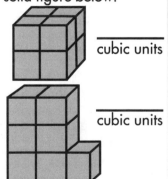

_____ cubic units

_____ cubic units

```
◄──┬───┬───★───┬───►
  12  13      14  15
```

The star best represents what number?

◯ 12.5

◯ 12.7

◯ 13.5

◯ 13.7

Solve.

8)‾6‾0‾0‾

6)‾3‾9‾0‾

Orange = 40 **Green** = 24
White = 16 **Purple** = 48
To correctly color the pie graph so that it matches the above data, each section must stand for the same number. Determine <u>that</u> number, then color the graph. Each part = _____

Tam's age is an even number less than 14. He is one half his sister's age. His sister's age is a number between 16 and 24.

How old is Tam? _____

How old is his sister?

_____

Casey's bead art set has 372 beads for each of 12 colors. She saw 23 more sets like hers in the craft store. Which is the best estimate for the number of beads in all the art sets?

◯ 80,000

◯ 70,000

◯ 60,000

◯ 50,000

1	5	9	1	5

If these cards are shuffled and placed face down, the chances of drawing a 1 are

_____ to the chances of drawing a 5, and _____ times greater than the chances of drawing a 9.

80

Math 4 today

Name _____

Test # 36

1

```
  345        4,254
x  47        9,897
           + 6,579
```

2

4⟌300

3

☑ ✗ ✗ ✗ ▲

▲ ▲ ○   If these cards
are shuffled and placed face
down, the chances of
drawing a ✗ are _____
to the chances of drawing a
▲ and _____ times
greater than drawing a ✓.

4

```
◄━┼━┼━┼━┼━┼━┼━┼━┼━┼━►
  8   9   10  11  12  13
```
A is positioned between 11 and 12

The letter **A** best represents what number?

- ◯ 11.9
- ◯ 10.5
- ◯ 11.5
- ◯ 10.7

5

Wayne is boxing fireworks for sale at his uncle's stand. Each box contains the same number. So far he has boxed 210 fireworks in 7 boxes. Which equation would tell how many fireworks are in each box?

- ◯ 210 + 7= ❑
- ◯ 210 - 7= ❑
- ◯ 210 x 7= ❑
- ◯ 210 ÷ 7= ❑

6

Artworks exhibited at the Children's Art Fairs
1995 = 25   color white
1996 = 20   color green
1997 = 40   color blue
1998 = 35   color red
Color the pie graph to match the above data by determining the value of each section.
Each part = _____

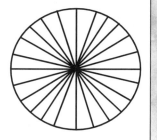

7

Mindy and her friends went to the county fair. They spent 1 hour and twenty minutes riding the rides. They played games at the booths for 45 minutes, visited the exhibits for a half hour, then went into the Fun House for fifteen minutes before going home. How long did Mindy and her friends stay at the fair?

8

Find the volume for the solid figures below.

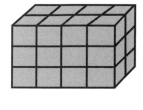

_____ cubic units   _____ cubic units

9

Which numeral has a lesser digit in the hundred thousands place than in the tens place?

- ◯ 5,836,170
- ◯ 8,208,957
- ◯ 6, 530,659
- ◯ 2,970,885

10

At the candy factory, the workers pack 47 chocolate delights in each box. They can pack about 53 boxes each hour. What is the best estimate of the number of chocolate delights packed in 8 hours?

- ◯ 20,000
- ◯ 21,000
- ◯ 22,000
- ◯ 23,000

Which numeral has a lesser digit in the thousands place than in the ten millions place?

⬭ 347,928,743

⬭ 562,147,812

⬭ 620,213,401

⬭ 754,563,928

A square has 4 lines of symmetry.

How many lines of symmetry does a pentagon have?

_____

What is the difference in length between a hiking trail 20,402 meters long and a trail 13,857 meters long?

Solve.

$$321 \times 52$$

$$12\frac{15}{30}$$

$$+ 6\frac{25}{30}$$

Add the decimals shown by each model.

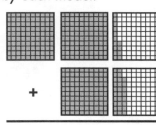

+

= _____

Tony's math grades are:

85, 92, 95, 81, 92

What is his average in math?

How can you make $1.27 using a minimal collection of these coins?

_____ nickels
_____ dimes
_____ pennies
using a minimal collection of these coins?

_____ quarters
_____ pennies

Shade in the next two squares to continue the pattern.

Continue counting.

995,985
995,990
995,995

_____
_____
_____
_____
_____
_____

Find the volume for each solid figure below:

_____ cubic units

_____ cubic units

The star best represents what number?

⬭ 13.25

⬭ 13.50

⬭ 13.75

⬭ 14.10

Solve.

$$50\overline{)4500}$$

$$25\frac{2}{12}$$

$$- 14\frac{10}{12}$$

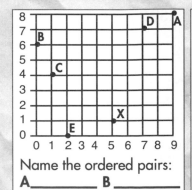

Name the ordered pairs:

A_____ B_____
C_____ D_____
E_____ X_____

The area of the dining table is an even number. The desk is a square. The coffee table's length is three times its width. The end table's area is one half of one of the other tables. Match the area to each table.

6 sq. ft. _____
20 sq. ft. _____
12 sq. ft. _____
16 sq. ft. _____

3,452,835 rounded to the nearest …

10 = _____

1,000 = _____

100,000 = _____

1,000,000 = _____

Subtract. Simplify the answer.

$$11\frac{3}{9} - \frac{4}{9} = \underline{\hspace{1cm}}$$

$$\frac{21}{5} - \frac{6}{5} = \underline{\hspace{1cm}}$$

$$17\frac{3}{24} - 8\frac{5}{24} = \underline{\hspace{1cm}}$$

1

$$\begin{array}{r} 345 \\ \times\ 32 \end{array}$$ $40\overline{)2800}$

2 Subtract and simplify.

$12\frac{3}{14} - 7\frac{10}{14} =$ _____

$\frac{24}{8} - \frac{20}{8} =$ _____

3 6,251,481 rounded to the nearest...

100 = _____

10,000 = _____

100,000 = _____

4 What is the difference in length between a highway 147,895 meters long and a highway 601,234 meters long?

5 What is Ray's average score in bowling?

Ray's Bowling Scores	
Game	Points Per Game
1	102
2	98
3	129
4	201
5	80

6 Continue counting.

895,680
895,780
895,880
895,980

_____
_____
_____
_____
_____
_____

7 Which numeral has a digit of greater value in the hundred thousands place than in the ten millions place?

⬯ 875,836,170
⬯ 861,508,957
⬯ 651,530,659
⬯ 280,190,885

8 How many lines of symmetry for each figure? Draw in the lines of symmetry.

____   ____   ____

9 How can you make $2.38 using a minimal collection of these coins?
quarters_____ nickles_____
pennies_____

using a minimal collection of these coins?

half-dollars_____ quarters_____
dimes _____ pennies _____

10

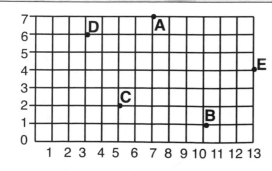

Name the ordered pairs.

A = _____   B = _____

C = _____   D = _____

E = _____

Name_____

In 1978, the most expensive coin was a $20.00 gold piece. Hal read that the gold piece sold for an approximate dollar amount that had an 8 in the tens place, a 4 in the thousands place, a 5 in the ones place, a 3 in the hundred thousands place. What was the price of the coin?

$_____.00

Label the lines;
I = intersecting
PA = parallel
P=perpendicular

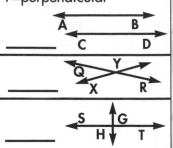

_____

_____

_____

The greatest oil gusher was at Spindletop, Texas in 1901. It yielded about 810,459 barrels of oil in 9 days. About how many barrels of oil did this oil gusher produce each day?

$$605 \times 85$$

$$20\overline{)453}$$

Subtract the decimals shown by each model.

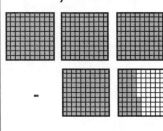

-

= _____

Circle the common factors for each number pair.

4, 16
2, 4, 8, 10, 16 , 20,

10, 20
2, 3, 4, 5 , 10, 20,

18, 36
2, 3, 4, 6, 9, 12 , 18,

Oscar earns $5.25 per hour working part time at the grocery store. Last week he worked 4 hours a day for 6 days. How much did Oscar earn last week?

---

9 , 11, 15, 23, 39, 71
What is the rule for the above pattern?
(hint: use 2 operations)

_____

_____

Japanese Cities Populations 1977	
Tokyo	8,112,000
Osaka	3,276,000
Yokohama	2,601,000
Sapporo	2,162,000
Nagoya	1,719,000

List the cities in order from least to greatest populations.

_____

_____

_____

Using the lines of symmetry, find the perimeter of this hexagon.

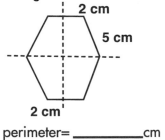

2 cm

5 cm

2 cm

perimeter=_____cm

The continent of Asia has a land mass of forty-three million, nine hundred seventy-five thousand square kilometers. This number is written as:

◯ **43,975,000**
◯ **430,975**
◯ **439,750,000**
◯ **43,975**

$$4.37 \quad\quad 9.82$$
$$6.22 \quad\quad 3.41$$
$$+ 4.50 \quad\quad + 7.25$$

$$9.82 \quad\quad 8.12$$
$$- 3.25 \quad\quad - 6.78$$

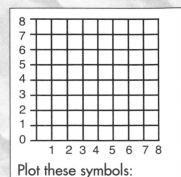

Plot these symbols:
✖ = (8,7)   ◆ = (0,2)
▲ = (4,6)   ■ = (5,1)

Popeye Pig ate over 100 peanuts which was twice as many peanuts as Pinky Pig ate. Pinky ate a number of peanuts that was divisible by 7. Petunia Pig ate 11 more peanuts than Pinky. The number she ate was an odd number between 60 and 70. How many peanuts did each pig eat?

Popeye _____
Pinky_____
Petunia _____

The world's largest park is the Wood Buffalo Park in Canada. It is 19,362 times larger than the world's oldest park in London which covers 577 acres. Which equation best estimates the size of the Canadian park?

◯ **21,400 x 700**
◯ **20,000 x 500**
◯ **19,000 x 600**
◯ **20,000 x 400**

$$9\frac{19}{42} + 17\frac{25}{42} = \underline{\quad}$$

$$52\frac{12}{30} - 25\frac{22}{30} = \underline{\quad}$$

$$31\frac{1}{15} - 18\frac{9}{15} = \underline{\quad}$$

1

$$\begin{array}{r} 403 \\ \times\ 75 \\ \hline \end{array}$$

$60\overline{)385}$

2

$$\begin{array}{r} 3.05 \\ 2.61 \\ +\ 9.85 \\ \hline \end{array}$$

$$\begin{array}{r} 12.21 \\ -\ 9.85 \\ \hline \end{array}$$

3 4, 17, 56, 173, 524
What is the rule for the pattern?
(hint: use 2 operations)

4 In square miles, the country of India has an area of one million, two hundred twenty-nine thousand, seven hundred thirty-seven.
This number is written:

◯ 12,297,037
◯ 1,229,737
◯ 122,973,007

5 During one week in August, the Icy Freeze Shop used 140,210 ice cubes to make snow cones. If the Icy Freeze Shop used the same number of ice cubes each day, how many ice cubes were used daily?

6 Plot the symbols.

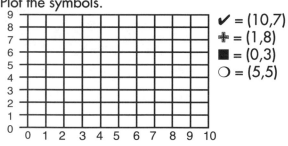

✔ = (10,7)
✚ = (1,8)
■ = (0,3)
◯ = (5,5)

7 Evan spent $9.48 a week to rent videos. How much did he spend in 8 weeks?

8 Using the lines of symmetry, find the perimeter of this figure.

perimeter =

_____ mm

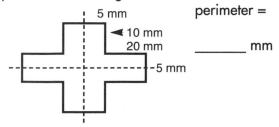

5 mm
◀ 10 mm
20 mm
5 mm

9 Scott was looking at a warehouse catalog for ordering music cassette tapes, compact disks, and albums. The number of items available through the catalog had a 7 in the ten thousands place, a 5 in the hundreds place, a 9 in the hundred thousands place, and a 6 in the ones place. How many items were in the catalog?

_____

10 In the 1890's, railroad passenger travel was estimated to be about 11,848,000 passenger miles. In 1974, the number of passenger miles was 67 times that amount. Which equation best estimates the number of passenger miles traveled in 1974?

◯ 1,890 x 11,000 million
◯ 60 x 11,000 million
◯ 70 x 12,000 million
◯ 60 x 10,000 million

Name _____

Susan read that one of the longest toy balloon flights achieved a record length in miles. The balloon traveled an approximate distance that had an 1 in the hundreds place, a 5 in the tens place, a 9 in the thousands place and a 7 in the hundredths place and a 5 in the tenths place. How far did the balloon travel?

_____ miles

Number each plane figure.
1. a pentagon with 2 right angles
2. a quadrilateral with 1 right angle
3. an equilateral triangle
4. a right triangle

One of the largest living trees, the General Sherman tree is a sequoia tree in California. It is about 272.3 feet tall. The tallest redwood tree is about 367.8 feet tall. What is the difference in height between the two trees?

Solve.

$$923 \times 381$$

$$50 \overline{)1532}$$

Solve.

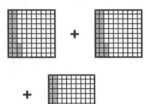

= 3 x .23 = _____

What is the greatest common factor for:

12 and 16 _____

20 and 30 _____

36 and 45 _____

How many?

8 hours = _____ minutes

3 days = _____ hours

1 hour = _____ seconds
one quarter hour = _____ minutes

1 year = _____ hours

Create your own pattern.

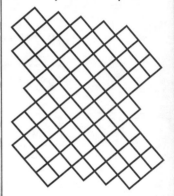

Write the decimals in order from least to greatest.

3.45   3.5   3.82
3.02   3.1   3.67

_____   _____

_____   _____

_____   _____

Use the grid to enlarge the top figure 2 times its size.

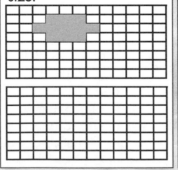

In 1970, a car, "The Blue Flame" achieved an average speed of six hundred twenty-seven and twenty-nine hundredths miles per hour. This number is written:

○ 62,729.0029
○ 627.29
○ 627.029

$$\begin{array}{r} 34.97 \\ 16.2 \\ + 54.03 \end{array}$$

$$\begin{array}{r} 30.02 \\ - 16.18 \end{array}$$

$$\begin{array}{r} 42.12 \\ - 29.9 \end{array}$$

$$\begin{array}{r} 19.02 \\ 73.69 \\ 13.5 \end{array}$$

Number of Girls & Boys Enrolled at Burns Elementary School

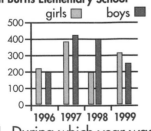

girls ▢   boys ▪

1. During which year was the enrollment for the girls and boys about the same?

Use the graph at the **left**.

2. In which years was the enrollment less for the girls than the boys?

_____   _____

3. In which year was the enrollment for the boys about 390? _____

4. In which years was the enrollment for the girls about 200?

_____   _____

Adrian has 4 collections, rocks, shells, stamps, and marbles. Each collection has between 20 and 50 items. What is a reasonable total for all the items in his collections?

○ 75
○ 520
○ 150

In a meter race, Alan ran 3 times as far as Cathy. Cathy ran one-half as far as David. David's total meters run was a multiple of 7 less than 50. Becky ran 21 times less than the number of meters run by Alan. How many meters did each child run?

Alan _____

Becky _____

Cathy _____

David _____

1

726
x 438

80)5,625

2

71.90
36.7
+ 19.09

31.04
- 17.18

3 Emil played hoops 5 times. Each time he made between 10 and 40 baskets. What is a reasonable total for the baskets made by Emil?

○ 205   ○ 185
○ 50   ○ 20

4 In 1965, an American aviator flew his plane at speeds of about 3331.5 kilometers per hour. In 1962, a Russian aviator flew his plane at about 2,680. 99 kilometers per hour. What is the difference in speed between the two flights?

_____ kph

5 Circle the common factors for the pairs of numerals.

10, 15   2, 5, 3,

24, 40   2, 3, 5, 6, 8, 10

6 Write the decimals in order from greatest to least.

7.28; 7.02; 7.82; 7.08; 7.8; 8.1

_____ _____ _____

_____ _____ _____

7 Manuel was reading that one of the tallest structures in the world was a radio tower in Poland. The tower's height in feet had a 1 in the hundreds place, a 2 in the tens place, a 2 in the thousands place and a eight in the tenths place. Write the height of the building.

8 Number each plane figure:
1. a pentagon with 2 right angles
2. a quadrilateral with 2 right angles
3. a right triangle

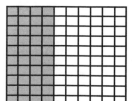

____   ____   ____

9 How many?

6 hours = _____ minutes

5 days = _____ hours

one quarter hour = _____ minutes

1 hour = _____ seconds

10 Use the models to multiply the decimals.

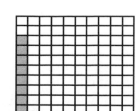 x 2 = _____

x 5 = _____

Which numeral has a 5 in the ten thousands place, a 3 in the hundreds place, an 8 in the millions place and a 6 in the hundredths place?

◯ 850, 308.60

◯ 8,005,308.30

◯ 8,057,308.06

◯ 85,360,016.6

Number each triangle.

1. right triangle
2. scalene
3. acute

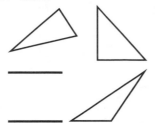

Each student in Mr. Hernandez's class brought $3.25 for the end of the year pizza party. The party cost $78.00. What information is needed to determine whether there would be enough money?

(Can you find the number for the missing information?)

$$\begin{array}{r} 145 \\ \times \boxed{} \\ \hline 2900 \end{array}$$

$$\boxed{}\,\overline{)\,2550}^{\;51}$$

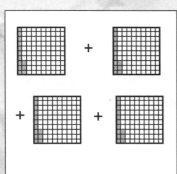

+

+   +

_____ x 4 = _____

If 30 is 4 times less than a number, which equation could be used to find the number?

◯ 30 x 4 = n

◯ 30 ÷ 4 = n

◯ 30 + 4 = n

◯ 30 - 4 = n

Ikito spends $4\frac{1}{2}$ hours practicing his violin each week. He has practiced for $1\frac{3}{4}$ hours this week. How many more minutes does he need to practice?

10	13	19	22
7	10	16	19

What two numbers are missing in this pattern?

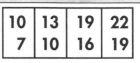

Write the decimals in order from greatest to least.

12.85   13.2   12.08
13.02   13.50 12.6

_____   _____

_____   _____

_____

Use the grid to enlarge the top figure 3 times its size.

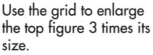

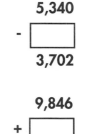

Match using the number line.

_____ 37. 21

_____ 35. 4

_____ 37. 89

_____ 36. 5

$$\begin{array}{r} 5,340 \\ - \boxed{} \\ \hline 3,702 \end{array}$$

$$\begin{array}{r} 9,846 \\ + \boxed{} \\ \hline 14,772 \end{array}$$

Average Minutes to Complete 1 K Race   Jim ▨   Ted ☐

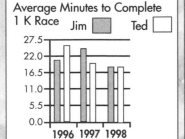

1996 1997 1998

Which chart to the right best matches the data on the above graph?

chart _____

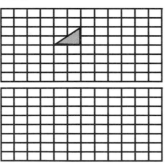

		Jim	Ted
	1996	20.2	25.5
A	1997	24.7	20.5
	1998	19.21	18.85
	1996	16.5	27.5
B	1997	20.7	20.5
	1998	11.21	12.85
	1996	22.0	25.5
C	1997	28.7	20.5
	1998	19.21	5.85

Each year Rita had between 21 and 45 classmates. What is a reasonable total for the number of classmates she had in grades one through six?

◯ 150

◯ 250

◯ 350

For a community food drive, Mrs. Witt needed to pack 438 cans of vegetables. She can pack 40 cans in each box. What is the least number of boxes she can use to pack all the cans?

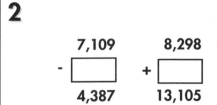

Math 4 today Name _____ **Test #40**

1

225
x [ ]
11,250

30
[ ])2100

2

7,109
- [ ]
4,387

8,298
+ [ ]
13,105

3

11	18	25	39
2	9	14	30

Which two numbers are missing from this pattern?

4

A   B   C D E

42   43   44   45

Match using the number line.

_____ 44.10   _____ 42.92

_____ 44.5   _____ 43.75

_____ 42.25

5

Several friends went to Six Flags Amusement Park. Their total entrance fee was $264.00. What information do you need to find out the entrance fee for each person?

(Can you find a reasonable number for the missing information?)

6

Average Miles On Road Race Video Game

55.0
49.5
44.0
38.5
33.0
27.5
22.0
16.5
11.0
5.5
0.0

1 2 3

Sam ☐
Joe ▨

Circle the chart that best matches the graph?

Game:	1	2	3
Sam	53.5	22.1	8.79
Joe	12.3	38.2	17.5

Game:	1	2	3
Sam	52.2	27.9	8.79
Joe	19.3	45.2	22.3

7

Paula's goal is to jog for 2 hours and 45 minutes a week. So far this week, she has jogged for three quarters of an hour. How many more minutes does she need to jog to meet her weekly goal?

8

Use the empty grid to enlarge this shape 2 times.

9

Which numeral has a 5 in the tens place, a 7 in the ten thousands place, a 6 in the millions place, and a 4 in the hundredths place?

◯ 5,760,401

◯ 6,270,052.04

◯ 5,670,219.4

◯ 6,870,059.40

10

Erin goes swimming between 52 and 105 times each summer. What would be a reasonable total of the times she has gone swimming over the last 6 years?

◯ 525

◯ 725

◯ 825

◯ 225

89

© Good Apple GA1659 Reproducible

Name the place and the value of the 4 in each number.

34,127 _____
value

_____
place name

41,980 _____
value

_____
place name

Iso means *bend. Equi* means *same. Ska* means *uneven.* Use the clues to number each triangle.
1. isosceles
2. equilateral
3. scalene

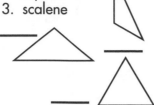

Soccer camp costs $125.00 per team. The team washed 50 cars to earn money for camp. What information is needed to determine whether they earned enough money?

(Can you find the number for the missing information?)

$$86\frac{25}{27}$$
$$+ 48\frac{11}{27}$$

$$73\frac{7}{49}$$
$$- 29\frac{14}{49}$$

Write the decimal for each model.

____ ____

If 120 is 3 times more than a number, which equation could be used to find the number?

○ **120 x 3 = n**

○ **120 ÷ 3 = n**

○ **120 + 3 = n**

○ **120 - 3 = n**

Fernando worked after school to save money for a video game that cost $63.00. At the end of 3 months, he had enough to buy the game. How much money did he save each month?

144	121	100	64
12	11	10	8

What two numbers are missing in this pattern?

Math Average
List the students in order from highest to lowest math average.

Cathy	81.55
Paul	97.2
Roberto	88.25
Hakeem	96.7
Leslie	92.5

1. _____
2. _____
3. _____
4. _____
5. _____

Enlarge the top figure 2 times.

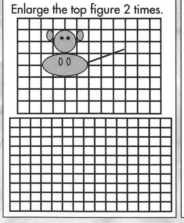

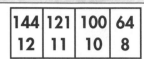

Match using the number line.
____ **73. 92**
____ **75. 75**
____ **73. 08**
____ **74. 42**

$$4,681$$
$$- \boxed{}$$
$$1,443$$

$$876$$
$$+ \boxed{}$$
$$1,862$$

Value of Mineral Produced Billions In Dollars

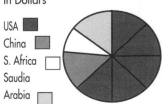

USA ■
China ■
S. Africa □
Saudia Arabia ■

Which chart to the right best matches the data on the above graph?
chart _____

	U.S.A.	62.27
A	China	16.7
	S. Africa	8.51
	Saudia Arabia	19.42
	U.S.A.	8.51
B	China	16.7
	S. Africa	62.27
	Saudia Arabia	19.42
	U.S.A.	19.42
C	China	8.51
	S. Africa	16.7
	Saudia Arabia	62.27

Movie Opening	$ Gross
Dino Island	$ 37,539.
Tidal Terror	$ 9,210.
Star Invasion	$ 69,510.

What is the best estimate of the money grossed by all three movies?

○ **$120,000**
○ **$155,000**
○ **$250,000**

The cooks at the Grand Hotel are preparing a special shrimp dish for their menu. They will need 729 shrimp. The shrimp comes in bulk packages of 80. What is the least number of packages the cooks can buy?

1

$62\frac{31}{60}$ $73\frac{3}{64}$

$+ 38\frac{29}{60}$ $- 28\frac{35}{64}$

2

5,802 − ▢ = 1,349

4,307 + ▢ = 11,464

3 What is the best estimate of the money grossed in ticket sales for all three concerts?

Ponytails Concert	$ Gross Ticket Sales
Houston	$21,135.
Chicago	$59,421.
Seattle	$77,982.

○ $160,000   ○ $150,000

○ $140,000   ○ $130,000

4 Ms. Alipour needed $236.00 to buy an air conditioner for the kennels at her pet grooming shop. She groomed 12 dogs. What information is needed to find out if this would be enough money to buy the air conditioner?

5 If 450 is 3 times more than a number, which equation could be used to find the number?

○ 450 x 3 = n

○ 450 + 3 = n

○ 450 ÷ 3 = n

○ 450 - 3 = n

6

Average Scores on Diving Competition	
Rudi	72.3
Brook	88.21
Lindsay	88.57
Milly	71.9
Cecily	72.71.

_____

_____

_____

_____

_____

List the competitors' names in order from the highest to lowest average score.

7 Name the place and the value for the 7 in each numeral below.

72,509 _____
value

_____
place name

29,709 _____
value

_____
place name

8 Match.

A. equilateral   B. isosceles   C. scalene

____   ____   ____

      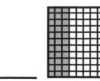

9 Tiffany worked at her father's florist shop after school to save money for a summer gymnastic camp. Tuition for the camp was $108.00. She was paid the same amount for each week she worked and at the end of 9 weeks she had enough money to pay the tuition. How much did she earn each week?

10 Write the decimal for each model.

____   ____   ____   ____

Name the place and the value of the 5 in each numeral.

520,347

_____
value

_____
place name

5,201,968

_____
value

_____
place name

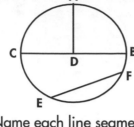

Name each line segment.

radius _____
chord _____
diameter _____

Alleha weighs 89 pounds. To find the weight of her baby brother, she held him as she weighed again. This time the scale showed 102 pounds. How much does Alleha's baby brother weigh?

Solve.

$$31,094$$
$$-\quad 867$$

$$20,532$$
$$-\quad 785$$

Shade in and write an equivalent decimal for each model.

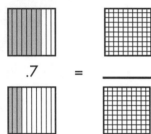

.7 = _____

.3 = _____

---

240 drivers competed in the 8 day road rally. On the average, how many drivers raced each day?

The spirit club sold banners to earn money for a party. They sold 108 banners at $3.00 each. How much money did the spirit club earn?

Tim and his friends designed paper airplanes. Their best model could fly 103 inches. The next day, they improved the model so it could fly 112 inches. If the improvement continues in this pattern, how far will the plane fly on the 5th day?

_____ inches

Use **>**, **<**, or **=**.

52.13 ☐ 52.3

10.10 ☐ 10.1

75.42 ☐ 75.49

23.08 ☐ 23.8

Each ☐ = 3 foot.
What is the perimeter of the shape? _____ ft.
the area? _____ sq. ft.

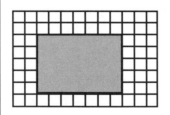

Match.
A. 74.2   B. 72.04
C. 72.4   D. 70.42

_____ seventy-two and four hundredths

_____ seventy and forty-two hundredths

_____ seventy-four and two tenths

_____ seventy-two and four tenths

$$215,743$$
$$315,094$$
$$+ 867,255$$

$$8,200,999$$
$$+ 12,836,487$$

Reforestation Project

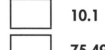

Park	Number of New Trees
King	
Ford	
Taft	
Bush	

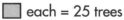 each = 25 trees

The forestry service wishes to plant 850 new trees in these 4 parks. Shade the graph to show how many more trees are needed in Bush Park to meet this goal.

---

wrapping papers

ribbons

Kalyn is wrapping gifts. Using the above ribbons and paper, how many different combinations can she make?

_____ different combinations

Round each numeral to the nearest tenth:

36.42 _____

92.19 _____

77.87 _____

14.64 _____

In the above group of flowers, the odds of picking a 🌸 over a ❀ are 3 to 1. What are the odds of picking a 🌸 over a ❀ ?

_____ to _____

Math 4 today

Name _____

Test #42

1

47,084
- 31,267

2

831,457
217,886
+ 504,108

---

3 Round each numeral to the nearest tenth.

84.12 _____
15.58 _____
27.07 _____

---

4 Match.
A. 94.4 B. 94.7 C. 94.07 D. 94.47

_____ ninety-four and seven hundredths
_____ ninety-four and seven tenths
_____ ninety-four and forty-seven hundredths
_____ ninety-four and four tenths

---

5 Andy wanted to find the weight of a pumpkin he bought. When he got on the scales alone, he weighed 92 pounds. When he weighed holding the pumpkin the scales read 110 pounds. How much did his pumpkin weigh?

6
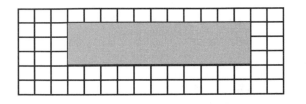

Park   Number of Bears Collared   Each ▨ = 20
Yellowstone
Yosemite
Smokey Mt.
Glacier

To study the habitats of bears, the park service plans to radio collar 620 bears in these 4 parks. Shade the graph to show how many more bears need to be collared in Yosemite to meet their total.

---

7 Papers

Designs

Pavet was designing covers for his journals. Using the above papers and designs, how many different combinations of covers can he make?

_____ different combinations

---

8 What is the perimeter of   Each ▨ = 4 feet
the shape? _____ ft.
the area? _____ sq. ft.

---

9 Name the place and the value for the **2** in each numeral below.

2,631,980 value _____
place name _____

8,2**1**9,443 value _____
place name _____

---

10   ☆ ☆ ☆ ☆ ○ ○ ○   ▼ ▼ ▼ ▼ ▼ ▼ ☐ ☐

The odds of drawing a ☆ over a ○ are 4 to 3 with the above group of shapes.

With the above group of shapes, the odds of drawing a ▼ over a ☐ are

_____ to _____

93

Complete the place value chart.

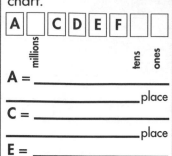

A		C	D	E	F		
millions | | | | | | tens | ones

A = _____

_____ place

C = _____

_____ place

E = _____

_____ place

Match.

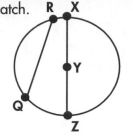

XY _____   A. diameter

QR _____   B. radius

XZ _____   C. chord

Each of the 26 students in art class has a set of 18 watercolor pens. How many watercolor pens do they have altogether?

Solve.

$$211,005 - 24,146$$

$$98,778 + 76,845$$

Write an equivalent decimal.

1.9 = _____

0.20 = _____

9.45 = _____

4.07 = _____

Complete the chart to find some multiples for each numeral.

x	4	6	8
2			
3			
4			
5			
6			
7			
8			
9			

Circle the common multiples.

Although this clock is missing the minute hand, what is the best estimate of the time it shows?

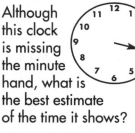

◯ 4:30

◯ 3:02

◯ 3:55

Ada was collecting plant specimens for a botany class. On the first day she collected 23 specimens. The next day, she collected 3 more specimens than on the first day. If she continues in the same pattern, how many plant specimens total will she have on the fifth day?

Use **>**, **<**, or **=**.

71.93 ☐ 71.930

1 8.2 ☐ 18.035

98.52 ☐ 98.541

43.17 ☐ 43.189

Each ☐ = 4 foot. What is the perimeter of the shape?   ft.
the area?   sq. ft.

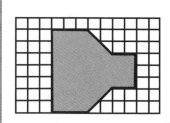

Write the number word for each numeral.

35.607 _____

_____

_____

29.35 _____

_____

_____

Solve.

$$5,421 \times 33$$

$$7\overline{)21,426}$$

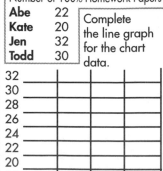

Number of 100% Homework Papers	
Abe	22
Kate	20
Jen	32
Todd	30

Complete the line graph for the chart data.

32
30
28
26
24
22
20
18

Abe Kate Jen Todd

♡ ♡ ♡ ♡

Using the colors red, pink, purple, and white only one time on each row, how many different colored rows of hearts can you make?

_____ different rows

Round each numeral to the nearest whole number:

21.032 _____

87.67 _____

45.02 _____

99.506 _____

7	7	7	7	7

3	3	3	3

If the above group of cards is shuffled and placed face down, compare the probability of picking a 7 to the probability of picking a 3 (expressed as a fraction using the greater than symbol).

_____ > _____

1

$$212,003 \\ -\ 87,136$$

2

$$7,214 \\ x\quad 25$$

3 Round each numeral to the nearest whole number.

98.345 _____

27.702 _____

82.027 _____

4 Each of the 34 children in the City Celebration Parade carried 9 flag shaped balloons. How many balloons were carried by all the children in the parade?

5 Complete the chart. Circle the common multiples of all 3 numbers.

x	2	3	4	5	6	7	8	9	10
3									
6									
9									

6 Use >, < or =.

39.43 ☐ 39.048

47.098 ☐ 47.98

81.3 ☐ 81.300

7 Complete the place value chart.

A B millions D E F G tens ones

A = _____ place

D = _____ place

F = _____ place

G = _____ place

8 Match.

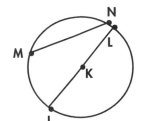

MN = _____

KL = _____

JL = _____

diameter, radius, chord

9

Although the minute hand is missing, what is the best estimate of the time shown on this clock?

◯ 11:05   ◯ 6:00

◯ 12:45   ◯ 11:58

10

Super Citizen Stars Earned		
Jeff	36	★
Mando	30	★
Lakina	33	★
Willy	24	★

Complete the line graph for the chart data.

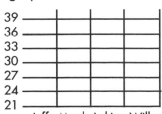

Math 4 today

If a 3 is followed by 8 zeros, the 3 is in the

_____
place.

If a 7 is followed by 6 zeros, the 7 is in the

_____
place.

If polygons are congruent, the corresponding or matching angles are also congruent. For example:

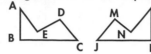

∠ABC ≅ ∠JKL

∠AED ≅ ∠ _____

∠BCD ≅ ∠ _____

Kevin's remote control bi-plane can fly 3.42 meters high. Danny's plane can fly 4.021 meters high. How much higher can Danny's plane fly?

$$345.043$$
$$- 127.127$$

$$358.79$$
$$+ 668.402$$

A pizza has 12 slices. Julio ate 8 slices. Which fraction describes the portion Julio ate?

○ $\frac{1}{2}$ ○ $\frac{3}{4}$ ○ $\frac{2}{3}$

Which fraction describes the portion of pizza that was left?

○ $\frac{1}{2}$ ○ $\frac{1}{3}$ ○ $\frac{1}{12}$

(6 x 2) x 5
is equivalent to
○ (6 x 2) + 5
○ (6 ÷ 2) x 5
○ 6 x (2 x 5)

(9 + 4) + 8
is equivalent to
○ (9 x 4) + 8
○ 9 + (4 + 8)
○ 9 x (8 x 4)

Although this clock is missing the minute hand, what is the best estimate of the time it shows?

○ **8:20**
○ **8:59**
○ **9:15**

Kalui caught 27 fish. On the first day, he sold 7 of them at the market. If each day after, he sells one less fish than on the day before, on what day will he have no fish left to sell?

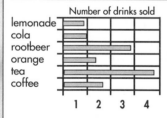

Number of drinks sold

lemonade
cola
rootbeer
orange
tea
coffee

1 2 3 4

List the drinks sold from least to greatest.

1._____   4._____
2._____   5._____
3._____   6._____

Which is a way to find the area of this shape?

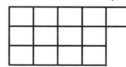

○ (5 + 4)+(4 - 1)
○ (5 x 1)+(5 x 2)
○ (4 x 3)+(1 x 1)
○ (5 + 3)+(4 + 3)

Write the number word for each numeral.

71.032 _____
_____
_____

12.05 _____
_____
_____

$$9,876$$
$$\times \quad 63$$

$$9\overline{)45,452}$$

Weekly Temperatures

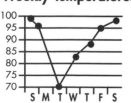

100
95
90
85
80
75
70
S M T W T F S

Write a sentence to summarize the graph data._____

_____

If $2n = 54 ÷ 9$

$n =$ ☐

If $5n = 26 + 4$

$n =$ ☐

If $3n = 30 - 3$

$n =$ ☐

Jiffy's Pizza is running a special of 2 pizzas for $15.00. Which would be a reasonable cost of 7 pizzas?

○ **$30.00**
○ **$40.00**
○ **$50.00**
○ **$60.00**

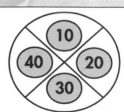

If all the colored circles on the dart board are the same size, the probability of hitting a 20 (expressed as a fraction) is: _____

1

582.74
+ 217.806
_____

2

3)27,182

3 Skinny the clown had 20 balloons to pass out at the circus. He gave the first child entering the big top 6 balloons. If he gives each of the next children 1 less than the child before, with which child will Skinny be out of balloons?

_____

4 Write the number word for each numeral:

24.017 _____
_____

10.51 _____
_____

30.6 _____
_____

5 Miss Tamira was measuring walls in the museum for a new tapestry exhibit. The west wall was 7.13 meters wide, and the north wall was 9.06 meters wide. How much wider was the north wall?

_____

6

Average Number of Days Precipitation for S. Carolina

Write a sentence to **summarize** the graph data.

_____
_____
_____
_____
_____

7

If $7n = 84 \div 12$; $n =$ ☐

If $5n = 100 - 25$; $n =$ ☐

If $9n = 27 + 18$; $n =$ ☐

8 Which shows a way to find the area of this shape?

○ (8 x 2) + (8 x 2)
○ (8 x 6)
○ (8 x 4) - (8 x 2)
○ (8 x 6) - (4 x 2)

9 If a 7 is followed by 4 zeros, the 7 is in the _____ place.

If a 2 is followed by 9 zeros, the 2 is in the _____ place.

10 Easy Feet Shoe Store is having a sale: 5 pair of shoes for $40.00. Mrs. Sans, Mrs. King, and Mrs. Boyd bought 12 pairs of shoes for their families. What would be a reasonable cost of the 12 pairs of shoes the women bought?

○ $50.00
○ $100.00
○ $150.00
○ $200.00

Math 4 today

Which numeral has a 4 in the ten billions place?

◯ 45,0872,501

◯ 421,704,623

◯ 475,189,080,225

◯ 248,095,667,120

Which are corresponding angles?

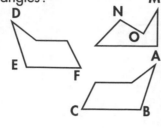

∠ _____ ≅ ∠ _____

Marquis had 50 jawbreaker candies. He wanted to keep two for his little brother and share the rest equally with 8 of his friends. How many jawbreakers will each of his friends receive?

Solve.

```
  121,092
-  95,095
```

```
  622,173
  415,669
+ 323,355
```

Mr. Prine bought a book of 36 stamps. He used nine to mail some letters. Which fraction describes the portion of stamps he used?

◯ $\frac{1}{2}$ ◯ $\frac{3}{4}$ ◯ $\frac{1}{4}$

What fraction of stamps was left?

◯ $\frac{1}{2}$ ◯ $\frac{3}{4}$ ◯ $\frac{1}{36}$

(9 x 3) + (9 x 5) is equivalent to

◯ 9 x (3 x 5)
◯ (9 x 9) + (3 x 5)
◯ 9 x (3 + 5)

(9 ÷ 3) + (15 ÷ 3) is equivalent to:

◯ (9 x 3) ÷5
◯ (9 + 15) ÷3
◯ (9 x 5) ÷ 6

Andrea bought 4 sets of fingernail tatoos for $3.25 a set including tax. She gave the clerk a $20. bill. How much change did Andrea receive?

Tyler went hiking in the forest. He carried a pack with 124 small pebbles. To help him find his way back, he dropped pebbles every 5 meters. At the first 5 meters, he dropped 4 pebbles. At 10 meters, he dropped 8 pebbles. If he continues dropping twice the number of pebbles, how far can he hike into the forest until he runs out of pebbles?

Average Daily Temperature °F

List the days in order from highest to lowest temperature.

1. _____   5. _____
2. _____   6. _____
3. _____   7. _____
4. _____

Which is a way to find the area of this shape?

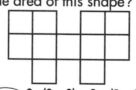

◯ 2 x(2 x 2) + 3 x (1 x 1)
◯ (2 + 2) + (2 + 2) + 12
◯ (5 x 2) + (5 x 2)
◯ (4 + 4) - 3

|◄—|—|—S—|—►|
63   64   65

Point S best represents which number?

◯ 65.2
◯ 64.2
◯ 64.6
◯ 64.9
◯ not here

Solve.

```
   315
x  214
```

```
22)675
```

Pat's Keyboarding Scores

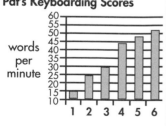

Write a sentence to **summarize** the graph data.

_____
_____

If $n + 5 = 6 \times 6$

$n = \boxed{}$

If $n - 4 = 30 + 4$

$n = \boxed{}$

If $n \div 2 = 12 \div 6$

$n = \boxed{}$

Carnival ride tickets cost 10 for $12.50. Which would be a reasonable cost for 25 tickets?

◯ $20.00
◯ $30.00
◯ $40.00
◯ not here

If you have one dice with the numbers **1, 2, 3, 4, 5**, and **6**. Expressed as a fraction, what is the probability of rolling a 2 if you roll 5 times.

_____

Math 4 today

1

$$572 \times 223$$

2

$$25\overline{)557}$$

3 At the video arcade, Ely can play 8 games for $3.00. Which would be a reasonable cost of 20 games?

⬭ $5.00   ⬭ $10.00
⬭ $15.00   ⬭ $20.00

4 Gillian bought 48 hair scrunchies on sale for $10.00. She wants to keep 6 for herself and give the rest to 7 of her friends. If she shares the scrunchies equally, how many will she give to each friend?

5 $(4 \times 3) + (4 \times 7)$ is equivalent to

⬭ $(4 + 7) \times 7$
⬭ $(4 + 4) \times (7 \times 7)$
⬭ $4 \times (7 + 3)$
⬭ $(4 \times 3) - 7$
⬭ **not here**

6 Jobs in Norway

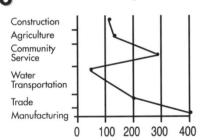

List the jobs in Norway from least to greatest number of workers.

1. _____
2. _____
3. _____
4. _____
5. _____
6. _____

7 Which numeral has a 9 in the hundred billions place?

⬭ **392,107,456,025**
⬭ **189,502,011,047**
⬭ **907,356**
⬭ **9,261,077,684**
⬭ **not here**

8

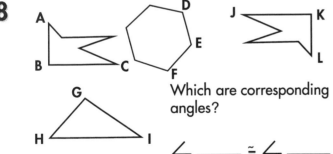

Which are corresponding angles?

∠ _____ ≅ ∠ _____

9 Tito bought 7 minature model sets. Each set costs $4.89 including tax. How much change will he receive if he gives the clerk $40.00?

10 Inez had a packet of stationery with 42 sheets of colored paper. She used 14 sheets to write letters to her penpals. What is the fraction for the portion of sheets she used?

⬭ $\frac{1}{2}$ ⬭ $\frac{1}{3}$ ⬭ $\frac{2}{7}$ ⬭ $\frac{4}{6}$

Write in expanded form:

2,310,107,900 =

_____

_____

_____

125,320,900 =

_____

_____

_____

Match:

1. cone   2. sphere
3. cylinder   4. cube
5. triangular prism
6. rectangular prism

---

240 fifth-graders were going on a field trip. 80 students can ride on each bus. How many buses will be needed for the field trip?

Solve.

    209
x 634

    572
x 468

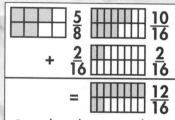

$\frac{5}{8}$ $\frac{10}{16}$

$+ \frac{2}{16}$ $\frac{2}{16}$

$= $ $\frac{12}{16}$

Complete this example:

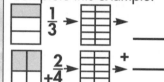

$\frac{1}{3} \rightarrow$ _____

$\frac{2}{4} \rightarrow$ _____ +

_____ =

Which numeral should replace the ? in each equation?

$(4.7 + 3.8) + 1.2 =$
    $4.7 + (3.8 + ?)$

? = _____

$8.2 + (0.71 + 9.36) =$
    $(8.2 + ?) + 9.36$

? = _____

Mrs. Yates bought 5 cans of asparagus spears that were on special at 10 for $8.00. She gave the clerk a $10 bill. How much change will she receive?

Font Town's community growth plan is illustrated in the above picture. If the town adds a new building and a new tree every two years, in ten years, Font Town will have

_____ buildings
_____ trees

Continue counting.
   2,895,600
   2,896,600
   2,897,600
   2,898,600

_____

_____

_____

_____

_____

If the perimeter of this fenced garden is 339 feet, what is the length of the missing side?

_____ feet

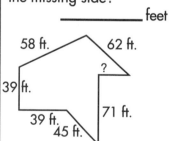

58 ft.   62 ft.

?

39 ft.

39 ft.

45 ft.   71 ft.

B

25   26   27

Point **B** best represents which number?

◯ **25.029**
◯ **25.321**
◯ **25.628**
◯ **25.989**
◯ **not here**

Solve.

$26\overline{)988}$

$87\overline{)423}$

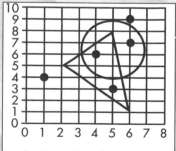

Which ordered pair is inside both the triangle and the circle?

_____

Fat Max, the cat, is twice as fat as Garfield. TubbyTabby is almost as big as Fat Max. Skinny Scat is thinner than Garfield but fatter than Bones. Use the back of this page and write conclusions to compare:
1. Tubby Tabby to Garfield.
2. Garfield to Fat Max.
3. Bones to Garfield.
4. Skinny Scat to Tubby Tabby.

The Ford family attended World on Parade. Each of the 8 exhibits they saw cost between $5.00 and $12.00 per family. What is a reasonable total spent by the Fords on visiting the exhibits?

◯ **$39.00**
◯ **$79.00**
◯ **$119.00**
◯ **not here**

If you have one dice with the numbers 1,2,3,4,5, and 6. Expressed as a fraction, what is the probability of rolling a double (2 of the same number) in 25 rolls?

_____

1

807
x 543

2

48)954

3

▼ ❑ ■ ✳ ● ○

Mary was creating a design using the above shapes. Every 3 minutes, she adds another ▼ and another ❑. How many ▼ and ❑ will be in her design after 30 minutes?

4

A

|――|――|――|――|――|――|――|
48   49   50   51

Point **A** is best represented by which numeral?

○ 49.457   ○ 49.589

○ 49.124   ○ 49.970

5

An old-fashioned steam train conducts scenic mountain tours. Each train car can hold 76 passengers. How many train cars are needed for a tour of 912 people?

6

Which ordered pair is inside the rectangle and the triangle?

_____

7

Natika bought 8 folders that were on sale for 12 for $4.68. She gave the clerk $10.00. How much change should she receive?

8

The perimeter of this shape is 349 feet. What is the length of the missing side?

93 ft.

37 ft.

35 ft.

?

48 ft.

27 ft.   86 ft.

_____ feet

9

$\frac{1}{4}$ → ⟶

$+\frac{2}{5}$ → ⟶

+ _____

= _____

10 Mr. Talbot bought 7 items at the discount store. Each item cost between $6.00 and $15.00. What is a reasonable total cost of Mr. Talbot's items?

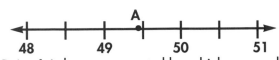

○ $14.00
○ $54.00
○ $74.00
○ $124.00
○ not here

Write in expanded form:

27,504,821 =

_____

_____

65,457 =

_____

_____

Which figures have only 1 line of symmetry?

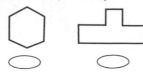

○   ○

○   ○

On a business trip in Canada, Mr. Yuma stopped several times to buy gas. His car held 12.4 liters when he filled up the first time. At his next gas stop, his car held 22.8 liters. The last time he stopped for gas, the car held 18.6 liters. How many liters of gas did his car use on the trip?

Solve.

$$3.9$$
$$\times\ 7$$

$$7.5$$
$$\times\ 9$$

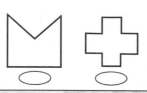

The above model shows:

○ $\frac{3}{6} > \frac{1}{2}$

○ $\frac{3}{6} < \frac{1}{2}$

○ $\frac{3}{6} = \frac{1}{2}$

$6^2 =$

○ 6 + 6

○ 6 x 6

○ 6 ÷ 6

$3^3 =$

○ 3 + 3

○ 3 + 3 + 3

○ 3 x 3 x 3

---

7 hours 34 minutes
- 2 hours 56 minutes
_____

5 hours 10 minutes
- 3 hours 25 minutes
_____

---

1   2

3

4

Use the grid below to shade in the 7th pattern.

Continue counting.
5,682,301
5,782,301
5,882,301
5,982,301

_____

_____

_____

If the area of this rectangular swimming pool is 84 square feet. What is the length of the missing side? _____ feet

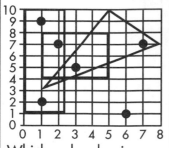

?

7 ft.

Nine hundred twenty-seven thousand, four hundred and sixty-two thousandths is written:

○ 927.462

○ 9,270.62

○ 927,400.6

○ 9,400,274.0062

○ **not here**

Solve.

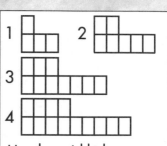

$8\overline{)72.80}$

$5\overline{)45.35}$

10
9
8
7
6
5
4
3
2
1
0
  0 1 2 3 4 5 6 7 8

Which ordered pairs are outside both the triangle and the square?

_____

Bossy Boots bossed around an average of 35 people during the school week. On Monday she bossed around 7 people, on Wednesday she bossed around 6 people, on Thursday she bossed around 4 people, and on Friday she bossed around 8 people. How many people did she boss around on Tuesday?

Tuesday _____ people

The Chicago O'Hare Airport has an average of 900,279 aircraft take-offs and landings per year. About how many aircraft take off or land at O'Hare each hour?

○ 7,500

○ 75,023

○ 750,230

○ **not here**

Hair Colors in Mr. Brock's Class
Blonde |||| |||
Brown |||| ||||
Red |||
Black |||| ||||
If one student was selected at random from Mr. Brock's class, what is the probability that the student would have blonde hair?

_____ out of _____

Math 4 today

1

$$4.7$$
$$\times\ 7$$

2

$$6\overline{)48.42}$$

3 In 1980, the crater of Mt. St. Helen's volcano enlarged 1,450 feet in 13 days due to the magma pressure. About how many feet did the crater enlarge per day?

- ⬭ **100 ft.**   ⬭ **200 ft.**
- ⬭ **300 ft.**   ⬭ **400 ft.**

4 Mr. Harp put 6.8 liters of cleaner in his pool on Monday. On Friday, he added 4.6 more liters of cleaner. On the following Monday, 8.9 liters of cleaner was needed. How many liters of cleaner did Mr. Harp put in his pool?

5

$9^2 =$
- ⬭ **9 + 9**
- ⬭ **9 x 2**
- ⬭ **9 x 9**

$7^5 =$
- ⬭ **7 + 7 + 7 + 7 + 7**
- ⬭ **7 x 5**
- ⬭ **7 x 7 x 7 x 7 x 7**

6 Continue counting.

    23,597,123 _____

    23,697,123 _____

    23,797,123 _____

    23,897,123 _____

_____

7 Write in expanded form:

89,403,276= _____

_____

_____

45,210= _____

_____

_____

8 Which figures have only 1 line of symmetry?

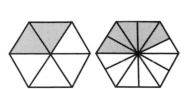

⬭   ⬭   ⬭   ⬭

9

    8 hours 21 minutes
-   3 hours 47 minutes

    5 hours 53 minutes
-   1 hour   17 minutes

10 The models show:

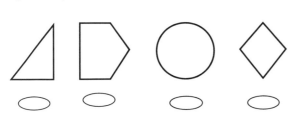

- ⬭ $\dfrac{2}{6} > \dfrac{5}{12}$
- ⬭ $\dfrac{2}{6} < \dfrac{5}{12}$
- ⬭ $\dfrac{2}{6} = \dfrac{5}{12}$

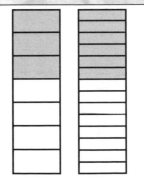

- ⬭ $\dfrac{3}{7} > \dfrac{6}{14}$
- ⬭ $\dfrac{3}{7} < \dfrac{6}{14}$
- ⬭ $\dfrac{3}{7} = \dfrac{6}{14}$

Steffi was reading about when the Jurassic Period of prehistoric life began. The number she read had an 8 in the ten millions place, and a 1 in the hundred millions place. Steffi found out that the Jurassic Period began

_____ years ago.

Match.
1. parallelogram
2. trapezoid
3. pentagon
4. quadrilateral
5. rhombus
6. octogon

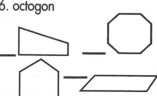

At Disney World, Nigel wanted to buy souvenirs for himself and his friends. He bought 2 caps for $8.00 each, 5 sets of Disney stamps for $6.00 a set, and 3 banners for $7.50. How much did Nigel spend on souvenirs?

Solve.

$$27.093 \times 25$$

$$13.521 \times 22$$

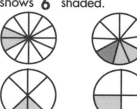
This model shows $\frac{1}{6}$ shaded. X the model below which also shows $\frac{1}{6}$ shaded.

$7^2 =$ _____

$5^3 =$ _____

$2^{10} =$ _____

$10^2 =$ _____

8 hours 54 minutes
+ 6 hours 28 minutes

12 hours 47 minutes
+ 13 hours 38 minutes

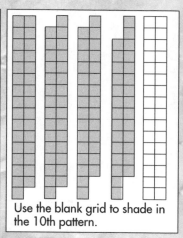

Use the blank grid to shade in the 10th pattern.

Write this group of numerals in order from least to greatest.

12,645.79   12,645.97
126,425.1   6,654.99
1,264,500.07

1. _____
2. _____
3. _____
4. _____
5. _____

Find the volume of this box.

_____ cubic cm

6 cm
10 cm
7 cm

Forty-one billion, two hundred million, sixty-three thousand, eight hundred and nine thousandths is written:

◯ 41,200,063,800.009
◯ 4,200,630,008.9
◯ 412,063,080.90
◯ 410,263,809,800.09
◯ not here

Solve.

$6 \overline{)48.84}$

$9 \overline{)720.36}$

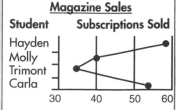

Magazine Sales

Student	Subscriptions Sold
Hayden	
Molly	
Trimont	
Carla	

Circle the graph to the right that best matches the data shown on the above graph.

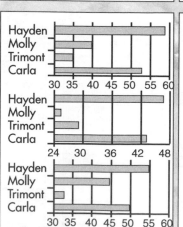

Light travels in a vacuum at the speed of 186,282 miles per second. Which is the best estimate of how fast light travels per minute?
(mpm = miles per minute)
◯ 1,000 mpm
◯ 3,000 mpm
◯ 5,000 mpm
◯ 10,000 mpm
◯ not here

Ms. Lee's Class' Favorite Sports
Baseball ⌿⌿⌿ ⌿⌿⌿ ||
Soccer ⌿⌿⌿ ⌿⌿⌿ ||||
Tennis |||
Swimming ⌿⌿⌿ ||

If one student was selected at random from Ms. Lee's class, what is the probability that the student's favorite sport would be either tennis or soccer?

_____ out of _____

1

$$34.021 \\ \times \quad 55$$

2

$$8\overline{)64.56}$$

3

Mr. Todds Class' Favorite Movies

Star Wars	ЖІ ЖІ ЖІ
Bat Man	ЖІ ЖІ
Toy Story	III
Babe	ЖІ III

The probability of a randomly selected student in Mr. Todd's class choosing the movie *Babe* is
_____ out of _____.

4 Fifty-nine billion, three hundred seventy-six million, two hundred eight thousand and one thousandth is written:

- ◯ 59,376,208.1
- ◯ 59,376,208,000.001
- ◯ 593,762,008.100
- ◯ 590,376,208.01

5 Holly was redecorating her room. She bought 3 sets of curtains for $13.98 a set, 4 throw pillows for $8.25 each, and 2 posters for $5.00 a piece. How much did Holly spend on redecorating her room?

6

Naper Family
Vacation Journal Entries

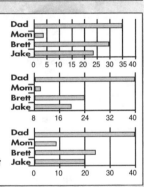

Circle the graph to the left that best matches the above graph.

7

$$9 \text{ hours } 35 \text{ minutes} \\ + \; 3 \text{ hours } 49 \text{ minutes}$$

$$15 \text{ hours } 28 \text{ minutes} \\ + \; 23 \text{ hours } 59 \text{ minutes}$$

8 Find the volume of each box.

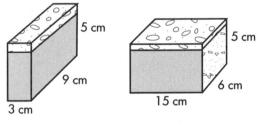

_____   _____

9 Henry's science project included riddles about space. One riddle said: The approximate distance in light years that the Andromeda Galaxy is from Earth is a number that has a 2 in the hundred thousands place, a 2 in the millions place. The Andromeda Galaxy is

_____ light years from Earth.

10 The Pacific is the largest and deepest ocean. Its deepest point is called Mariana Trench which is 36,198 feet below the surface. What is the best estimate of this depth in inches?

- ◯ 100,000 inches
- ◯ 200,000 inches
- ◯ 300, 000 inches
- ◯ 400,000 inches
- ◯ not here

Math 4 today

To which place have the pairs of numerals been rounded?

1,256	1,300

_____
place

27,230	30,000

_____
place

Which pairs of figures are NOT congruent?

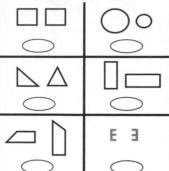

A delivery truck is hauling 7 crates of boxed stereo speakers. Each box contains 12 speakers and each crate contains 8 boxes. How many stereo speakers is the delivery truck hauling?

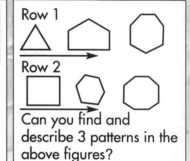

$$31.222$$
$$\times \quad .11$$

$$18.007$$
$$\times \quad .42$$

Add and simplify.

$$\frac{1}{2} + \frac{2}{5} = \underline{\hspace{1cm}}$$

$$\frac{2}{8} + \frac{2}{32} = \underline{\hspace{1cm}}$$

$$\frac{4}{9} - \frac{1}{6} = \underline{\hspace{1cm}}$$

$$\frac{5}{7} - \frac{3}{5} = \underline{\hspace{1cm}}$$

If 7 times a number is 84, which equation could be used to find the number?

○ $84 \times 7 = n$

○ $84 \div 7 = n$

○ $84 + 7 = n$

○ $84 - 7 = n$

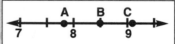

Sunscreen	2 for $1.40
Shampoo	4 for $4.00
Insect candles	8 for $16.00

The items above are sold only in multiples of 2, 4, or 6. Stacy wants to buy an equal number of the items to take with her to camp. What is the least number of each she can buy, and how much will she spend?

Row 1

Row 2

Can you find and describe 3 patterns in the above figures?

_____
_____

Write this group of numerals in order from greatest to least.

254,005.092   2,545.2
2,545.002   25,405.01
254,000.97

1. _____
2. _____
3. _____
4. _____
5. _____

Find the missing dimension.
The volume is 90 cubic cm.

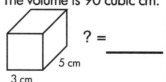

? = _____
5 cm
3 cm

The volume is 100 cubic cm.

2 cm
10 cm
? = _____

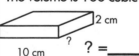

Which point best represents:

$$\frac{65}{7} \underline{\hspace{1cm}} \qquad \frac{39}{5} \underline{\hspace{1cm}}$$

$$\frac{68}{8} \underline{\hspace{1cm}}$$

Solve.

$$9\overline{)1.026}$$

$$12\overline{)25.08}$$

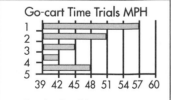

Go-cart Time Trials MPH

Cody clocked his go-cart 5 times and graphed the speeds in miles per hour. What is the average of his three best time trials?

_____ mph

Devon planted pumpkin vines. He noticed that for every 5 inches the vine grew, it also grew 3 new leaves. If the vine grows $2\frac{1}{2}$ inches every three days, how many leaves will the pumpkin vine have in 30 days?

Ken found that the Sears Tower has 110 stories and is 1,454 feet tall. He used his calculator to find the height of each story which was 13.218181818 feet. Rounded to the nearest hundreth, how tall is each story in the Sears Tower?

_____ feet

Wes wanted to find out the probability of tossing a dime and a penny and having them both land on heads. He made a chart of the possible outcomes.

Dime	Penny	Outcomes
heads {	tails	= H T
	heads	= H H
tails {	tails	= T T
	heads	= T H

Expressed as a fraction, what is the probability of tossing 2 heads?

© Good Apple GA1659 Reproducible

1

$$55.204$$
$$\times \quad .22$$

2

$$7\overline{)1.89}$$

3 Simeon wanted to find the tax on a $23.00 remote control car. He multiplied the cost by the tax rate of .08236 and found that the tax would be $1.89428. Rounded to the nearest tenth how much tax will Simeon pay?

4 In Bessie's Gift Shop, the clerk is arranging shadow boxes on wall shelves. There are 6 wall shelf units with 9 shelves per unit. If the clerk places 15 shadow boxes on each shelf, how many shadow boxes will be on display in the gift shop?

5 If 9 times a number is 126. Which equation can be used to find the number n ?

- ⬭ $126 + 9 = n$
- ⬭ $126 - 9 = n$
- ⬭ $126 \times 9 = n$
- ⬭ $126 \div 9 = n$

6 Write this group of numerals in order from greatest to least.

7,845.639   1._____

17,845.69   2._____

71,485.063   3._____

7,845.6   4._____

71,485.603   5._____

7 To which place have the pairs of numerals been rounded?

$6,725 \longrightarrow 7,000$

_____ place

$92,345 \longrightarrow 92,350$

_____ place

8 Which pairs of figures are NOT congruent?

⬭

S s

⬭

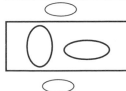

⬭

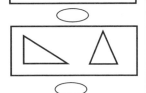

⬭

9

air mattress	3 for $12.00
waterproof matches	12 boxes for $7.20
5 g. propane bottles	2 for $7.00

Julio wants to purchase an equal number of the above items to take on a 3-week hiking trip. The items are sold only in multiples of 2, 3, and 12. What is the least number he can purchase of each and how much will he spend? _____

10 Add or subtract and simplify if needed.

$$\frac{2}{3} + \frac{5}{6} = \underline{\hspace{1cm}} \qquad \frac{1}{3} + \frac{8}{9} = \underline{\hspace{1cm}} \qquad \frac{4}{9} - \frac{1}{3} = \underline{\hspace{1cm}}$$

Math 4 today

To which place have the pairs of numerals been rounded?

26.429 → 26.430

_____
place

41.623 → 42.0

_____
place

Label: F = flip   T = turn

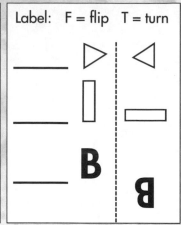

A craft store received 12 cartons of ribbon. There are 25 spools of ribbon in each carton and each spool holds 329 inches of ribbon. How many inches of ribbon are contained in each carton?

Solve.

$$4.18 \times 2.32$$

$$.705 \times 1.20$$

Add or subtract. Simpfy.

$2\frac{1}{8} + 5\frac{1}{3} =$ _____

$5\frac{2}{3} - 2\frac{2}{9} =$ _____

$2\frac{1}{4} + 5\frac{9}{10} =$ _____

$7\frac{1}{8} - 5\frac{5}{12} =$ _____

Complete the equations.

$(9 \times 8) \div 6 = 3 \times \boxed{}$

$3 \times \boxed{} = 4 \times \boxed{}$

$100 - 75 = 5 \times \boxed{}$

Soda   18 for $12.00
Plastic Cups   9 for $2.00
Chips   3 bags for $3.00

Mrs. MacLaren wants to buy an equal number of the above items for the school picnic. The items are sold only in multiples of 3, 9, and 18. What is the least number of each she can purchase, and how much will she spend on the items?

What is the rule?

$\frac{3}{6} \rightarrow 1$

$\frac{6}{18} \rightarrow \frac{15}{18}$

$\frac{1}{7} \rightarrow \frac{9}{14}$

$\frac{3}{5} \rightarrow 1\frac{1}{10}$

(Hint: add ?)

_____

_____

Use > or <.

25.037 $\boxed{}$ 25.307

9,267.52 $\boxed{}$ 9,263.88

32,947.1 $\boxed{}$ 3,297.9

985.269 $\boxed{}$ 985.264

1,007.057 $\boxed{}$ 1,007.02

By using the line of symmetry, what is the length of line segment FG?

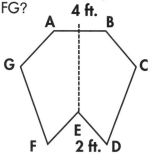

Which point best represents:

$\frac{79}{7}$ _____ $\frac{121}{9}$ _____

$\frac{154}{12}$ _____

Solve.

$39\overline{)163.8}$

$84\overline{)530.88}$

Highest Recorded Temperature Degrees Fahrenheit

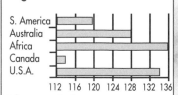

The total degrees Fahrenheit for the 3 highest temperatures is

_____ °F.

A garden maze is built in the shape of a hexagon inside an octagon. Each side, both inner and outer, have vined arches for doorways. Each arch is made of 12 gourd vines. How many gourd vines are in the maze? (Hint: draw a picture.)

Mr. Rodriguez travels from Boston to Salt Lake City, a distance of about 4,848.821 miles round trip. On the average, he makes this trip 9.25 times a year. Rounded to the nearest tenth of a mile, how far does he travel each year?

A   B

Spinner
A   B   Possible Outcomes
1 { 1   1,1
      2   1,2
      3   1,3
2   1   2,1

(Continue the chart if needed on the back)
What is the probability of spinning a 2 on both spinners?

1

$$\begin{array}{r} 139 \\ \times\ .25 \\ \hline \end{array}$$

2

$$48\overline{)124.8}$$

3

$\frac{2}{6} \rightarrow 1$	$\frac{1}{2} \rightarrow 1\frac{1}{6}$
$\frac{4}{15} \rightarrow \frac{14}{15}$	$\frac{2}{7} \rightarrow \frac{20}{21}$

What is the rule?

4

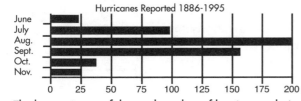

Which point best represents:

$\frac{98}{15}$ ____ $\frac{43}{9}$ ____ $\frac{104}{20}$ ____ $\frac{65}{9}$ ____

5 Lotty's Fruit Drink Cafe ordered 27 cases of drink mixes. Each case holds 24 boxes and each box contains 250 individual packets of fruit drink mix. How many individual packets of fruit drink mix are in each case?

6

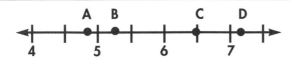

Hurricanes Reported 1886-1995

The best estimate of the total number of hurricanes during the 3 highest frequency months is:

- ⬭ 200
- ⬭ 400
- ⬭ 300
- ⬭ 500

7 Cobblestone walls surround an oriental garden built in the shape of a triangle. These walls are inside another square shaped wall. From the outside going in there is a door on every wall. Each door has a 12 board slatted gate. How many boards are in the garden gates?
(Hint: draw a picture.)

8

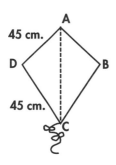

45 cm.

45 cm.

Using the line of symmetry, what is the length of line segment AB?

_____

9 To which place have the pairs of numerals been rounded?

35.087 → 35.1

_____ place

10.621 → 11.0

_____ place

10 Mrs. Kline spends an average of $173.82 per week on groceries. Rounded to the nearest dollar, about how much does she spend each year? (52 weeks = year)

- ⬭ $9,040.64
- ⬭ $9,050.00
- ⬭ $9,039.00
- ⬭ $9,100.00
- ⬭ not here

Using the numerals 2-9 one time each in the patterns below, create the greatest and least number possible.

greatest numeral:

_ _ _ _ _ _ . _ _ _ _

least numeral:

_ _ _ _ _ _ . _ _ _ _

Label: F = flip T = turn

_____

_____

_____

Kim bought party favors. Underline the equation that shows how to find the total number of items she bought if she purchased 8 bags of 23 balloons, 7 packs of 12 party hats, and 15 packages of 4 gumballs.

$(8 + 23) \times (7 + 12) \times (15 + 4)$

$(8 \times 23) \times (7 \times 12) \times (15 \times 4)$

$(8 \times 23) + (7 \times 12) + (15 \times 4)$

Solve.

$$\begin{array}{r} 12.52 \\ \times\ 8.4 \\ \hline \end{array}$$

$$\begin{array}{r} 560.903 \\ +\ 429.598 \\ \hline \end{array}$$

A ratio is used to compare two quantities.

▲ ▲ ■ ■ ■ ○
□ □ □ □ □ □ ★

example: ▲ compared to ❏ is 2 to 6 or $\frac{2}{6}$ or 2:6.

Write the ratios for:

★ to ■ = _____

○ to ▲ = _____

■ to ❏ = _____

Prime numbers have only 2 factors. Composite numbers have more than two factors. Label each numeral below as P (prime) or C (composite).

12_____   7_____

33_____   25_____

5_____   111_____

An adult hippopotamus eats about 130 pounds of vegetable matter per day. How many pounds of vegetable matter would a hippotamus eat during the month of July?

* About how many tons of food would this be?

What is the rule?

$\frac{6}{20}$ → $\frac{2}{20}$

$\frac{2}{3}$ → $\frac{7}{15}$

$\frac{1}{2}$ → $\frac{3}{10}$

$\frac{7}{12}$ → $\frac{23}{60}$

_____

Use > or <

$.25 \times 4$ ☐ $.012 \times 12$

$23.65 - .89$ ☐ $21.60 + .97$

$69.12 \div 3$ ☐ $23.91 \times .2$

$.45 \times .45$ ☐ $.26 + .26$

For a 4th of July Celebration the city used 3,500 meters of red, white, and blue crepe paper to decorate the park pavilion. How many kilometers of crepe paper did they use?

How many centimeters of crepe paper would this be?

Write the numeral for: twenty-seven billion, four hundred ninety-two million, eight

_____

six hundred fifty million, one hundred two thousand, five hundred

_____

Solve.

$97\overline{)340.664}$

$$\begin{array}{r} 621.027 \\ -\ 518.634 \\ \hline \end{array}$$

Whales   Length in feet

Minke
Bowhead
Gray
Killer
Blue
Fin
Sei

25   50   75   100

Which whales measure over 50 feet in length?

_____

_____

A Medieval Castle's first story is in the shape of an octagon, the second story in the shape of a hexagon, and the third story in the shape of a square. On each level, each corner has a merlon with 8 openings where the castle's defenders could set their weapons. How many such openings are in this castle?

A B

If basket A can hold 125 apples, about how many of basket B would be needed to fill basket A?

◯ 1

◯ 2

◯ 10

◯ 20

$1\frac{1}{4} + 2\frac{3}{4} =$ _____

$7\frac{2}{3} + 3\frac{8}{9} =$ _____

$9\frac{1}{3} - 2\frac{2}{3} =$ _____

$6 - 1\frac{4}{12} =$ _____

1

$$\begin{array}{r} 10.5 \\ \times\ 9.37 \\ \hline \end{array}$$

$$\begin{array}{r} \frac{6}{9} \\ +\ \frac{5}{7} \\ \hline \end{array}$$

2

$$13\overline{)377.65}$$

3

A   B

If bag A can hold 215 marbles, how many of bag B would it take to fill bag A?

◯ $1\frac{1}{2}$ ◯ 3   ◯ $5\frac{1}{2}$

4 For the PTA banquet, Ms. Kim bought 8 cases of 12 pack sodas, 15 cartons of 10 pack juice drinks, and 4 boxes of 4 can juice concentrate. Which equation shows how to find the total number of drinks she bought?

◯ (8 x 12) + (15 x 10) + (4 x 4)

◯ (8 + 12) + (15 + 10) + (4 + 4)

◯ 8 x (12 + 15) x 10 + (4 x 4)

5 Prime numbers have only 2 factors. Composite numbers have more than two factors. Label each numeral below as P (prime) or C (composite).

36 _____   9 _____

73 _____   67 _____

13 _____   204 _____

6 Use **>** or **<**.

.35 x 8 ☐ 5.23 + .078

82.061-74.359 ☐ 49.49 ÷ 7

.962 x .53 ☐ .978 x .67

7 Using the numerals 0,2,4,6,8,9,7,5 one time each in the patterns below, create the greatest and least number possible.

greatest numeral:

__ __ __ __ __ . __ __ __

least numeral:

__ __ __ __ __ . __ __ __

8 Label: F = flip   T = turn

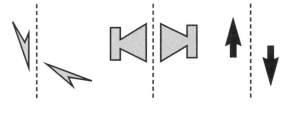

___   ___   ___

9 Camels that graze in the Sahara may go all winter without water, but in the summer they may drink 19 liters of water a day. How many liters of water might a camel drink during 3 weeks in the summer?

10

The ratio of 🐧 to 🐧 is 7:1. What is the ratio of:

🐟 to 🦞 = _____

🐠 to 🐧 = _____

Which numeral has a digit of lesser value in the hundred thousands place than in the hundreds place?

○ 75,462,190
○ 369,502,431
○ 2,156,287,302
○ 8,032,265,299

Give the number of vertices, faces, and edges.

V	F	E

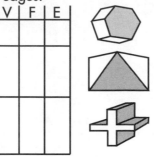

Dennis bought 15 stamp albums for $1.35 each and 4 baseball card sets for $6.89 a piece. Eric bought 6 comic books for $2.45 each and 7 packs of model seals for $4.76 each. What is the difference in the amount of change due the boys if they both gave the cashier $50.00?

```
    45.521
 1,259.0
   786.099
+ 57,877.02


  78,866.039
- 31,427.06
```

Equivalent fractions name equal ratios. For example

2:3 or $\frac{2}{3}$ is the same as

4:6 or $\frac{4}{6}$

Can you list other equal ratios for **2:3**?

___ ___

Complete the factor tree to find the prime factorization.

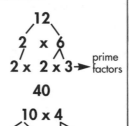

```
        12
      2 × 6
    2 × 2 × 3 → prime factors

        40
      10 × 4
    __ × __ × __
```

A hummingbird's wings beat about 68.9 times a second. How many beats is this per hour?

* About how many beats would this be per day?

24.859
24.874
24.889
24.904

Continue the pattern.

_____
_____
_____
_____
_____

Planets	Equatorial Diameter in Kilometers
Saturn	120,660
Earth	12,756
Uranus	51,810
Jupiter	142,800
Neptune	49,528

List the planets in order from least to greatest diameter.
1. _____
2. _____
3. _____
4. _____
5. _____

The highway department painted a new stripe on $7\frac{1}{2}$ kilometers of highway. The paint truck carried enough paint for 500 meters. How many times did the truck need to refill to paint the new stripe?

*How many dekameters long was the stripe?

Write the numeral for:

six hundred seventy-one billion, five hundred three million, eighty-two thousand, thirty-four

_____

three billion, two hundred nine thousand, six hundred forty-seven

_____

To multiply fractions, multiply the numerators, then multiply the denominators.

$\frac{2}{3} \times \frac{2}{3} = \frac{4}{9}$

$\frac{1}{7} \times \frac{6}{8} = $ _____

$\frac{4}{5} \times \frac{6}{10} = $ _____

$\frac{3}{8} \times \frac{5}{7} = $ _____

Licks to the center of a Tootsie Roll Pop™   Boys ■   Girls □

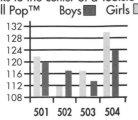

```
132
128
124
120
116
112
108
    501  502  503  504
```

What is the difference in the total number of licks taken by the girls and the total number of licks taken by the boys? _____

The 7 Dwarfs measured their heights. Sleepy is taller than Grumpy. Dopey is taller than Sneezy. Doc is not as tall as Sneezy. Bashful is taller than Grumpy but not as tall as Sleepy. Happy is shorter than Doc. Which dwarf is the tallest?

_____

the shortest? _____
in the middle? _____

A   B

If page A holds 362 stamps, about how many stamps would be needed to fill page B?

○ 500
○ 1,000
○ 1,500
○ 2,000

$8 - 5\frac{6}{10} = $ _____

$3\frac{7}{20} - 1\frac{2}{5} = $ _____

$9\frac{10}{16} + 3\frac{7}{8} = $ _____

$6\frac{11}{15} + 5\frac{4}{5} = $ _____

1

```
     .057          4
  2,188.8         18
   792.396
+ 45,237.0         6
               +  12
```

2 Multiply. Write the product in simplest terms.

$$\frac{3}{10} \times \frac{7}{8} =$$

$$\frac{9}{12} \times \frac{5}{7} =$$

3 Continue the pattern.

39.452 _____

39.562 _____

39.672 _____

39.782 _____

4 Write the numeral for:

fifty-one million, nine hundred seventy-eight thousand, four hundred

_____

sixty billion, twenty-five million, three hundred six thousand, eighteen

_____

5 Trenda bought 5 sets of deco-nails for $3.50 a set and 12 hair clips for $2.00 a piece. Lisha bought 8 bangle bracelets for $2.34 each and 4 pair of earrings for $5.00 a pair. What is the difference in the amount of change due the girls if they both give the cashier $50.00?

6 Watermelon Seed Spittin' Contest
Distance in Inches

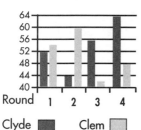

Clyde and Clem competed in the Annual Seed Spittin' Contest. Who won?

_____

by how many inches?

_____

Clyde ■   Clem ▢

7 The Lazies got tired of yawning and began arguing about who is the laziest person in the family. Shut-eye is lazier than Lulu but not as lazy as Tuckered. Snoozy is lazier than Slug but not as lazy as Sleepy. Slug is almost as lazy as Tuckered. Who is the laziest?

_____

8 Mr. Hernandez is rebuilding the fence around his grazing pasture. The perimeter of the pasture is $8\frac{1}{2}$ kilometers. His pickup can haul enough lumber for fencing 250 meters at a time. How many loads of lumber will he need to haul to complete the fence?

9 Which numeral has a digit of lesser value in the hundred thousands place than in the billions place?

◯   124,560,738,016

◯   3,689,920,315

◯   78,565,830,716

◯   342,189,375,002

◯   not here

10 Complete the factor trees.

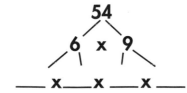

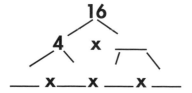

Math 4 today

Name the place and the value of the 9 in each numeral.

79,462,150

_____

3,872.109

_____

2,159,476

_____

Give the number of vertices, faces, and edges.

V	F	E

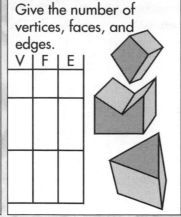

Yesenia needed to do a 840 word research paper for science. After typing 3 pages of her report, she had her computer do a line count. Each page had 15 lines with an average of 14 words per line. Show how to find the number of pages she still needs to type.

$6\frac{3}{8}$ $12\frac{5}{7}$

$2\frac{1}{4}$ $+8\frac{2}{3}$

$+7\frac{9}{16}$

$13\frac{1}{4}$

$-4\frac{2}{3}$

Molly needs 2 teaspoons of cooking oil to make 6 fudge cakes. Complete the ratio chart to see how much cooking oil is needed to make other quantities of fudge cakes.

teaspoons of oil

2					
3	6	18	30	54	100

fudge cakes

Complete the factor tree to find the prime factorization.

63

_ x _
_ x _ x _ prime factors

44

_ x _
_ x _ x _ prime factors

Tinker's Toy Store Sale

Item	Regular Price	Sale Price
Nerf Football	$4.89	$3.99
Super Soaker	$32.15	$29.79
Models	$7.49	$5.19

How much money can Ted save by buying 2 Nerf Footballs, 1 Super Soaker, and 3 Models at the sale prices?

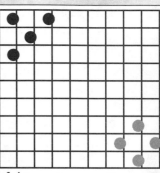

If this pattern continues what will the center row look like?

Kilometer, meter, inch, foot, mile, yard, centimeter, and milimeter. List the units of standard and metric measures in order from least to greatest.

1. _____ 6. _____
2. _____ 7. _____
3. _____ 8. _____
4. _____
5. _____

In Jules Verne's *Twenty Thousand Leagues Under the Sea*, Captain Nemo takes a submarine voyage. A nautical league = 5.556 kilometers or about 3.452 miles. How many kilometers deep did Captain Nemo's sub descend?

How many miles?_____

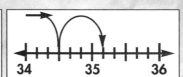

34   35   36

This number line shows:

◯ $34 + 1\frac{1}{2} = 35\frac{1}{2}$

◯ $34\frac{1}{2} + \frac{5}{8} = 35\frac{1}{8}$

◯ $34\frac{3}{4} + 1 = 35\frac{3}{4}$

Multiply. Write the product in simplest terms.

$\frac{9}{15} \times \frac{3}{10} =$ _____

$\frac{3}{8} \times \frac{4}{5} =$ _____

$\frac{6}{30} \times \frac{2}{100} =$ _____

Active Volcanic Sites

Indonesia 130
Phillipines 100
Iceland 25
Japan 33
Chile 25

Of the active volcanic sites shown Indonesia and the Phillipines have...

◯ less than one half
◯ more than one half
◯ about one third

Animal Speeds Miles Per Hour

Cheetah	70
Elk	45
Zebra	40
Rabbit	35
Black Mamba Snake	20
Chicken	9

The answer is...
5 times as fast
What is the question?

_____
_____
_____

B

A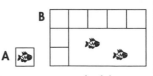

If aquarium A holds 57 fish, about how many fish would aquarium B hold?

◯ 500
◯ 1,000
◯ 1,500
◯ 2,000

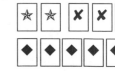

If these cards are shuffled and placed face down what is the probability of drawing a

	in 1 draw	in 60 draws
☆		
✗		
◆		

1

$$5\frac{5}{8} \quad 23\frac{9}{12} \quad 10\frac{1}{5}$$

$$3\frac{7}{16} \quad +5\frac{6}{8} \quad -3\frac{3}{4}$$

$$+4\frac{3}{4}$$

2 Multiply. Write the product in simplest terms.

$$\frac{4}{32} \times \frac{1}{2} = \underline{\hspace{1.5cm}}$$

$$\frac{2}{9} \times \frac{4}{6} = \underline{\hspace{1.5cm}}$$

3
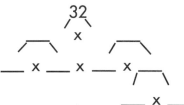
A   B

If 97 popped popcorn kernels fit into bucket A, about how many kernels can bucket B hold?

4 Elan is collecting baseball cards. His goal is to collect 2,000 cards. He already has 3 baseball card albums. Each album has 24 pages and each page holds 16 cards. Show how to find out how many more baseball cards Elan needs to meet his goal.

_____

5 Complete the factor tree.

```
          32
         /
        x
      /  \        /  \
  __ x __ x __  x
                 /  \
              __ x __
```

6 List the units of standard and metric measures in order from greatest to least.

| meter |
| inch |
| kilometer |
| mile |
| centimeter |
| foot |
| millimeter |
| yard |

_____
_____
_____
_____
_____
_____
_____
_____

7 Name the place and the value of the 5 in each numeral.

52,178,096 _____

8,523,746 _____

340,096.852 _____

8 Give the number of vertices, faces, and edges for each figure.

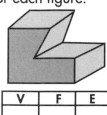

V	F	E

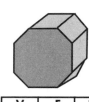

V	F	E

9

Martin's Music and More Sale		
Item	**Regular Price**	**Sale Price**
Cassettes	$6.73	$4.97
Blank Videos	$8.29	$7.79
Select CD's	$13.88	$11.99

How much money can be saved by buying 3 cassettes, 2 blank videos, and 1 CD at the sale prices?

10 The Old Steamers N' Gauge Model Train Club uses 15 sections of track to complete 3 rail layouts. Complete the ratio chart to find how much track is needed for other layouts.

Sections of Track

	15			
1	3	9	15	50

rail layouts

Math 4 today

Name_____

#54

Name the place and the value of the 3 in each numeral.

1,372,650,919

_____

3,107,254,041

_____

9,876.532

_____

Label each pair of figures.
S = similar *and/or*
C = congruent

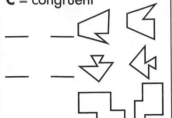

__ __

__ __

__ __

Circle the shapes that have only right angles.

The fireworks supply house delivered 856 sparklers, 494 bottle rockets, and 7 boxes of 125 Roman candles. Show how to find the number of firework assortment packages that can be made if 25 items are in each package.

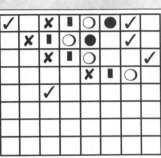

$$4,325.672 + \boxed{}$$
$$\overline{5,010.649}$$

$$8\frac{4}{5} + 3\frac{4}{6} = \boxed{}$$

$$15\frac{2}{9} - \frac{7}{8} = \boxed{}$$

Mr. Eugene makes 6 quarts of his special homemade ice cream by adding 4 eggs to his other secret ingredients. Complete the ratio chart to see how many eggs are needed for more ice cream.

eggs

	4				
3	6	18	30	120	8½

quarts of ice cream

Math Path

$462 \div 3 =$ _____ $\times 7 =$

_____ $+ 22 =$ _____

$\div 50 =$ _____ $- 2 =$

_____ $\times 20$

$=$ _____ $\times 9^2 =$

$\div (9 \times 5) =$ _____

$- (129 \times 2) =$ _____

Connie's Crafts

ITEM	PRICE
Colored Yarn	$5.00
Glass Beads	$3.00
Picture Frame	$7.50

Mrs. Wells purchased some items and received $1.50 in change from a $20.00 bill. What did Mrs. Wells buy?

_____

_____

_____

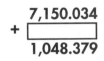

What is the pattern?

Which row if any will be blank?

Circle the larger unit of measure in each pair. If they are equal, circle both.

5 dm.   1 m.

500 mm.   50 cm.

100 m.   1 km.

100 cm.   1 m.

2000 g.   1 kg.

Measuring Circles

π = pi = 3.14

circumference = diameter $\times \pi$

area = $\pi \times$ radius^2

Find the circumference and the area of the circle below.

circumference =

_____mm.

12mm

area=

_____mm.

97   98   99

This number line shows:

◯ $97 + 1\frac{1}{2} = 98\frac{1}{2}$

◯ $99\frac{1}{2} - \frac{5}{8} = 98\frac{1}{8}$

◯ $98\frac{7}{8} - 1\frac{3}{4} = 97\frac{1}{8}$

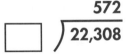

$$7,150.034 + \boxed{}$$
$$\overline{1,048.379}$$

$$\boxed{}\overline{)22,308}\quad 572$$

U.S.A. Endangered Species

Fish

Clams

Birds

Mammals

50 55 60 65 70 75

The answer is about 23. What is the question?

_____

_____

◄── continued

Answer: 139
Question?_____

_____

_____

_____

Answer: 97
Question?_____

Tara completed 9 oil paintings. The shortest time she took to complete a painting was 3 weeks and the longest time she needed was 12 weeks. What is a reasonable estimate of the time it took to complete all 9 paintings?

◯ **57 weeks**

◯ **114 weeks**

◯ **27 weeks**

Complete the chart to show the the probability of spinning a

	in 1 spin	in 40 spins
●		
○		
●		

Name _____

1

3,652.809
+ [   ]
5,003.475

459
x [   ]
37,179

2

[   ]) 17,296   368

3 Complete the chart to show the probability of spinning ...

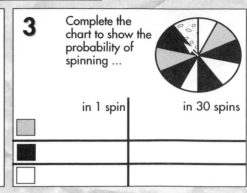

	in 1 spin	in 30 spins
▨		
■		
□		

4

[number line from 52 to 55 with an arrow curving left]

The number line shows:

◯ $54\frac{1}{8} - 1\frac{1}{2} = 52\frac{5}{8}$ ◯ $54\frac{2}{8} - 1\frac{1}{4} = 52\frac{1}{2}$

◯ $52 + 2 = 54$ ◯ $54 - 2 = 52$

5 From a flood relief, Baker City received 309 dry goods, 452 drinks, and 36 cases of canned goods holding 124 cans each. Show how many food boxes the volunteers can pack so that each box has 55 items.

6 Write a question for each answer.

Recorded. Exceptional Lifespans of Animals

[bar graph with categories: dog, cow, monkey, hippo, chicken, bear; x-axis: Number of Years 20 24 28 32 36 40 44 48 52]

1. About twice as many years as the dog.

2. About 10 years longer.

7

Susie's Sweet Shoppe	
Item	Price
Gummi Yummies (bag)	$4.82
Chocolate Delights (box)	$10.33
Slurpy Sundae	$3.99

Pave and Margo bought some goodies at the Sweet Shoppe and received $1.87 change from $25.00. What did they buy?

8 Find the area and circumference of each circle.
$\pi = 3.14$ Area $= \pi R^2$ Circumference $= D \times \pi$

A [circle with 22 mm]

B [circle with 10 mm]

	Circle	A	B
Area:		___	___
Circumference:		___	___

9 Name the place and the value of the **2** in each numeral.

2**3**1,178,096 _____

3,0**2**9,541 _____

103,400.10**2** _____

10 Since their club began, the Quick Quilters have completed 13 quilts. The American Flag quilt took them 18 weeks to complete which was their longest time. A baby quilt took them only 5 weeks to finish. What is a reasonable estimate of the time it took to complete all 13 quilts?

◯ **16 weeks**

◯ **60 weeks**

◯ **160 weeks**

◯ **1,160 weeks**

◯ **not here**

Which numeral has a 3 in the hundreds place?
- ⬭ 231
- ⬤ 390
- ⬭ 803
- ⬭ 730

Which shape is a triangle?

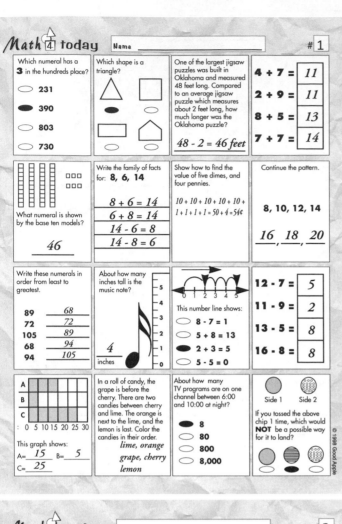

One of the largest jigsaw puzzles was built in Oklahoma and measured 48 feet long. Compared to an average jigsaw puzzle which measures about 2 feet long, how much longer was the Oklahoma puzzle?

$48 - 2 = 46$ feet

$4 + 7 = \boxed{11}$
$2 + 9 = \boxed{11}$
$8 + 5 = \boxed{13}$
$7 + 7 = \boxed{14}$

What numeral is shown by the base ten models?

$\underline{46}$

Write the family of facts for: 8, 6, 14

$8 + 6 = 14$
$6 + 8 = 14$
$14 - 6 = 8$
$14 - 8 = 6$

Show how to find the value of five dimes, and four pennies.

$10 + 10 + 10 + 10 + 10 + 1 + 1 + 1 + 1 = 50 + 4 = 54¢$

Continue the pattern.

8, 10, 12, 14

$\underline{16}$, $\underline{18}$, $\underline{20}$

Write these numerals in order from least to greatest.

89	68
72	72
105	89
68	94
94	105

About how many inches tall is the music note?

$\underline{4}$ inches

This number line shows:
- ⬭ 8 - 7 = 1
- ⬭ 5 + 8 = 13
- ⬤ 2 + 3 = 5
- ⬭ 5 - 5 = 0

$12 - 7 = \boxed{5}$
$11 - 9 = \boxed{2}$
$13 - 5 = \boxed{8}$
$16 - 8 = \boxed{8}$

This graph shows:
A = $\underline{15}$ B = $\underline{5}$
C = $\underline{25}$

In a roll of candy, the grape is before the cherry. There are two candies between cherry and lime. The orange is next to the lime, and the lemon is last. Color the candies in their order.

lime, orange grape, cherry lemon

About how many TV programs are on one channel between 6:00 and 10:00 at night?
- ⬤ 8
- ⬭ 80
- ⬭ 800
- ⬭ 8,000

Side 1   Side 2

If you tossed the above chip 1 time, which would NOT be a possible way for it to land?

© 1998 Good Apple

1
$8 + 5 = \boxed{13}$
$9 + 2 = \boxed{11}$
$6 + 7 = \boxed{13}$

2
$15 - 8 = \boxed{7}$
$14 - 5 = \boxed{9}$
$17 - 9 = \boxed{8}$

3 About how many pieces of mail would 1 family receive in a day?
- ⬭ 6000
- ⬭ 600
- ⬭ 60
- ⬤ 6

4 One of the largest beds was built in 1430 in Belgium. This bed was 19 feet long. Today, an average bed is about 6 feet long. How much longer was the bed built in 1430?

$19 - 6 = 13$ feet

5 Write the family of facts for 3, 6, and 9.

$3 + 6 = 9$
$6 + 3 = 9$
$9 - 6 = 3$
$9 - 3 = 6$

6 Write these numerals in order from least to greatest.

50	50
65	65
89	79
85	85
79	89

7 Which numeral has a 2 in the tens place?
- ⬤ 921
- ⬭ 192
- ⬭ 2
- ⬭ 209

8 Which shape is a triangle?

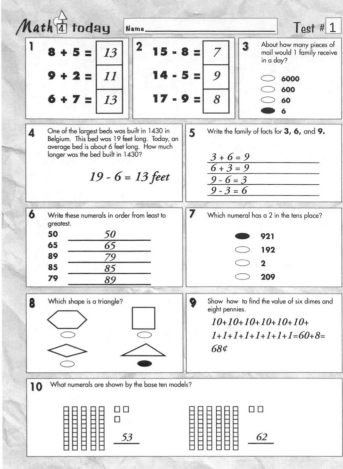

9 Show how to find the value of six dimes and eight pennies.

$10 + 10 + 10 + 10 + 10 + 10 + 1 + 1 + 1 + 1 + 1 + 1 + 1 + 1 = 60 + 8 = 68¢$

10 What numerals are shown by the base ten models?

$\underline{53}$ $\underline{62}$

© 1998 Good Apple

In 673

the $\underline{7}$ is in the tens place.
the $\underline{6}$ is in the hundreds place.
the $\underline{3}$ is in the ones place.

Which shape best represents a cube?

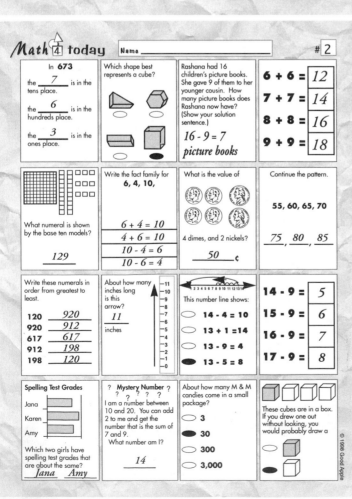

Rashana had 16 children's picture books. She gave 9 of them to her younger cousin. How many picture books does Rashana now have? (Show your solution sentence.)

$16 - 9 = 7$ picture books

$6 + 6 = \boxed{12}$
$7 + 7 = \boxed{14}$
$8 + 8 = \boxed{16}$
$9 + 9 = \boxed{18}$

What numeral is shown by the base ten models?

$\underline{129}$

Write the fact family for 6, 4, 10,

$6 + 4 = 10$
$4 + 6 = 10$
$10 - 4 = 6$
$10 - 6 = 4$

What is the value of

4 dimes, and 2 nickels?

$\underline{50}$ ¢

Continue the pattern.

55, 60, 65, 70

$\underline{75}$, $\underline{80}$, $\underline{85}$

Write these numerals in order from greatest to least.

120	920
920	912
617	617
912	198
198	120

About how many inches long is this arrow?

$\underline{11}$ inches

This number line shows:
- ⬭ 14 - 4 = 10
- ⬭ 13 + 1 = 14
- ⬭ 13 - 9 = 4
- ⬤ 13 - 5 = 8

$14 - 9 = \boxed{5}$
$15 - 9 = \boxed{6}$
$16 - 9 = \boxed{7}$
$17 - 9 = \boxed{8}$

Spelling Test Grades

Jana
Karen
Amy

Which two girls have spelling test grades that are about the same?

$\underline{Jana}$ $\underline{Amy}$

? Mystery Number ?
? ? ? ? ?
I am a number between 10 and 20. You can add 2 to me and get the number that is the sum of 7 and 9. What number am I?

$\underline{14}$

About how many M & M candies come in a small package?
- ⬭ 3
- ⬤ 30
- ⬭ 300
- ⬭ 3,000

These cubes are in a box. If you drew one out without looking, you would probably draw a

© 1998 Good Apple

1
$5 + 5 = \boxed{10}$
$9 + 9 = \boxed{18}$
$7 + 7 = \boxed{14}$

2
$11 - 9 = \boxed{2}$
$13 - 4 = \boxed{9}$
$15 - 9 = \boxed{6}$

3 Continue the pattern.

35, 40, 45, 50

$\underline{55}$, $\underline{60}$, $\underline{65}$

4

This number line shows:
- ⬭ 9 + 9 = 18
- ⬤ 17 - 8 = 9
- ⬭ 8 + 5 = 13
- ⬭ 17 - 10 = 7

5 Nina bought 17 peppermints. She shared 8 of them with her friend. How many peppermints does Nina now have?

$17 - 8 = 9$ peppermints

6 Fourth Grade's Favorite Pets

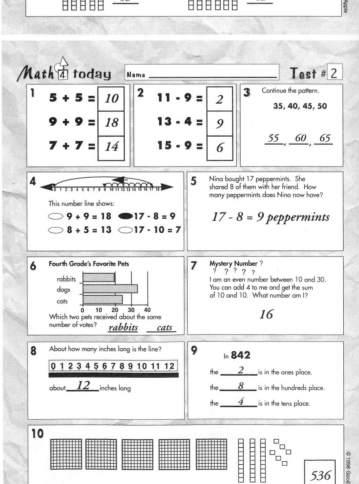

rabbits
dogs
cats

Which two pets received about the same number of votes? $\underline{rabbits}$ $\underline{cats}$

7 Mystery Number ?
? ? ? ? ?
I am an even number between 10 and 30. You can add 4 to me and get the sum of 10 and 10. What number am I?

$\underline{16}$

8 About how many inches long is the line?

`0 1 2 3 4 5 6 7 8 9 10 11 12`

about $\underline{12}$ inches long

9 In 842

the $\underline{2}$ is in the ones place.
the $\underline{8}$ is in the hundreds place.
the $\underline{4}$ is in the tens place.

10

What numeral is shown by the base ten models?

$\boxed{536}$

© 1998 Good Apple

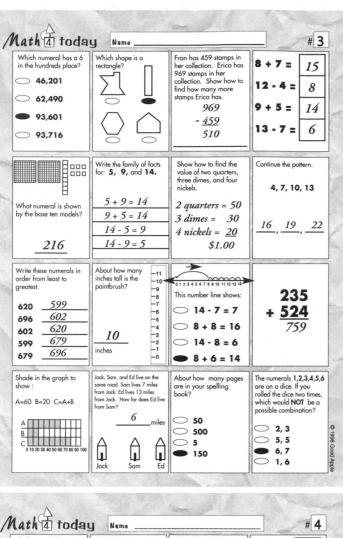

Math 4 today — Name _____ #3

- Which numeral has a 6 in the hundreds place?
  - 46,201
  - 62,490
  - ● 93,601
  - 93,716
- Which shape is a rectangle?
- Fran has 459 stamps in her collection. Erica has 969 stamps in her collection. Show how to find how many more stamps Erica has.
  $$969 - 459 = 510$$
- 8 + 7 = 15
- 12 - 4 = 8
- 9 + 5 = 14
- 13 - 7 = 6
- What numeral is shown by the base ten models? **216**
- Write the family of facts for: **5, 9, and 14.**
  - 5 + 9 = 14
  - 9 + 5 = 14
  - 14 - 5 = 9
  - 14 - 9 = 5
- Show how to find the value of two quarters, three dimes, and four nickels.
  - 2 quarters = 50
  - 3 dimes = 30
  - 4 nickels = 20
  - $1.00
- Continue the pattern. 4, 7, 10, 13 ... 16, 19, 22
- Write these numerals in order from least to greatest. 620 / 599, 696 / 602, 602 / 620, 599 / 679, 679 / 696
- About how many inches tall is the paintbrush? 10 inches
- This number line shows:
  - 14 - 7 = 7
  - 8 + 8 = 16
  - 14 - 8 = 6
  - ● 8 + 6 = 14
- 235 + 524 = 759
- Shade in the graph to show: A=60 B=20 C=A+B
- Jack, Sam, and Ed live on the same road. Sam lives 7 miles from Jack. Ed lives 13 miles from Jack. How far does Ed live from Sam? 6 miles
- About how many pages are in your spelling book?
  - 50
  - 500
  - 5
  - ● 150
- The numerals 1,2,3,4,5,6 are on a dice. If you rolled the dice two times, which would be **NOT** be a possible combination?
  - 2, 3
  - 5, 5
  - ● 6, 7
  - 1, 6

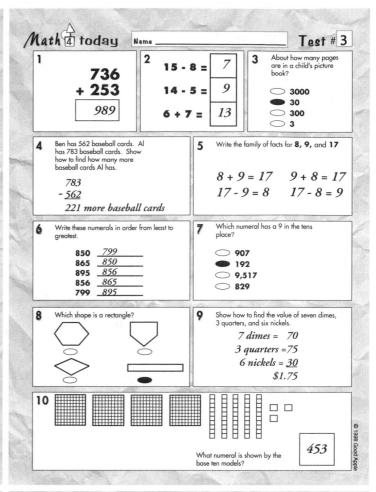

Math 4 today — Name _____ Test #3

1. 736 + 253 = 989
2. 15 - 8 = 7, 14 - 5 = 9, 6 + 7 = 13
3. About how many pages are in a child's picture book?
   - 3000
   - ● 30
   - 300
   - 3
4. Ben has 562 baseball cards. Al has 783 baseball cards. Show how to find how many more baseball cards Al has.
   $$783 - 562 = 221 \text{ more baseball cards}$$
5. Write the family of facts for **8, 9, and 17.**
   - 8 + 9 = 17   9 + 8 = 17
   - 17 - 9 = 8   17 - 8 = 9
6. Write these numerals in order from least to greatest. 850 / 799, 865 / 850, 895 / 856, 856 / 865, 799 / 895
7. Which numeral has a 9 in the tens place?
   - 907
   - ● 192
   - 9,517
   - 829
8. Which shape is a rectangle?
9. Show how to find the value of seven dimes, 3 quarters, and six nickels.
   - 7 dimes = 70
   - 3 quarters = 75
   - 6 nickels = 30
   - $1.75
10. What numeral is shown by the base ten models? 453

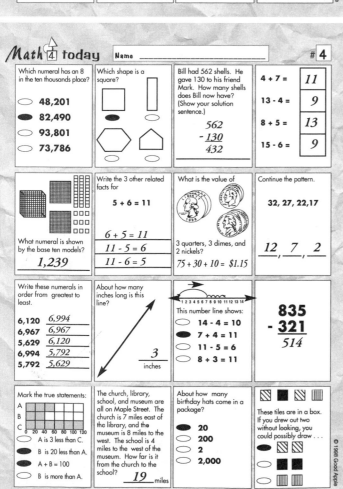

Math 4 today — Name _____ #4

- Which numeral has an 8 in the ten thousands place?
  - 48,201
  - ● 82,490
  - 93,801
  - 73,786
- Which shape is a square?
- Bill had 562 shells. He gave 130 to his friend Mark. How many shells does Bill now have? (Show your solution sentence.)
  $$562 - 130 = 432$$
- 4 + 7 = 11
- 13 - 4 = 9
- 8 + 5 = 13
- 15 - 6 = 9
- What numeral is shown by the base ten models? **1,239**
- Write the 3 other related facts for 5 + 6 = 11
  - 6 + 5 = 11
  - 11 - 5 = 6
  - 11 - 6 = 5
- What is the value of 3 quarters, 3 dimes, and 2 nickels? 75 + 30 + 10 = $1.15
- Continue the pattern. 32, 27, 22, 17 ... 12, 7, 2
- Write these numerals in order from greatest to least. 6,120 / 6,994, 6,967 / 6,967, 5,629 / 6,120, 6,994 / 5,792, 5,792 / 5,629
- About how many inches long is this line? 3 inches
- This number line shows:
  - 14 - 4 = 10
  - ● 7 + 4 = 11
  - 11 - 5 = 6
  - 8 + 3 = 11
- 835 - 321 = 514
- Mark the true statements:
  - A is 3 less than C.
  - ● B is 20 less than A.
  - ● A + B = 100
  - B is more than A.
- The church, library, school, and museum are all on Maple Street. The church is 7 miles east of the library, and the museum is 8 miles to the west. The school is 4 miles to the west of the museum. How far is it from the church to the school? 19 miles
- About how many birthday hats come in a package?
  - ● 20
  - 200
  - 2
  - 2,000
- These tiles are in a box. If you drew out two without looking, you could possibly draw ...

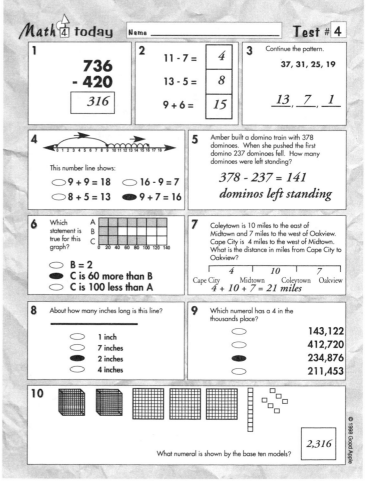

Math 4 today — Name _____ Test #4

1. 736 - 420 = 316
2. 11 - 7 = 4, 13 - 5 = 8, 9 + 6 = 15
3. Continue the pattern. 37, 31, 25, 19 ... 13, 7, 1
4. This number line shows:
   - 9 + 9 = 18   16 - 9 = 7
   - 8 + 5 = 13   ● 9 + 7 = 16
5. Amber built a domino train with 378 dominoes. When she pushed the first domino 237 dominoes fell. How many dominoes were left standing?
   $$378 - 237 = 141 \text{ dominos left standing}$$
6. Which statement is true for this graph?
   - B = 2
   - ● C is 60 more than B
   - C is 100 less than A
7. Coleytown is 10 miles to the east of Midtown and 7 miles to the west of Oakview. Cape City is 4 miles to the west of Midtown. What is the distance in miles from Cape City to Oakview?
   Cape City — 4 — Midtown — 10 — Coleytown — 7 — Oakview
   4 + 10 + 7 = 21 miles
8. About how many inches long is this line?
   - 1 inch
   - 7 inches
   - ● 2 inches
   - 4 inches
9. Which numeral has a 4 in the thousands place?
   - 143,122
   - 412,720
   - ● 234,876
   - 211,453
10. What numeral is shown by the base ten models? 2,316

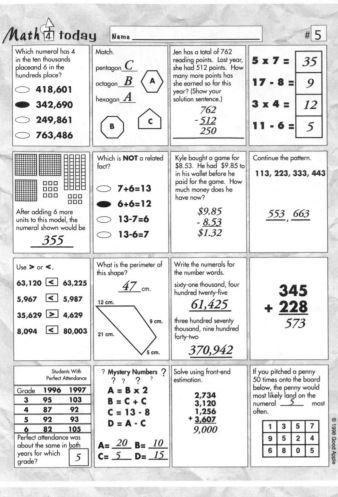

Which numeral has 4 in the ten thousands place and 6 in the hundreds place?
- ○ 418,601
- ● 342,690
- ○ 249,861
- ○ 763,486

Match.
pentagon _C_
octagon _B_
hexagon _A_

(shapes A hexagon, B octagon, C pentagon)

Jen has a total of 762 reading points. Last year, she had 512 points. How many more points has she earned so far this year? (Show your solution sentence.)

762
- 512
250

5 x 7 = | 35
17 - 8 = | 9
3 x 4 = | 12
11 - 6 = | 5

(grid model) **After adding 6 more units to this model, the numeral shown would be _355_**

Which is NOT a related fact?
- ○ 7+6=13
- ● 6+6=12
- ○ 13-7=6
- ○ 13-6=7

Kyle bought a game for $8.53. He had $9.85 to in his wallet before he paid for the game. How much money does he have now?

$9.85
- 8.53
$1.32

Continue the pattern.

113, 223, 333, 443

_553_ , _663_

Use > or <.

63,120 [<] 63,225
5,967 [<] 5,987
35,629 [>] 4,629
8,094 [<] 80,003

What is the perimeter of this shape?
_47_ cm.
12 cm.
9 cm.
21 cm.
5 cm.

Write the numerals for the number words.

sixty-one thousand, four hundred twenty-five
_61,425_

three hundred seventy thousand, nine hundred forty-two
_370,942_

345
+ 228
573

Students With Perfect Attendance		
Grade	1996	1997
3	95	103
4	87	92
5	92	93
6	82	105

Perfect attendance was about the same in both years for which grade? [5]

? Mystery Numbers ?
? ? ?
A = B x 2
B = C + C
C = 13 - 8
D = A - C
A= _20_ B= _10_
C= _5_ D= _15_

Solve using front-end estimation.

2,734
3,120
1,256
+ 3,607
9,000

If you pitched a penny 50 times onto the board below, the penny would most likely land on the numeral _5_ most often.

1	3	5	7
9	5	2	4
6	8	0	5

© 1998 Good Apple

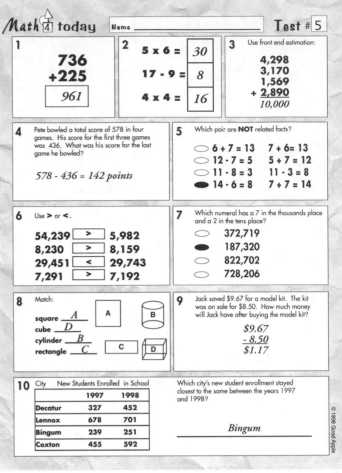

1
736
+225
961

2
5 x 6 = | 30
17 - 9 = | 8
4 x 4 = | 16

3 Use front end estimation:
4,298
3,170
1,569
+ 2,890
10,000

4 Pete bowled a total score of 578 in four games. His score for the first three games was 436. What was his score for the last game he bowled?

578 - 436 = 142 points

5 Which pair are NOT related facts?
- ○ 6 + 7 = 13   7 + 6= 13
- ○ 12 - 7 = 5   5 + 7 = 12
- ○ 11 - 8 = 3   11 - 3 = 8
- ● 14 - 6 = 8   7 + 7 = 14

6 Use > or <.
54,239 [>] 5,982
8,230 [>] 8,159
29,451 [<] 29,743
7,291 [>] 7,192

7 Which numeral has a 7 in the thousands place and a 2 in the tens place?
- ○ 372,719
- ● 187,320
- ○ 822,702
- ○ 728,206

8 Match:
square _A_
cube _D_
cylinder _B_
rectangle _C_

9 Jack saved $9.67 for a model kit. The kit was on sale for $8.50. How much money will Jack have after buying the model kit?

$9.67
- 8.50
$1.17

10
City	New Students Enrolled in School	
	1997	1998
Decatur	327	452
Lennox	678	701
Bingum	239	251
Coxton	455	592

Which city's new student enrollment stayed closest to the same between the years 1997 and 1998?

Bingum

© 1998 Good Apple

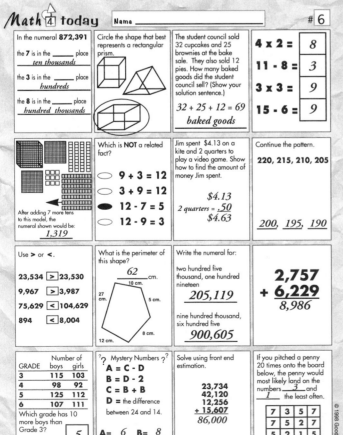

In the numeral 872,391
the 7 is in the _ten thousands_ place
the 3 is in the _hundreds_ place
the 8 is in the _hundred thousands_ place

Circle the shape that best represents a rectangular prism.

The student council sold 32 cupcakes and 25 brownies at the bake sale. They also sold 12 pies. How many baked goods did the student council sell? (Show your solution sentence.)

32 + 25 + 12 = 69
baked goods

4 x 2 = | 8
11 - 8 = | 3
3 x 3 = | 9
15 - 6 = | 9

(grid model) **After adding 7 more tens to this model, the numeral shown would be: _1,319_**

Which is NOT a related fact?
- ○ 9 + 3 = 12
- ○ 3 + 9 = 12
- ● 12 - 7 = 5
- ○ 12 - 9 = 3

Jim spent $4.13 on a kite and 2 quarters to play a video game. Show how to find the amount of money Jim spent.

$4.13
2 quarters = .50
$4.63

Continue the pattern.

220, 215, 210, 205

_200_, _195_, _190_

Use > or <.

23,534 [>] 23,530
9,967 [>] 3,987
75,629 [<] 104,629
894 [<] 8,004

What is the perimeter of this shape?
_62_ cm.
10 cm.
27 cm.
5 cm.
8 cm.
12 cm.

Write the numeral for:

two hundred five thousand, one hundred nineteen
_205,119_

nine hundred thousand, six hundred five
_900,605_

2,757
+ 6,229
8,986

	Number of	
GRADE	boys	girls
3	115	103
4	98	92
5	125	112
6	107	111

Which grade has 10 more boys than Grade 3? [5]

? Mystery Numbers ?
A = C - D
B = D - 2
C = B + B
D = the difference between 24 and 14.
A= _6_ B= _8_
C= _16_ D= _10_

Solve using front end estimation.

23,734
42,120
12,256
+ 15,607
86,000

If you pitched a penny 20 times onto the board below, the penny would most likely land on the numbers _3_ and _1_ the least often.

7	3	5	7
7	5	2	7
5	2	1	5

© 1998 Good Apple

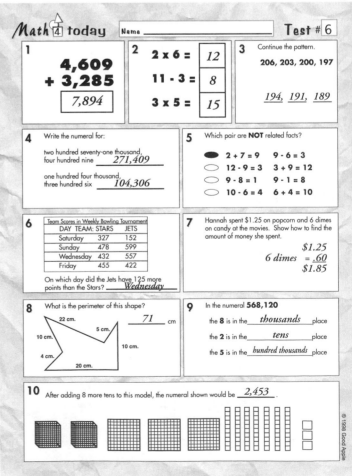

1
4,609
+ 3,285
7,894

2
2 x 6 = | 12
11 - 3 = | 8
3 x 5 = | 15

3 Continue the pattern.
206, 203, 200, 197
_194_, _191_, _189_

4 Write the numeral for:
two hundred seventy-one thousand, four hundred nine _271,409_
one hundred four thousand, three hundred six _104,306_

5 Which pair are NOT related facts?
- ● 2 + 7 = 9   9 - 6 = 3
- ○ 12 - 9 = 3   3 + 9 = 12
- ○ 9 - 8 = 1   9 - 1 = 8
- ○ 10 - 6 = 4   6 + 4 = 10

6
Team Scores in Weekly Bowling Tournament		
DAY	TEAM: STARS	JETS
Saturday	327	152
Sunday	478	599
Wednesday	432	557
Friday	455	422

On which day did the Jets have 125 more points than the Stars? _Wednesday_

7 Hannah spent $1.25 on popcorn and 6 dimes on candy at the movies. Show how to find the amount of money she spent.

$1.25
6 dimes = .60
$1.85

8 What is the perimeter of this shape?
_71_ cm
22 cm.
5 cm.
10 cm.
10 cm.
4 cm.
20 cm.

9 In the numeral 568,120
the 8 is in the _thousands_ place
the 2 is in the _tens_ place
the 5 is in the _hundred thousands_ place

10 After adding 8 more tens to this model, the numeral shown would be _2,453_.

© 1998 Good Apple

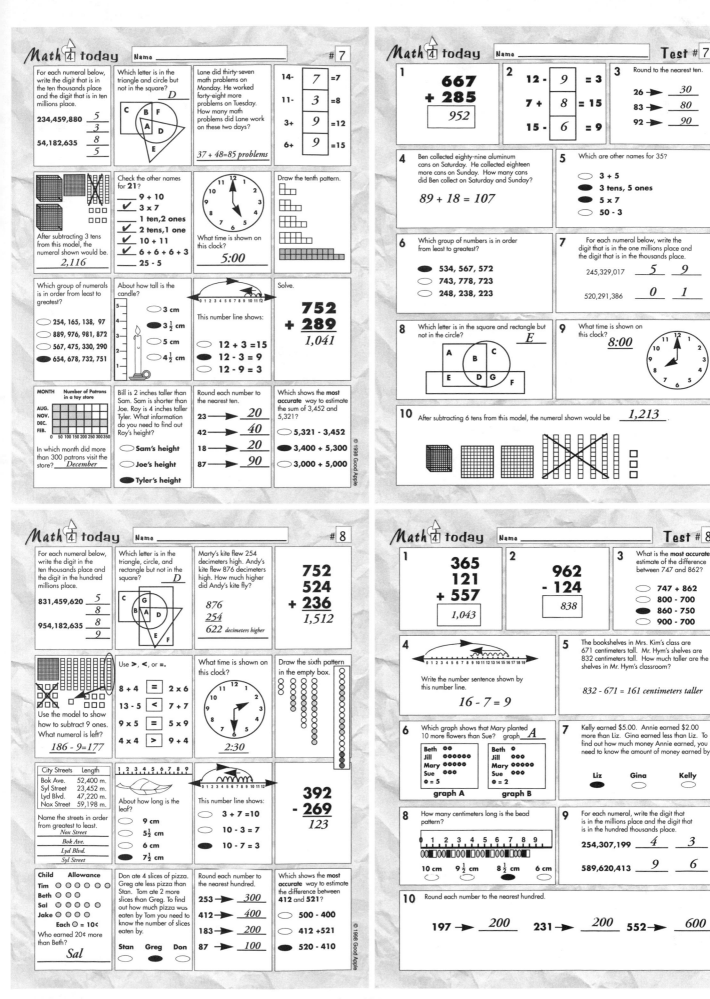

Math 4 today — #7

For each numeral below, write the digit that is in the ten thousands place and the digit that is in ten millions place.

234,459,880 — 5, 3
54,182,635 — 8, 5

Which letter is in the circle but not in the square? — D

Lane did thirty-seven math problems on Monday. He worked forty-eight more problems on Tuesday. How many math problems did Lane work on these two days?

37 + 48 = 85 problems

14 - 7 = 7
11 - 3 = 8
3 + 9 = 12
6 + 9 = 15

After subtracting 3 tens from this model, the numeral shown would be. — 2,116

Check the other names for 21?
- 9 + 10
- ✔ 3 x 7
- 1 ten, 2 ones
- ✔ 2 tens, 1 one
- ✔ 10 + 11
- ✔ 6 + 6 + 6 + 3
- 25 - 5

What time is shown on this clock? — 5:00

Draw the tenth pattern.

Which group of numerals is in order from least to greatest?
- 254, 165, 138, 97
- 889, 976, 981, 872
- 567, 475, 330, 290
- ⬤ 654, 678, 732, 751

About how tall is the candle?
- 3 cm
- ⬤ 3½ cm
- 5 cm
- 4½ cm

This number line shows:
- 12 + 3 = 15
- ⬤ 12 - 3 = 9
- 12 - 9 = 3

Solve. 752 + 289 = 1,041

MONTH / Number of Patrons in a toy store
AUG. NOV. DEC. FEB.
0 50 100 150 200 250 300 350

In which month did more than 300 patrons visit the store? — December

Bill is 2 inches taller than Sam. Sam is shorter than Joe. Roy is 4 inches taller than Tyler. What information do you need to find out Roy's height?
- Sam's height
- Joe's height
- ⬤ Tyler's height

Round each number to the nearest ten.
23 → 20
42 → 40
18 → 20
87 → 90

Which shows the most accurate way to estimate the sum of 3,452 and 5,321?
- 5,321 - 3,452
- ⬤ 3,400 + 5,300
- 3,000 + 5,000

© 1998 Good Apple

Math 4 today — Test #7

1. 667 + 285 = 952

2. 12 - 9 = 3 ; 7 + 8 = 15 ; 15 - 6 = 9

3. **Round to the nearest ten.**
26 → 30
83 → 80
92 → 90

4. **Ben collected eighty-nine aluminum cans on Saturday. He collected eighteen more cans on Sunday. How many cans did Ben collect on Saturday and Sunday?**
89 + 18 = 107

5. **Which are other names for 35?**
- 3 + 5
- ⬤ 3 tens, 5 ones
- ⬤ 5 x 7
- 50 - 3

6. **Which group of numbers is in order from least to greatest?**
- ⬤ 534, 567, 572
- 743, 778, 723
- 248, 238, 223

7. **For each numeral below, write the digit that is in the one place and the digit that is in the thousands place.**
245,329,017 — 5, 9
520,291,386 — 0, 1

8. **Which letter is in the square and rectangle but not in the circle?** — E

9. **What time is shown on this clock?** — 8:00

10. **After subtracting 6 tens from this model, the numeral shown would be** — 1,213

© 1998 Good Apple

Math 4 today — #8

For each numeral below, write the digit that is in the ten thousands place and the digit in the hundred millions place.
831,459,620 — 5, 8
954,182,635 — 8, 9

Which letter is in the triangle, circle, and rectangle but not in the square? — D

Marty's kite flew 254 decimeters high. Andy's kite flew 876 decimeters high. How much higher did Andy's kite fly?
876 - 254 = 622 decimeters higher

752 + 524 + 236 = 1,512

Use the model to show how to subtract 9 ones. What numeral is left?
186 - 9 = 177

Use >, <, or =.
8 + 4 = 2 x 6
13 - 5 < 7 + 7
9 x 5 = 5 x 9
4 x 4 > 9 + 4

What time is shown on this clock? — 2:30

Draw the sixth pattern in the empty box.

City Streets / Length
Bok Ave. — 52,400 m.
Syl Street — 23,452 m.
Lyd Blvd. — 47,220 m.
Nox Street — 59,198 m.

Name the streets in order from greatest to least.
Nox Street
Bok Ave.
Lyd Blvd.
Syl Street

About how long is the leaf?
- 9 cm
- 5½ cm
- 6 cm
- ⬤ 7½ cm

This number line shows:
- 3 + 7 = 10
- 10 - 3 = 7
- ⬤ 10 - 7 = 3

392 - 269 = 123

Child / Allowance
Tim ○○○○○○
Beth ○○○
Sal ○○○○○○○○
Jake ○○○○
Each ○ = 10¢

Who earned 20¢ more than Beth? — Sal

Don ate 4 slices of pizza. Greg ate less pizza than Stan. Tom ate 2 more slices than Greg. To find out how much pizza was eaten by Tom you need to know the number of slices eaten by.
- Stan
- ⬤ Greg
- Don

Round each number to the nearest hundred.
253 → 300
412 → 400
183 → 200
87 → 100

Which shows the most accurate way to estimate the difference between 412 and 521?
- 500 - 400
- 412 + 521
- ⬤ 520 - 410

© 1998 Good Apple

Math 4 today — Test #8

1. 365 + 121 + 557 = 1,043

2. 962 - 124 = 838

3. **What is the most accurate estimate of the difference between 747 and 862?**
- 747 + 862
- 800 - 700
- ⬤ 860 - 750
- 900 - 700

4. **Write the number sentence shown by this number line.**
16 - 7 = 9

5. **The bookshelves in Mrs. Kim's class are 671 centimeters tall. Mr. Hym's shelves are 832 centimeters tall. How much taller are the shelves in Mr. Hym's classroom?**
832 - 671 = 161 centimeters taller

6. **Which graph shows that Mary planted 10 more flowers than Sue?** graph — A

graph A: Beth ○○○ / Jill ○○○○○ / Mary ○○○○○ / Sue ○○○ ; ○ = 5
graph B: Beth ○○ / Jill ○○○○○ / Mary ○○○○○ / Sue ○○ ; ○ = 1

7. **Kelly earned $5.00. Annie earned $2.00 more flowers than Liz. Gina earned less than Liz. To find out how much money Annie earned, you need to know the amount of money earned by**
- ⬤ Liz
- Gina
- Kelly

8. **How many centimeters long is the bead pattern?**
- 10 cm
- 9½ cm
- ⬤ 8½ cm
- 6 cm

9. **For each numeral, write the digit that is in the millions place and the digit that is in the hundred thousands place.**
254,307,199 — 4, 3
589,620,413 — 9, 6

10. **Round each number to the nearest hundred.**
197 → 200
231 → 200
552 → 600

© 1998 Good Apple

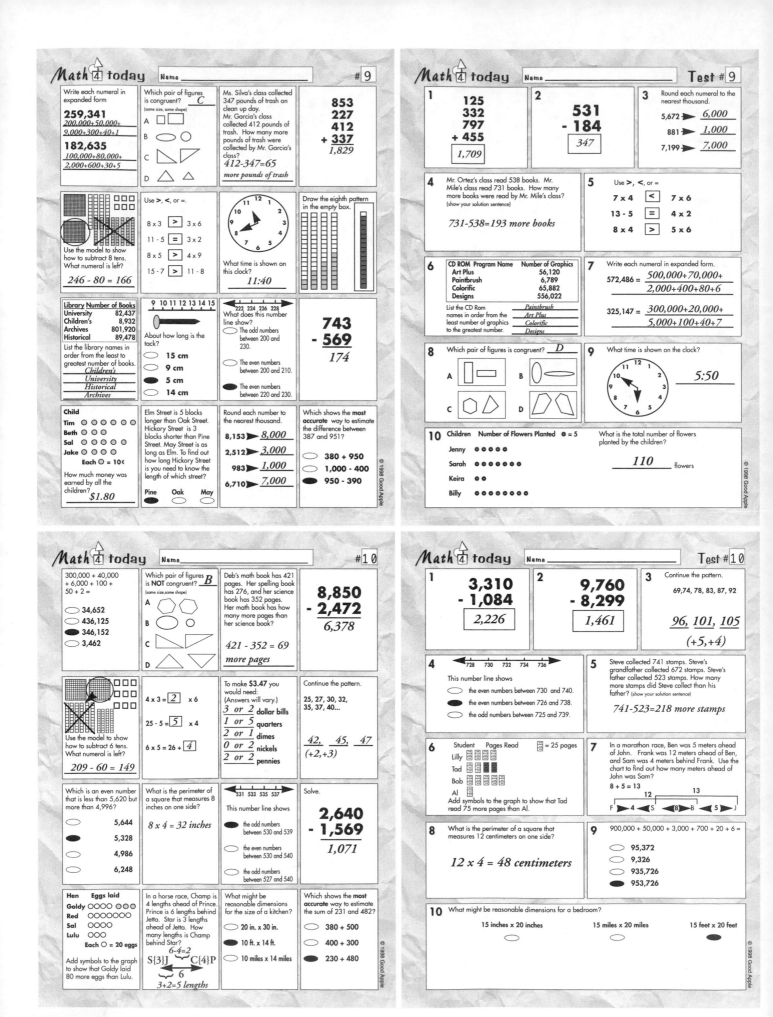

Math 4 today — Name _____ #9

Write each numeral in expanded form.

259,341
200,000+50,000+
9,000+300+40+1

182,635
100,000+80,000+
2,000+600+30+5

Which pair of figures is congruent? C
(some size, some shape)
A ☐ ☐
B ⬭ ⬭
C △ △
D △ △

Ms. Silva's class collected 347 pounds of trash on clean up day. Mr. Garcia's class collected 412 pounds of trash. How many more pounds of trash were collected by Mr. Garcia's class?
412-347=65
more pounds of trash

```
  853
  227
  412
+ 337
-----
1,829
```

Use the model to show how to subtract 8 tens. What numeral is left?
246 - 80 = 166

Use >, <, or =.
8 x 3 > 3 x 6
11 - 5 = 3 x 2
8 x 5 > 4 x 9
15 - 7 > 11 - 8

What time is shown on this clock?
11:40

Draw the eighth pattern in the empty box.

Library	Number of Books
University	82,437
Children's	8,932
Archives	801,920
Historical	89,478

List the library names in order from the least to greatest number of books.
Children's
University
Historical
Archives

9 10 11 12 13 14 15
About how long is the tack?
○ 15 cm
○ 9 cm
● 5 cm
○ 14 cm

222 224 226 228
What does this number line show?
○ The odd numbers between 200 and 230.
○ The even numbers between 200 and 210.
● The even numbers between 220 and 230.

```
 743
-569
----
 174
```

Child				
Tim	○	○	○	○ ○
Beth	○	○	○	
Sal	○	○	○	
Jake	○	○	○	

Each ○ = 10¢
How much money was earned by all the children? $1.80

Elm Street is 5 blocks longer than Oak Street. Hickory Street is 3 blocks shorter than Pine Street. May Street is as long as Elm. To find out how long Hickory Street is you need to know the length of which street?
Pine Oak May
(Pine is filled in)

Round each number to the nearest thousand.
8,153 → 8,000
2,512 → 3,000
983 → 1,000
6,710 → 7,000

Which shows the **most accurate** way to estimate the difference between 387 and 951?
○ 380 + 950
○ 1,000 - 400
● 950 - 390

© 1998 Good Apple

Math 4 today — Name _____ Test #9

1
```
 125
 332
 797
+455
----
1,709
```

2
```
 531
-184
----
 347
```

3 Round each numeral to the nearest thousand.
5,672 → 6,000
881 → 1,000
7,199 → 7,000

4 Mr. Ortez's class read 538 books. Mr. Mile's class read 731 books. How many more books were read by Mr. Mile's class? (show your solution sentence)
731-538=193 more books

5 Use >, <, or =.
7 x 4 < 7 x 6
13 - 5 = 4 x 2
8 x 4 > 5 x 6

6
CD ROM Program Name	Number of Graphics
Art Plus	56,120
Paintbrush	6,789
Colorific	65,882
Designs	556,022

List the CD Rom names in order from the least number of graphics to the greatest number.
Paintbrush
Art Plus
Colorific
Designs

7 Write each numeral in expanded form.
572,486 = 500,000+70,000+ 2,000+400+80+6
325,147 = 300,000+20,000+ 5,000+100+40+7

8 Which pair of figures is congruent? D
A ▭ ▭
B ⬭ ⬭
C ⬠ ⬠
D ▱ ▱

9 What time is shown on the clock?
5:50

10
Children	Number of Flowers Planted	❀ = 5
Jenny	❀❀❀❀❀	
Sarah	❀❀❀❀❀❀❀	
Keira	❀❀	
Billy	❀❀❀❀❀❀❀	

What is the total number of flowers planted by the children?
110 flowers

© 1998 Good Apple

Math 4 today — Name _____ #10

300,000 + 40,000 + 6,000 + 100 + 50 + 2 =
○ 34,652
○ 436,125
● 346,152
○ 3,462

Which pair of figures is NOT congruent? B
(some size, some shape)
A ⬠ ⬠
B ⬭ ○
C △ △
D △ △

Deb's math book has 421 pages. Her spelling book has 276, and her science book has 352 pages. Her math book has how many more pages than her science book?
421 - 352 = 69 more pages

```
 8,850
-2,472
------
 6,378
```

Use the model to show how to subtract 6 tens. What numeral is left?
209 - 60 = 149

4 x 3 = 2 x 6
25 - 5 = 5 x 4
6 x 5 = 26 + 4

To make $3.47 you would need:
(Answers will vary.)
3 or 2 dollar bills
1 or 5 quarters
2 or 1 dimes
0 or 2 nickels
2 or 2 pennies

Continue the pattern.
25, 27, 30, 32, 35, 37, 40...
42, 45, 47
(+2,+3)

Which is an even number that is less than 5,620 but more than 4,996?
○ 5,644
● 5,328
○ 4,986
○ 6,248

What is the perimeter of a square that measures 8 inches on one side?
8 x 4 = 32 inches

531 533 535 537
This number line shows
● the odd numbers between 530 and 539
○ the even numbers between 530 and 540
○ the odd numbers between 527 and 540

Solve.
```
 2,640
-1,569
------
 1,071
```

Hen	Eggs laid
Goldy	○○○○ ○○○
Red	○○○○○○○
Sal	○○○○
Lulu	○○○

Each ○ = 20 eggs
Add symbols to the graph to show that Goldy laid 80 more eggs than Lulu.

In a horse race, Champ is 4 lengths ahead of Prince. Prince is 6 lengths behind Jetta. Star is 3 lengths ahead of Jetta. How many lengths is Champ behind Star?
6-4=2
S{3}J ⌣ C{4}P
6
3+2=5 lengths

What might be reasonable dimensions for the size of a kitchen?
○ 20 in. x 30 in.
● 10 ft. x 14 ft.
○ 10 miles x 14 miles

Which shows the **most accurate** way to estimate the sum of 231 and 482?
○ 380 + 500
○ 400 + 300
● 230 + 480

© 1998 Good Apple

Math 4 today — Name _____ Test #10

1
```
 3,310
-1,084
------
 2,226
```

2
```
 9,760
-8,299
------
 1,461
```

3 Continue the pattern.
69,74, 78, 83, 87, 92
96, 101, 105
(+5,+4)

4
728 730 732 734 736
This number line shows
○ the even numbers between 730 and 740.
● the even numbers between 726 and 738.
○ the odd numbers between 725 and 739.

5 Steve collected 741 stamps. Steve's grandfather collected 672 stamps. Steve's father collected 523 stamps. How many more stamps did Steve collect than his father? (show your solution sentence)
741-523=218 more stamps

6
Student	Pages Read	▤ = 25 pages
Lilly	▤▤▤▤	
Tad	▤▤▤	
Bob	▤▤▤▤▤	
Al	▤	

Add symbols to the graph to show that Tad read 75 more pages than Al.

7 In a marathon race, Ben was 5 meters ahead of John. Frank was 12 meters ahead of Ben, and Sam was 4 meters behind Frank. Use the chart to find out how many meters ahead of John was Sam?
8 + 5 = 13
F ◄ 4 ► S ◄ {8} ► B ◄ 5 ► J
12
13

8 What is the perimeter of a square that measures 12 centimeters on one side?
12 x 4 = 48 centimeters

9 900,000 + 50,000 + 3,000 + 700 + 20 + 6 =
○ 95,372
○ 9,326
○ 935,726
● 953,726

10 What might be reasonable dimensions for a bedroom?
○ 15 inches x 20 inches
○ 15 miles x 20 miles
● 15 feet x 20 feet

© 1998 Good Apple

© 1998 Good Apple   122

Worksheet #11 (top left)

What is the value of the 5 in each numeral?
Example: 35,622 __5,000__

34,652 __50__
436,125 __5__
356,102 __50,000__
3,562 __500__

Match.
A — pentagon __B__
B — quadrilateral __D__
C — octagon __C__
D — hexagon __A__

Joe scored 1,243 points on a video game. Matt's score was 1,458 and David's score was 985. Show how to find the difference between David's score and Joe's score.
1,243
- 985
258 points

Solve.
4,706
- 3,438
1,268

Use the model to show how to subtract 8 ones. What numeral is left?
303 - 8 = 295

8 × 3 =
(__5__ × 3) + (__3__ × 3)
(8, 0, 7, 1; 6, 2; 4, 4)
7 × 4 =
(__3__ × 4) + (__4__ × 4)
(2, 5; 7, 0; 6, 1)
9 × 6 =
(__5__ × 6) + (__4__ × 6)

To make $2.83 you would need: (Answers will vary.)
__2, 2, 1__ dollar bills
__3, 2, 6__ quarters
__0, 3, 0__ dimes
__1, 0, 6__ nickels
__3, 3, 3__ pennies

Continue the pattern by shading in the figure below.

Which is an odd number that is more than 7,821 but less than 10,000?
○ 9,340
○ 10,351
○ 1,975
● 8,243

What is the perimeter of a rectangle that measures 27 inches on one side and 56 inches on the other side?
27 + 27 + 56 + 56 = 166 inches

97,435 is read
○ ninety thousand, four hundred three five.
● ninety-seven thousand, four hundred thirty-five.
○ ninety-seven thousand, three hundred five.

Solve.
9,901
- 2,569
7,332

Favorite Pizza
Each △ = 2 votes
▨ cheese
▥ pepperoni
▦ bacon
How many votes for:
Pepperoni Pizza __10__
Cheese Pizza __12__

A phone company wants to create some new area codes. Each new area code will have 3 numbers. Using the digits 1,5, and 7 only once in each code, how many new codes can the phone company create?
(show your work on the back)
157, 175, 517, 571, 715, 751
__6__ new area codes

About how many gallons of gasoline can a car hold?
○ 2 gallons
● 20 gallons
○ 200 gallons
○ 2,000 gallons

| 4 | 7 | 3 | 4 | 2 |
These cards are shuffled and placed face down after each turn. You draw 1 card, look at it, and return it to the deck. After drawing for 10 times, you would probably draw a the most often. __4__

Test #11 (top right)

1
9,402
- 1,027
8,375

2
5,705
- 2,299
3,406

3 About how many gallons of water would it take to fill the kitchen sink?
● 3
○ 30
○ 300
○ 3,000

4 Rob, Sid, and Mark read 3 books each. The total number of pages Rob read was 2,134. Mark's total was 1,087 and Sid read a total of 876 pages. Show how to find the difference between the number of pages Sid read and the number of pages Rob read.
2,134-876=1,258

5 5 × 7 =
(__3__ × 7) + (__2__ × 7)
(0,5; 1,4;)
9 × 4 =
(__5__ × 4) + (__4__ × 4)
(0,9; 1,8; 2,7; 3,6;)

6 Which is an even number that is more than 8,234 but less than 9,933?
● 8,328
○ 9,641
○ 9,944

7 What is the value of the 8 in each numeral?
85,231 __80,000__
12,890 __800__
8,725,231 __8,000,000__

8 Match.
hexagon __B__
pentagon __A__
quadrilateral __C__
octagon __D__

9 To make $4.94, you would need: (Answers will vary.)
__4, 4__ dollar bills
__3, 2__ quarters
__1, 4__ dimes
__1, 0__ nickels
__4, 4__ pennies

10 Use the model to show how to subtract 5 ones. What number is left? 403-5= 398

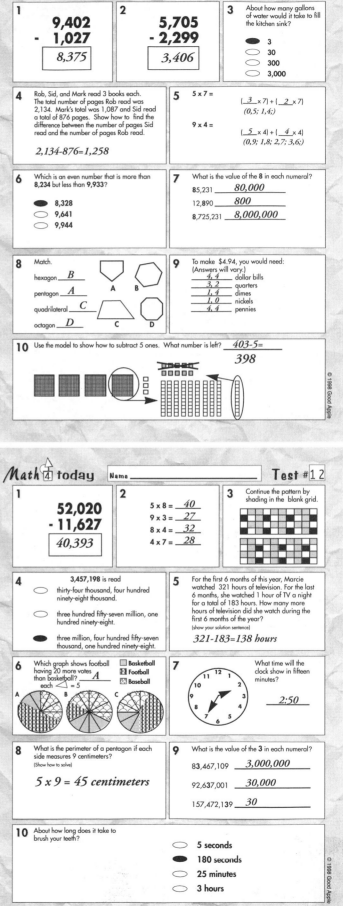

Worksheet #12 (bottom left)

What is the value of the 2 in each numeral?
Example: 35,620 __20__
234,651 __200,000__
436,102 __2__
2,356,109 __2,000,000__
23,562 __20,000__

By definition, which shape could be considered a:
A — pentagon __C__
B — quadrilateral __A__
C — octagon __B__
D — hexagon __D__

Ms. Baker weighed 174 pounds before she went on a diet. She lost 4 pounds a week for 12 weeks for a total of 48 pounds lost on the diet. How much does Ms. Baker now weigh?
174 - 48 = 126 lbs.

Solve.
94,020
- 13,438
80,582

Draw a base ten model to show this numeral:
2,485

7 × 5 =
(__5__ × 5) + (__2__ × 5)
(7, 0; 1, 6; 3, 4)
6 × 7 =
(__2__ × 7) + (__4__ × 7)
(6, 0; 1, 5; 3, 3)
12 × 8 =
(__10__ × 6) + (__2__ × 6)
(12,0;11;1,9;3;8,4;7,5;6,6)

What time will this clock show in fifteen minutes?
7:35

Continue the pattern by shading in the figure below.

Which numeral would go in the empty box?
342, 344, ☐ , 348
○ 351
○ 340
○ 345
● 346

What is the perimeter of an octagon that measures 4 inches on each side?
8 × 4 = 32 inches

2,597,401 is read:
● two million, five hundred ninety-seven thousand, four hundred one
○ twenty-five thousand, five hundred nine, four hundred one
○ two hundred fifty thousand ninety-seven, four hundred one

7 × 4 = __28__
8 × 5 = __40__
6 × 6 = __36__
3 × 9 = __27__
4 × 8 = __32__

Favorite Colors
Each △ = 3 votes
▨ red __21__
▥ blue __9__
▦ purple __15__
How many more votes for: Red than...
Purple? __6__
Blue? __12__

Using a red, blue, green, and yellow block only once in each row, how many 4 block patterns can you make that have a red block in the first position? (Show your work on the back.)
__6__ block patterns
** Bonus: How many patterns can be made in all?

About how long does it take to listen to a song?
○ 3 seconds
● 3 minutes
○ 30 minutes
○ 3 hours

Shade in the spinner which would give you the best chance of landing on the number 3?

Test #12 (bottom right)

1
52,020
- 11,627
40,393

2
5 × 8 = __40__
9 × 3 = __27__
8 × 4 = __32__
4 × 7 = __28__

3 Continue the pattern by shading in the blank grid.

4 3,457,198 is read
○ thirty-four thousand, four hundred ninety-eight thousand.
○ three hundred fifty-seven million, one hundred ninety-eight.
● three million, four hundred fifty-seven thousand, one hundred ninety-eight.

5 For the first 6 months of this year, Marcie watched 321 hours of television. For the last 6 months, she watched 1 hour of TV a night for a total of 183 hours. How many more hours of television did she watch during the first 6 months of the year?
(show your solution sentence)
321-183=138 hours

6 Which graph shows football having 20 more votes than basketball? __A__
▢ Basketball
▨ Football
▨ Baseball
each △ = 5

7 What time will the clock show in fifteen minutes?
2:50

8 What is the perimeter of a pentagon if each side measures 9 centimeters? (Show how to solve)
5 × 9 = 45 centimeters

9 What is the value of the 3 in each numeral?
83,467,109 __3,000,000__
92,637,001 __30,000__
157,472,139 __30__

10 About how long does it take to brush your teeth?
○ 5 seconds
● 180 seconds
○ 25 minutes
○ 3 hours

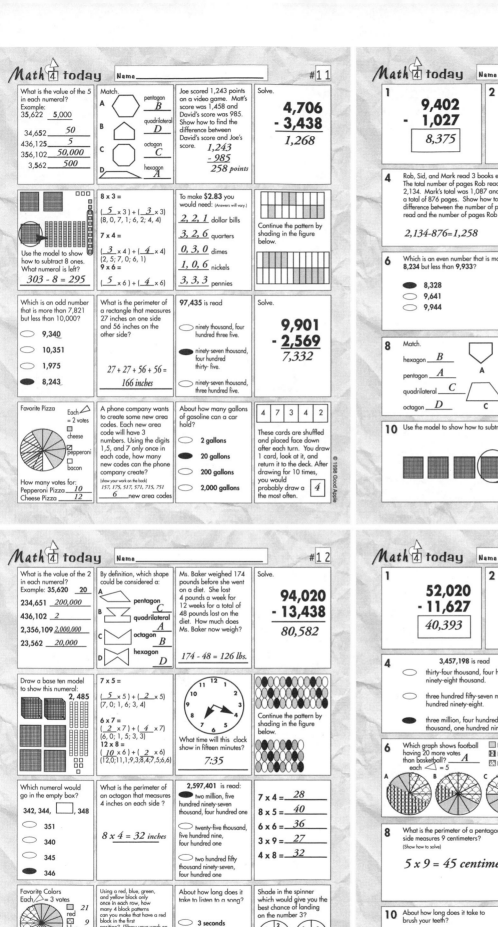

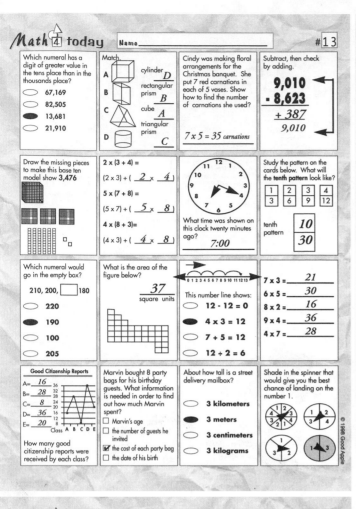

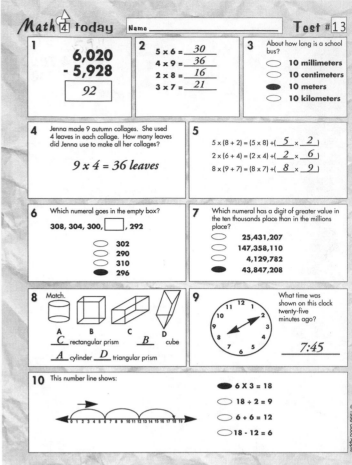

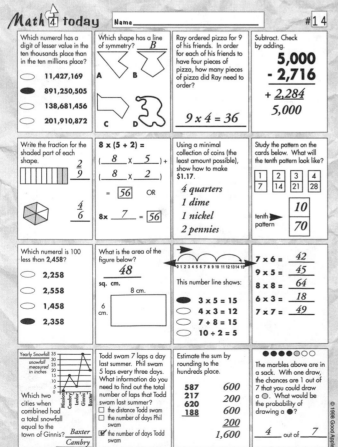

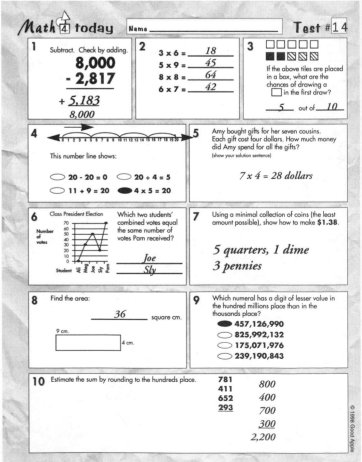

Math 4 today — #13

Name _____

Which numeral has a digit of greater value in the tens place than in the thousands place?
- ○ 67,169
- ○ 82,505
- ● 13,681
- ○ 21,910

Match.
A — cylinder — *D*
B — rectangular prism — *B*
C — cube — *A*
D — triangular prism — *C*

Cindy was making floral arrangements for the Christmas banquet. She put 7 red carnations in each of 5 vases. Show how to find the number of carnations she used?
7 x 5 = 35 carnations

Subtract, then check by adding.
9,010 − 8,623
+ 387
9,010

Draw the missing pieces to make this base ten model show 3,476

2 x (3 + 4) =
(2 x 3) + (*2* x *4*)
5 x (7 + 8) =
(5 x 7) + (*5* x *8*)
4 x (8 + 3)=
(4 x 3) + (*4* x *8*)

What time was shown on this clock twenty minutes ago?
7:00

Study the pattern on the cards below. What will the tenth pattern look like?

1	2	3	4
3	6	9	12

tenth pattern: 10 / 30

Which numeral would go in the empty box?
210, 200, ___, 180
- ○ 220
- ● 190
- ○ 100
- ○ 205

What is the area of the figure below?
37 square units

This number line shows:
- ○ 12 − 12 = 0
- ● 4 x 3 = 12
- ○ 7 + 5 = 12
- ○ 12 ÷ 2 = 6

7 x 3 = *21*
6 x 5 = *30*
8 x 2 = *16*
9 x 4 = *36*
4 x 7 = *28*

Good Citizenship Reports
A = *16*
B = *28*
C = *8*
D = *36*
E = *20*

How many good citizenship reports were received by each class?

Marvin bought 8 party bags for his birthday guests. What information is needed in order to find out how much Marvin spent?
- ☐ Marvin's age
- ☐ the number of guests he invited
- ☑ the cost of each party bag
- ☐ the date of his birth

About how tall is a street delivery mailbox?
- ○ 3 kilometers
- ● 3 meters
- ○ 3 centimeters
- ○ 3 kilograms

Shade in the spinner that would give you the best chance of landing on the number 1.

© 1998 Good Apple

Math 4 today — Test #13

Name _____

1. 6,020 − 5,928 = 92

2.
5 x 6 = 30
4 x 9 = 36
2 x 8 = 16
3 x 7 = 21

3. About how long is a school bus?
- ○ 10 millimeters
- ○ 10 centimeters
- ● 10 meters
- ○ 10 kilometers

4. Jenna made 9 autumn collages. She used 4 leaves in each collage. How many leaves did Jenna use to make all her collages?
9 x 4 = 36 leaves

5.
5 x (8 + 2) = (5 x 8) + (5 x 2)
2 x (6 + 4) = (2 x 4) + (2 x 6)
8 x (9 + 7) = (8 x 7) + (8 x 9)

6. Which numeral goes in the empty box?
308, 304, 300, ___, 292
- ○ 302
- ○ 290
- ○ 310
- ● 296

7. Which numeral has a digit of greater value in the ten thousands place than in the millions place?
- ○ 25,431,207
- ○ 147,358,110
- ○ 4,129,782
- ● 43,847,208

8. Match.
A — *C* rectangular prism — *B* cube
— *A* cylinder — *D* triangular prism

9. What time was shown on this clock twenty-five minutes ago?
7:45

10. This number line shows:
- ● 6 X 3 = 18
- ○ 18 ÷ 2 = 9
- ○ 6 + 6 = 12
- ○ 18 − 12 = 6

© 1998 Good Apple

Math 4 today — #14

Name _____

Which numeral has a digit of lesser value in the ten thousands place than in the ten millions place?
- ○ 11,427,169
- ● 891,250,505
- ○ 138,681,456
- ○ 201,910,872

Which shape has a line of symmetry? *B*

Ray ordered pizza for 9 of his friends. In order for each of his friends to have four pieces of pizza, how many pieces of pizza did Ray need to order?
9 x 4 = 36

Subtract. Check by adding.
5,000 − 2,716
+ 2,284
5,000

Write the fraction for the shaded part of each shape.
2/9
4/6

8 x (5 + 2) =
(8 x 5) + (8 x 2)
= 56 OR
8 x 7 = 56

Using a minimal collection of coins (the least amount possible), show how to make $1.17.
4 quarters
1 dime
1 nickel
2 pennies

Study the pattern on the cards below. What will the tenth pattern look like?

1	2	3	4
7	14	21	28

tenth pattern: 10 / 70

Which numeral is 100 less than 2,458?
- ○ 2,258
- ○ 2,558
- ○ 1,458
- ● 2,358

What is the area of the figure below?
48 sq. cm.
8 cm.
6 cm.

This number line shows:
- ● 3 x 5 = 15
- ○ 4 x 3 = 12
- ○ 7 + 8 = 15
- ○ 10 ÷ 2 = 5

7 x 6 = *42*
9 x 5 = *45*
8 x 8 = *64*
6 x 3 = *18*
7 x 7 = *49*

Yearly Snowfall
Which two cities when combined had a total snowfall equal to the town of Ginnis?
Baxter
Cambry

Todd swam 7 laps a day last summer. Phil swam 5 laps every three days. What information do you need to find out the total number of laps that Todd swam last summer?
- ☐ the distance Todd swam
- ☐ the number of days Phil swam
- ☑ the number of days Todd swam

Estimate the sum by rounding to the hundreds place.
587 → 600
217 → 200
620 → 600
188 → 200
1,600

The marbles above are in a sack. With one draw, the chances are 1 out of 7 that you could draw a ○. What would be the probability of drawing a ●?
4 out of 7

© 1998 Good Apple

Math 4 today — Test #14

Name _____

1. Subtract. Check by adding.
8,000 − 2,817
+ 5,183
8,000

2.
3 x 6 = 18
5 x 9 = 45
8 x 8 = 64
6 x 7 = 42

3. If the above tiles are placed in a box, what are the chances of drawing a ☐ in the first draw?
5 out of 10

4. This number line shows:
- ○ 20 − 20 = 0
- ○ 20 ÷ 4 = 5
- ○ 11 + 9 = 20
- ● 4 x 5 = 20

5. Amy bought gifts for her seven cousins. Each gift cost four dollars. How much money did Amy spend for all the gifts? (show your solution sentence)
7 x 4 = 28 dollars

6. Class President Election. Which two students' combined votes equal the same number of votes Pam received?
Joe
Sly

7. Using a minimal collection of coins (the least amount possible), show how to make $1.38.
5 quarters, 1 dime
3 pennies

8. Find the area:
36 square cm.
9 cm.
4 cm.

9. Which numeral has a digit of lesser value in the hundred millions place than in the thousands place?
- ● 457,126,990
- ○ 825,992,132
- ○ 175,071,976
- ○ 239,190,843

10. Estimate the sum by rounding to the hundreds place.
781 → 800
411 → 400
652 → 700
293 → 300
2,200

© 1998 Good Apple

© 1998 Good Apple

124

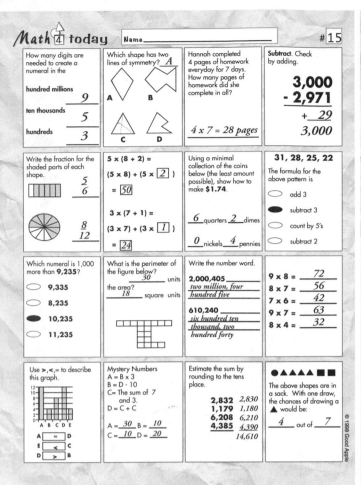

Math 4 today — Name _____ #15

How many digits are needed to create a numeral in the

hundred millions __9__

ten thousands __5__

hundreds __3__

Which shape has two lines of symmetry? _A_

A, B, C, D (shapes)

Hannah completed 4 pages of homework everyday for 7 days. How many pages of homework did she complete in all?

4 x 7 = 28 pages

Subtract. Check by adding.

3,000
- 2,971

+ 29

3,000

Write the fraction for the shaded parts of each shape.

5/6

8/12

5 x (8 + 2) =
(5 x 8) + (5 x [2]) = [50]

3 x (7 + 1) =
(3 x 7) + (3 x [1]) = [24]

Using a minimal collection of the coins below (the least amount possible), show how to make $1.74.

6 quarters 2 dimes

0 nickels 4 pennies

31, 28, 25, 22
The formula for the above pattern is

○ add 3
● subtract 3
○ count by 5's
○ subtract 2

Which numeral is 1,000 more than 9,235?

○ 9,335
○ 8,235
● 10,235
○ 11,235

What is the perimeter of the figure below?

30 units
the area? 18 square units

Write the number word.

2,000,405 *two million, four hundred five*

610,240 *six hundred ten thousand, two hundred forty*

9 x 8 = 72
8 x 7 = 56
7 x 6 = 42
9 x 7 = 63
8 x 4 = 32

Use >, <, = to describe this graph.

(bar graph A B C D E)

A [=] D
E [<] C
D [>] B

Mystery Numbers
A = B x 3
B = D - 10
C = The sum of 7 and 3.
D = C + C

A _30_ B _10_
C _10_ D _20_

Estimate the sum by rounding to the tens place.

2,832 2,830
1,179 1,180
6,208 6,210
4,385 4,390
         14,610

(shapes: ●○▲▲▲■■)

The above shapes are in a sack. With one draw, the chances of drawing a ▲ would be:

4 out of 7

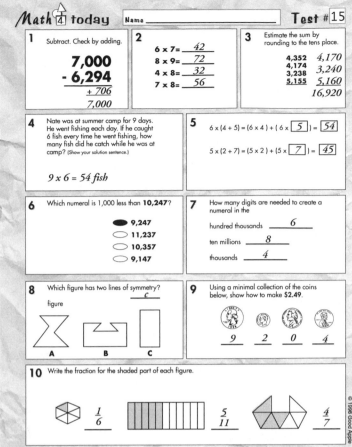

Math 4 today — Name _____ Test #15

1. Subtract. Check by adding.

7,000
- 6,294

+ 706

7,000

2.
6 x 7 = _42_
8 x 9 = _72_
4 x 8 = _32_
7 x 8 = _56_

3. Estimate the sum by rounding to the tens place.

4,352 4,170
4,174 3,240
3,238 5,160
5,155 16,920

4. Nate was at summer camp for 9 days. He went fishing each day. If he caught 6 fish every time he went fishing, how many fish did he catch while he was at camp? (Show your solution sentence.)

9 x 6 = 54 fish

5.
6 x (4 + 5) = (6 x 4) + (6 x [5]) = [54]

5 x (2 + 7) = (5 x 2) + (5 x [7]) = [45]

6. Which numeral is 1,000 less than 10,247?

● 9,247
○ 11,237
○ 10,357
○ 9,147

7. How many digits are needed to create a numeral in the

hundred thousands __6__

ten millions __8__

thousands __4__

8. Which figure has two lines of symmetry? figure _c_

A, B, C (shapes)

9. Using a minimal collection of the coins below, show how to make $2.49.

(coins) 9 2 0 4

10. Write the fraction for the shaded part of each figure.

1/6   5/11   4/7

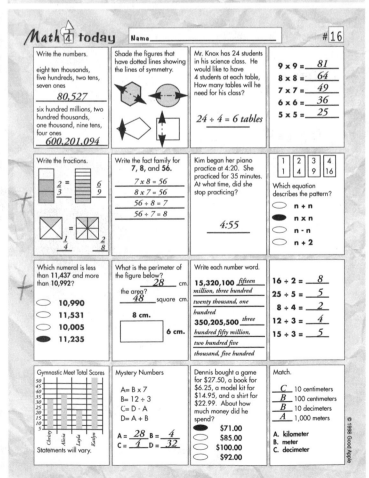

Math 4 today — Name _____ #16

Write the numbers.

eight ten thousands, five hundreds, two tens, seven ones
80,527

six hundred millions, two hundred thousands, one thousand, nine tens, four ones
600,201,094

Shade the figures that have dotted lines showing the lines of symmetry.

(figures)

Mr. Knox has 24 students in his science class. He would like to have 4 students at each table. How many tables will he need for his class?

24 ÷ 4 = 6 tables

9 x 9 = 81
8 x 8 = 64
7 x 7 = 49
6 x 6 = 36
5 x 5 = 25

Write the fractions.

2/3 = 6/9

1/4 = 2/8

Write the fact family for 7, 8, and 56.

7 x 8 = 56
8 x 7 = 56
56 ÷ 8 = 7
56 ÷ 7 = 8

Kim began her piano practice at 4:20. She practiced for 35 minutes. At what time did she stop practicing?

4:55

(number grid 1 2 3 4 / 1 4 9 16)

Which equation describes the pattern?

○ n + n
● n x n
○ n - n
○ n + 2

Which numeral is less than 11,437 and more than 10,992?

○ 10,990
○ 11,531
○ 10,005
● 11,235

What is the perimeter of the figure below?

28 cm.
the area? 48 square cm.

8 cm. / 6 cm.

Write each number word.

15,320,100 *fifteen million, three hundred twenty thousand, one hundred*

350,205,500 *three hundred fifty million, two hundred five thousand, five hundred*

16 ÷ 2 = 8
25 ÷ 5 = 5
8 ÷ 4 = 2
12 ÷ 3 = 4
15 ÷ 3 = 5

Gymnastic Meet Total Scores

(bar graph: Christy, Alicia, Layla, Katlyn)

Statements will vary.

Mystery Numbers

A= B x 7
B= 12 ÷ 3
C= D - A
D= A + B

A _28_ B _4_
C _1_   D _32_

Dennis bought a game for $27.50, a book for $6.25, a model kit for $14.95, and a shirt for $22.99. About how much money did he spend?

○ $71.00
○ $85.00
● $100.00
○ $92.00

Match.

_C_ 10 centimeters
_B_ 100 centimeters
_B_ 10 decimeters
_A_ 1,000 meters

A. kilometer
B. meter
C. decimeter

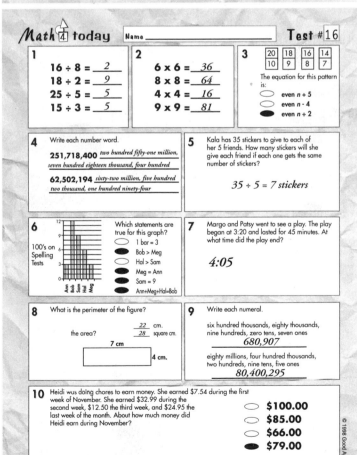

Math 4 today — Name _____ Test #16

1.
16 ÷ 8 = _2_
18 ÷ 2 = _9_
25 ÷ 5 = _5_
15 ÷ 3 = _5_

2.
6 x 6 = _36_
8 x 8 = _64_
4 x 4 = _16_
9 x 9 = _81_

3.
(20 18 16 14 / 10 9 8 7)

The equation for this pattern is:

○ even n + 5
○ even n - 4
● even n ÷ 2

4. Write each number word.

251,718,400 *two hundred fifty-one million, seven hundred eighteen thousand, four hundred*

62,502,194 *sixty-two million, five hundred two thousand, one hundred ninety-four*

5. Kala has 35 stickers to give to each of her 5 friends. How many stickers will she give each friend if each one gets the same number of stickers?

35 ÷ 5 = 7 stickers

6.
(bar graph — 100's on Spelling Tests — Ann, Bob, Sam, Hal, Meg)

Which statements are true for this graph?

○ 1 bar = 3
● Bob > Meg
○ Hal > Sam
● Meg = Ann
○ Sam = 9
○ Ann+Meg+Hal=Bob

7. Margo and Patsy went to see a play. The play began at 3:20 and lasted for 45 minutes. At what time did the play end?

4:05

8. What is the perimeter of the figure?

the area? 22 cm. / 28 square cm.

7 cm / 4 cm.

9. Write each numeral.

six hundred thousands, eighty thousands, nine hundreds, zero tens, seven ones
680,907

eighty millions, four hundred thousands, two hundreds, nine tens, five ones
80,400,295

10. Heidi was doing chores to earn money. She earned $7.54 during the first week of November. She earned $32.99 during the second week, $12.50 the third week, and $24.95 the last week of the month. About how much money did Heidi earn during November?

○ $100.00
○ $85.00
○ $66.00
● $79.00

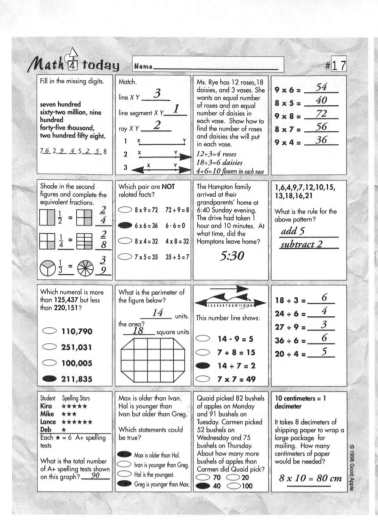

Fill in the missing digits.

seven hundred sixty-two million, nine hundred forty-five thousand, two hundred fifty eight.

7 6 2, 9 4 5, 2 5 8

Match.

line X Y   _3_
line segment X Y   _1_
ray X Y   _2_

1 X———Y
2 X———Y→
3 ←X———Y→

Ms. Rye has 12 roses, 18 daisies, and 3 vases. She wants an equal number of roses and an equal number of daisies in each vase. Show how to find the number of roses and daisies she will put in each vase.

12÷3=4 roses
18÷3=6 daisies
4+6=10 flowers in each vase

9 x 6 = _54_
8 x 5 = _40_
9 x 8 = _72_
8 x 7 = _56_
9 x 4 = _36_

Shade in the second figures and complete the equivalent fractions.

$\frac{1}{2}$ = _2_/_4_

$\frac{1}{4}$ = _2_/_8_

$\frac{1}{3}$ = _3_/_9_

Which pair are NOT related facts?

◯ 8 x 9 = 72   72 ÷ 9 = 8
● 6 x 6 = 36   6 - 6 = 0
◯ 8 x 4 = 32   4 x 8 = 32
◯ 7 x 5 = 35   35 ÷ 5 = 7

The Hampton family arrived at their grandparents' home at 6:40 Sunday evening. The drive had taken 1 hour and 10 minutes. At what time, did the Hamptons leave home?

5:30

1,6,4,9,7,12,10,15, 13,18,16,21

What is the rule for the above pattern?

add 5
subtract 2

Which numeral is more than 125,437 but less than 220,151?

◯ 110,790
◯ 251,031
◯ 100,005
● 211,835

What is the perimeter of the figure below?
_14_ units.
the area?
_18_ square units

←1 2 3 4 5 6 7 8 9 10 11 12 13 14→
This number line shows:

◯ 14 - 9 = 5
◯ 7 + 8 = 15
● 14 ÷ 7 = 2
◯ 7 x 7 = 49

18 ÷ 3 = _6_
24 ÷ 6 = _4_
27 ÷ 9 = _3_
36 ÷ 6 = _6_
20 ÷ 4 = _5_

Student	Spelling Stars
Kira	★★★★★
Mike	★★★
Lance	★★★★★★
Deb	★

Each ★ = 6 A+ spelling tests

What is the total number of A+ spelling tests shown on this graph? _90_

Max is older than Ivan. Hal is younger than Ivan but older than Greg.

Which statements could be true?

● Max is older than Hal.
◯ Ivan is younger than Greg.
◯ Hal is the youngest.
◯ Greg is younger than Max.

Quaid picked 82 bushels of apples on Monday and 91 bushels on Tuesday. Carmen picked 52 bushels on Wednesday and 75 bushels on Thursday. About how many more bushels of apples than Carmen did Quaid pick?

◯ 70   ◯ 20
● 40   ◯ 100

10 centimeters = 1 decimeter

It takes 8 decimeters of shipping paper to wrap a large package for mailing. How many centimeters of paper would be needed?

_8 x 10 = 80 cm_

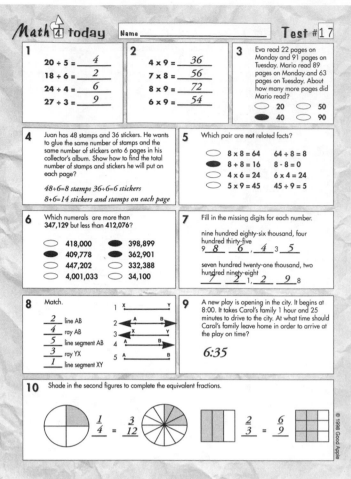

1
20 ÷ 5 = _4_
18 ÷ 6 = _2_
24 ÷ 4 = _6_
27 ÷ 3 = _9_

2
4 x 9 = _36_
7 x 8 = _56_
8 x 9 = _72_
6 x 9 = _54_

3 Eva read 22 pages on Monday and 91 pages on Tuesday. Mario read 89 pages on Monday and 63 pages on Tuesday. About how many more pages did Mario read?

◯ 20   ◯ 50
● 40   ◯ 90

4 Juan has 48 stamps and 36 stickers. He wants to glue the same number of stamps and the same number of stickers onto 6 pages in his collector's album. Show how to find the total number of stamps and stickers he will put on each page?

48÷6=8 stamps 36÷6=6 stickers
8+6=14 stickers and stamps on each page

5 Which pair are **not** related facts?

◯ 8 x 8 = 64   64 ÷ 8 = 8
● 8 + 8 = 16   8 - 8 = 0
◯ 4 x 6 = 24   6 x 4 = 24
◯ 5 x 9 = 45   45 ÷ 9 = 5

6 Which numerals are more than 347,129 but less than 412,076?

◯ 418,000   ● 398,899
● 409,778   ● 362,901
◯ 447,202   ◯ 332,388
◯ 4,001,033   ◯ 34,100

7 Fill in the missing digits for each number.

nine hundred eighty-six thousand, four hundred thirty-five
9 _8_ 6, _4_ 3 _5_

seven hundred twenty-one thousand, two hundred ninety-eight
_7_ 2 _1_, 2 9 _8_

8 Match.

_2_ line AB
_4_ ray AB
_5_ line segment AB
_3_ ray YX
_1_ line segment XY

1 X———Y
2 A———B→
3 ←X———Y→
4 ←A———B
5 A———B

9 A new play is opening in the city. It begins at 8:00. It takes Carol's family 1 hour and 25 minutes to drive to the city. At what time should Carol's family leave home in order to arrive at the play on time?

6:35

10 Shade in the second figures to complete the equivalent fractions.

$\frac{1}{4}$ = $\frac{3}{12}$

$\frac{2}{3}$ = $\frac{6}{9}$

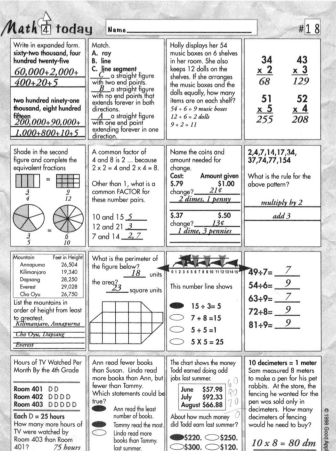

Write in expanded form.
sixty-two thousand, four hundred twenty-five
_60,000+2,000+_
_400+20+5_

two hundred ninety-one thousand, eight hundred fifteen
_200,000+90,000+_
_1,000+800+10+5_

Match.
A. ray
B. line
C. line segment

_C_ a straight figure with two end points.
_B_ a straight figure with no end points that extends forever in both directions.
_A_ a straight figure with one end point extending forever in one direction.

Holly displays her 54 music boxes on 6 shelves in her room. She also keeps 12 dolls on the shelves. If she arranges the music boxes and the dolls equally, how many items are on each shelf?

54 ÷ 6 = 9 music boxes
12 ÷ 6 = 2 dolls
9 + 2 = 11

34   43
x 2   x 3
68   129

51   52
x 5   x 4
255   208

Shade in the second figure and complete the equivalent fractions.

_3_/_4_ = _9_/_12_

_3_/_5_ = _6_/_10_

A common factor of 4 and 8 is 2 ... because 2 x 2 = 4 and 2 x 4 = 8.

Other than 1, what is a common FACTOR for these number pairs?

10 and 15 _5_
12 and 21 _3_
7 and 14 _2,7_

Name the coins and amount needed for change.

Cost:	Amount given
$.79	$1.00

change? _21¢_
2 dimes, 1 penny

| $.37 | $.50 |
change? _13¢_
1 dime, 3 pennies

2,4,7,14,17,34, 37,74,77,154

What is the rule for the above pattern?

multiply by 2
add 3

Mountain	Feet in Height
Annapurna	26,504
Kilimanjaro	19,340
Dapsang	28,250
Everest	29,028
Cho Oyu	26,750

List the mountains in order of height from least to greatest.

Kilimanjaro, Annapurna
Cho Oyu, Dapsang
Everest

What is the perimeter of the figure below?
_18_ units
the area?
_23_ square units

←0 1 2 3 4 5 6 7 8 9 10 11 12 13 14 15→
This number line shows

● 15 ÷ 3 = 5
◯ 7 + 8 = 15
◯ 5 ÷ 5 = 1
◯ 5 X 5 = 25

49÷7= _7_
54÷6= _9_
63÷9= _7_
72÷8= _9_
81÷9= _9_

Hours of TV Watched Per Month By the 4th Grade

Room 401 D D
Room 402 D D D D
Room 403 D D D D D

Each D = 25 hours
How many more hours of TV were watched by Room 403 than Room 401? _75 hours_

Ann read fewer books than Susan. Linda read more books than Ann, but fewer than Tammy. Which statements could be true?

◯ Ann read the least number of books.
● Tammy read the most.
◯ Linda read more books than Tammy last summer.

The chart shows the money Todd earned doing odd jobs last summer.

June	$57.98	60
July	$92.33	90
August	$66.88	70

About how much money did Todd earn last summer?

● $220.   ◯ $250.
◯ $300.   ◯ $120.

10 decimeters = 1 meter

Sam measured 8 meters to make a pen for his pet rabbits. At the store, the fencing he wanted for the pen was sold only in decimeters. How many decimeters of fencing would he need to buy?

_10 x 8 = 80 dm_

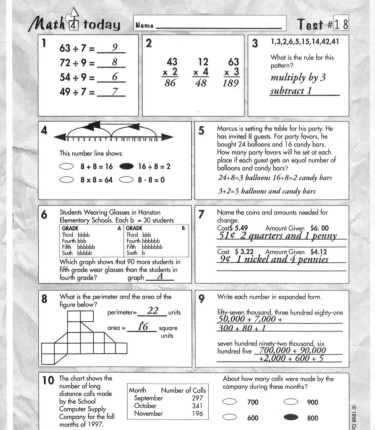

1
63 ÷ 7 = _9_
72 ÷ 9 = _8_
54 ÷ 9 = _6_
49 ÷ 7 = _7_

2
43   12   63
x 2   x 4   x 3
86   48   189

3 1,3,2,6,5,15,14,42,41

What is the rule for this pattern?

multiply by 3
subtract 1

4
←0 1 2 3 4 5 6 7 8 9 10 11 12 13 14→
This number line shows:

◯ 8 + 8 = 16   ● 16 ÷ 8 = 2
◯ 8 x 8 = 64   ◯ 8 - 8 = 0

5 Marcus is setting the table for his party. He has invited 8 guests. For party favors, he bought 24 balloons and 16 candy bars. How many party favors will he set at each place if each guest gets an equal number of balloons and candy bars?

24÷8=3 balloons 16÷8=2 candy bars
3+2=5 balloons and candy bars

6 Students Wearing Glasses in Hanston Elementary Schools. Each b = 30 students

GRADE	A	GRADE	B
Third	bbbb	Third	bbb
Fourth	bbb	Fourth	bbbbbb
Fifth	bbbbbb	Fifth	bbbbbbb
Sixth	bbbbb	Sixth	b

Which graph shows that 90 more students in fifth grade wear glasses than the students in fourth grade? graph _A_

7 Name the coins and amounts needed for change.

Cost$ 5.49   Amount Given $6.00
51¢ 2 quarters and 1 penny

Cost $ 3.22   Amount Given $4.12
9¢ 1 nickel and 4 pennies

8 What is the perimeter and the area of the figure below?

perimeter= _22_ units
area = _16_ square units

9 Write each number in expanded form.

fifty-seven thousand, three hundred eighty-one
_50,000 + 7,000 +_
_300 + 80 + 1_

seven hundred ninety-two thousand, six hundred five
_700,000 + 90,000_
_+2,000 + 600 + 5_

10 The chart shows the number of long distance calls made by the School Computer Supply Company for the fall months of 1997.

Month	Number of Calls
September	297
October	341
November	196

About how many calls were made by the company during these months?

◯ 700   ◯ 900
◯ 600   ● 800

Math 4 today — #19

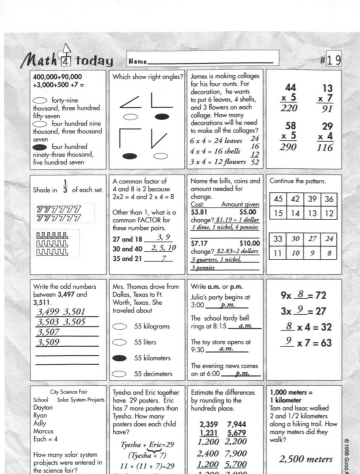

400,000+90,000 +3,000+500 +7 =
- forty-nine thousand, three hundred fifty-seven
- four hundred nine thousand, three thousand seven
- ● four hundred ninety-three thousand, five hundred seven

Which show right angles?

James is making collages for his four aunts. For decoration, he wants to put 6 leaves, 4 shells, and 3 flowers on each collage. How many decorations will he need to make all the collages?
6 x 4 = 24 leaves 24
4 x 4 = 16 shells 16
3 x 4 = 12 flowers 12
52

44 x 5 = 220   13 x 7 = 91
58 x 5 = 290   29 x 4 = 116

Shade in $\frac{1}{3}$ of each set.

A common factor of 4 and 8 is 2 because 2x2 = 4 and 2 x 4 = 8. Other than 1, what is a common FACTOR for these number pairs?
27 and 18 _3, 9_
30 and 40 _2, 5, 10_
35 and 21 _7_

Name the bills, coins and amount needed for change.
Cost: Amount given
$3.81 $5.00
change? $1.19 = 1 dollar 1 dime, 1 nickel, 4 pennies
$7.17 $10.00
change? $2.83 = 2 dollars 3 quarters, 1 nickel, 3 pennies

Continue the pattern.
| 45 | 42 | 39 | 36 |
| 15 | 14 | 13 | 12 |

| 33 | 30 | 27 | 24 |
| 11 | 10 | 9 | 8 |

Write the odd numbers between 3,497 and 3,511.
3,499 3,501
3,503 3,505
3,507
3,509

Mrs. Thomas drove from Dallas, Texas to Ft. Worth, Texas. She traveled about
- 55 kilograms
- 55 liters
- ● 55 kilometers
- 55 decimeters

Write a.m. or p.m.
Julio's party begins at 3:00 _p.m._
The school tardy bell rings at 8:15 _a.m._
The toy store opens at 9:30 _a.m._
The evening news comes on at 6:00 _p.m._

9x _8_ = 72
3x _9_ = 27
_8_ x 4 = 32
_9_ x 7 = 63

City Science Fair
School   Solar System Projects
Dayton
Ryan
Adly
Marcus
Each = 4
How many solar system projects were entered in the science fair? _58_

Tyesha and Eric together have 29 posters. Eric has 7 more posters than Tyesha. How many posters does each child have?
Tyesha + Eric=29
(Tyesha + 7)
11 + (11 + 7)=29
Tyesha = 11 Eric = 18

Estimate the differences by rounding to the hundreds place.
2,359 7,944
1,231 5,679
1,200 2,200
2,400 7,900
1,200 5,700
1,200 2,000

1,000 meters = 1 kilometer
Tam and Issac walked 2 and 1/2 kilometers along a hiking trail. How many meters did they walk?
2,500 meters

Math 4 today — Test #19

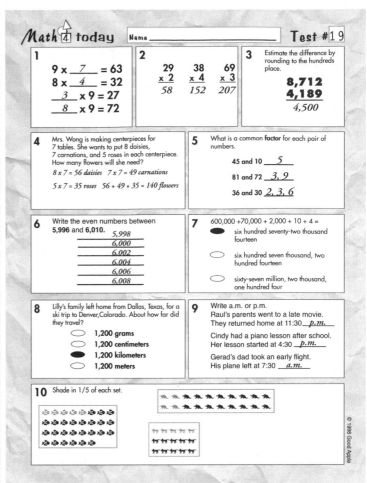

1
9 x _7_ = 63
8 x _4_ = 32
_3_ x 9 = 27
_8_ x 9 = 72

2
29 x 2 = 58   38 x 4 = 152   69 x 3 = 207

3 Estimate the difference by rounding to the hundreds place.
8,712
4,189
4,500

4 Mrs. Wong is making centerpieces for 7 tables. She wants to put 8 daisies, 7 carnations, and 5 roses in each centerpiece. How many flowers will she need?
8 x 7 = 56 daisies 7 x 7 = 49 carnations
5 x 7 = 35 roses 56 + 49 + 35 = 140 flowers

5 What is a common **factor** for each pair of numbers.
45 and 10 _5_
81 and 72 _3, 9_
36 and 30 _2, 3, 6_

6 Write the even numbers between 5,996 and 6,010.
5,998
6,000
6,002
6,004
6,006
6,008

7 600,000 +70,000 + 2,000 + 10 + 4 =
- ● six hundred seventy-two thousand fourteen
- six hundred seven thousand, two hundred fourteen
- sixty-seven million, two thousand, one hundred four

8 Lilly's family left home from Dallas, Texas, for a ski trip to Denver, Colorado. About how far did they travel?
- 1,200 grams
- 1,200 centimeters
- ● 1,200 kilometers
- 1,200 meters

9 Write a.m. or p.m.
Raul's parents went to a late movie. They returned home at 11:30 _p.m._
Cindy had a piano lesson after school. Her lesson started at 4:30 _p.m._
Gerad's dad took an early flight. His plane left at 7:30 _a.m._

10 Shade in 1/5 of each set.

Math 4 today — #20

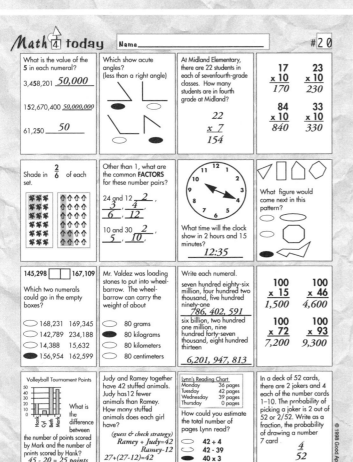

1 What is the value of the 5 in each numeral?
3,458,201 _50,000_
152,670,400 _50,000,000_
61,250 _50_

2 Which show acute angles? (less than a right angle)

3 At Midland Elementary, there are 22 students in each of seven fourth-grade classes. How many students are in fourth grade at Midland?
22
x 7
154

4
17 x 10 = 170   23 x 10 = 230
84 x 10 = 840   33 x 10 = 330

5 Shade in $\frac{2}{6}$ of each set.

6 Other than 1, what are the common **FACTORS** for these number pairs?
24 and 12 _2, 3, 4, 6, 12_
10 and 30 _2, 5, 10_

7 What time will the clock show in 2 hours and 15 minutes? _12:35_

8 What figure would come next in this pattern?

9 145,298 [ ] 167,109
Which two numerals could go in the empty boxes?
- 168,231 169,345
- 142,789 234,188
- 14,388 15,632
- ● 156,954 162,599

10 Mr. Valdez was loading stones to put into wheelbarrow. The wheelbarrow can carry the weight of about
- 80 grams
- ● 80 kilograms
- 80 kilometers
- 80 centimeters

11 Write each numeral.
seven hundred eighty-six million, four hundred two thousand, five hundred ninety-one
786, 402, 591
six billion, two hundred one million, nine hundred forty-seven thousand, eight hundred thirteen
6, 201, 947, 813

12
100 x 15 = 1,500   100 x 46 = 4,600
100 x 72 = 7,200   100 x 93 = 9,300

13 Volleyball Tournament Points — What is the difference between the number of points scored by Mark and the number of points scored by Hank?
45 - 20 = 25 points

14 Judy and Ramey together have 42 stuffed animals. Judy has 12 fewer animals than Ramey. How many stuffed animals does each girl have?
(guess & check strategy)
Ramey + Judy=42
Ramey-12
27+(27-12)=42
Ramey=27 Judy=15

15 Lynn's Reading Chart
Monday   36 pages
Tuesday   42 pages
Wednesday 39 pages
Thursday   0 pages
How could you estimate the total number of pages Lynn read?
- 42 ÷ 4
- 42 - 39
- ● 40 x 3
- 20 x 4

16 In a deck of 52 cards, there are 2 jokers and 4 each of the number cards 1–10. The probability of picking a joker is 2 out of 52 or 2/52. Write as a fraction, the probability of drawing a number 7 card.
$\frac{4}{52}$

Math 4 today — Test #20

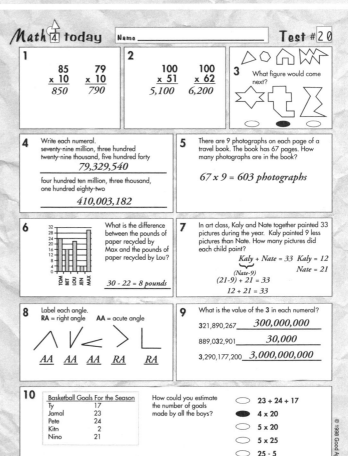

1
85 x 10 = 850   79 x 10 = 790

2
100 x 51 = 5,100   100 x 62 = 6,200

3 What figure would come next?

4 Write each numeral.
seventy-nine million, three hundred twenty-nine thousand, five hundred forty
79,329,540
four hundred ten million, three thousand, one hundred eighty-two
410,003,182

5 There are 9 photographs on each page of a travel book. The book has 67 pages. How many photographs are in the book?
67 x 9 = 603 photographs

6 What is the difference between the pounds of paper recycled by Max and the pounds of paper recycled by Lou?
30 - 22 = 8 pounds
(TOM BET LOU JEN MAX)

7 In art class, Kaly and Nate together painted 33 pictures during the year. Kaly painted 9 less pictures than Nate. How many pictures did each child paint?
Kaly + Nate = 33 Kaly = 12
(Nate-9) Nate = 21
(21-9) + 21 = 33
12 + 21 = 33

8 Label each angle. RA = right angle AA = acute angle
AA AA AA RA RA

9 What is the value of the 3 in each numeral?
321,890,267 _300,000,000_
889,032,901 _30,000_
3,290,177,200 _3,000,000,000_

10 Basketball Goals For the Season
Ty 17
Jamal 23
Pete 24
Kitn 2
Nino 21
How could you estimate the number of goals made by all the boys?
- 23 + 24 + 17
- ● 4 x 20
- 5 x 20
- 5 x 25
- 25 - 5

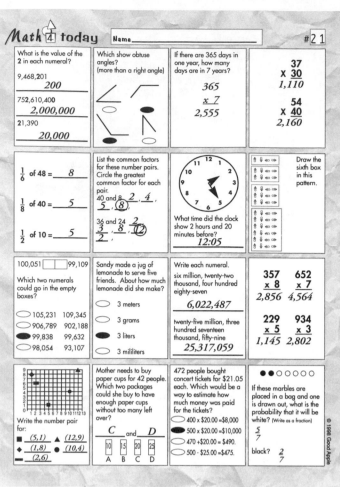

What is the value of the 2 in each numeral?
9,468,201 → 200
752,610,400 → 2,000,000
21,390 → 20,000

Which show obtuse angles? (more than a right angle)

If there are 365 days in one year, how many days are in 7 years?
365 × 7 = 2,555

37 × 30 = 1,110
54 × 40 = 2,160

1/6 of 48 = 8
1/8 of 40 = 5
1/2 of 10 = 5

List the common factors for these number pairs. Circle the greatest common factor for each pair.
40 and 8: 2, 4, / 5, (8)
36 and 24: 3, 8, (12) / 2

What time did the clock show 2 hours and 20 minutes before? 12:05

Draw the sixth box in this pattern.

100,051 □ 99,109 **Which two numerals could go in the empty boxes?**
○ 105,231 109,345
○ 906,789 902,188
● 99,838   99,632
○ 98,054   93,107

Sandy made a jug of lemonade to serve five friends. About how much lemonade did she make?
○ 3 meters
○ 3 grams
● 3 liters
○ 3 milliliters

Write each numeral.
six million, twenty-two thousand, four hundred eighty-seven
6,022,487
twenty-five million, three hundred seventeen thousand, fifty-nine
25,317,059

357 × 8 = 2,856   652 × 7 = 4,564
229 × 5 = 1,145   934 × 3 = 2,802

Write the number pair for:
■ (5,1) ▲ (12,9)
♦ (1,8) ● (10,4)
▬ (2,6)

Mother needs to buy paper cups for 42 people. Which two packages could she buy to have enough paper cups without too many left over?
C and D
10(A) 15(B) 20(C) 25(D)

472 people bought concert tickets for $21.05 each. Which would be a way to estimate how much money was paid for the tickets?
○ 400 x $20.00 =$8,000
● 500 x $20.00 =$10,000
○ 470 +$20.00 = $490.
○ 500 - $25.00 =$475.

If these marbles are placed in a bag and one is drawn out, what is the probability that it will be white? (Write as a fraction)
5/7
black? 2/7

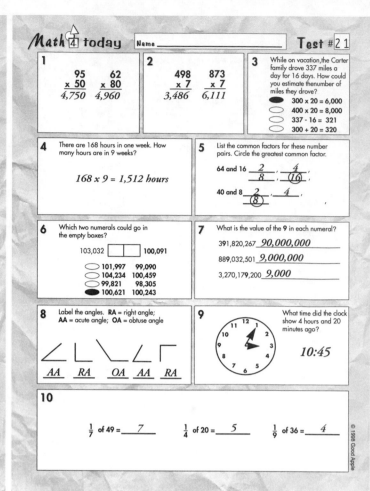

1. 95 × 50 = 4,750   62 × 80 = 4,960

2. 498 × 7 = 3,486   873 × 7 = 6,111

3. While on vacation, the Carter family drove 337 miles a day for 16 days. How could you estimate the number of miles they drove?
● 300 x 20 = 6,000
○ 400 x 20 = 8,000
○ 337 - 16 = 321
○ 300 + 20 = 320

4. There are 168 hours in one week. How many hours are in 9 weeks?
168 × 9 = 1,512 hours

5. List the common factors for these number pairs. Circle the greatest common factor.
64 and 16: 2, 4, (16)
40 and 8: 2, 4, (8)

6. Which two numerals could go in the empty boxes?
103,032 □ 100,091
○ 101,997 99,090
○ 104,234 100,459
○ 99,821   98,305
● 100,621 100,243

7. What is the value of the 9 in each numeral?
391,820,267 → 90,000,000
889,032,501 → 9,000,000
3,270,179,200 → 9,000

8. Label the angles. RA = right angle; AA = acute angle; OA = obtuse angle
AA RA OA AA RA

9. What time did the clock show 4 hours and 20 minutes ago? 10:45

10. 1/7 of 49 = 7   1/4 of 20 = 5   1/9 of 36 = 4

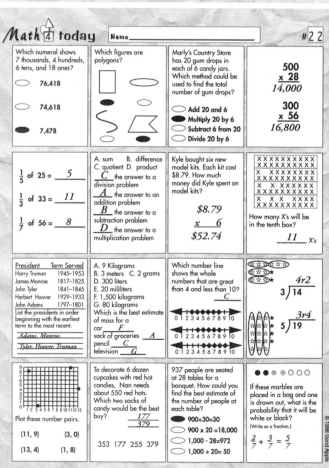

Which numeral shows 7 thousands, 4 hundreds, 6 tens, and 18 ones?
○ 76,418
○ 74,618
● 7,478

Which figures are polygons?

Marly's Country Store has 20 gum drops in each of 6 candy jars. Which method could be used to find the total number of gum drops?
○ Add 20 and 6
● Multiply 20 by 6
○ Subtract 6 from 20
○ Divide 20 by 6

500 × 28 = 14,000
300 × 56 = 16,800

1/5 of 25 = 5
1/3 of 33 = 11
1/7 of 56 = 8

A. sum   B. difference   C. quotient   D. product
C the answer to a division problem
A the answer to an addition problem
B the answer to a subtraction problem
D the answer to a multiplication problem

Kyle bought six new model kits. Each kit cost $8.79. How much money did Kyle spend on model kits?
$8.79 × 6 = $52.74

How many X's will be in the tenth box? 11 X's

President	Term Served
Harry Truman	1945-1953
James Monroe	1817-1825
John Tyler	1841-1845
Herbert Hoover	1929-1933
John Adams	1797-1801

List the presidents in order beginning with the earliest term to the most recent.
Adams, Monroe
Tyler, Hoover, Truman

A. 9 Kilograms B. 3 meters C. 2 grams D. 300 liters E. 20 milliliters F. 1,500 kilograms G. 80 kilograms
Which is the best estimate of mass for a
car F
sack of groceries A
pencil C
television G

Which number line shows the whole numbers that are great than 4 and less than 10? C

4r2 3)14
3r4 5)19

Plot these number pairs.
(11, 9) (3, 0)
(13, 4) (1, 8)

To decorate 6 dozen cupcakes with red hot candies, Nan needs about 550 red hots. Which two sacks of candy would be the best buy?
177 / 379
353 177 255 379

937 people are seated at 28 tables for a banquet. How could you find the best estimate of the number of people at each table?
● 900÷30=30
○ 900 x 20 =18,000
○ 1,000 - 28 =972
○ 1,000 ÷20= 50

If these marbles are placed in a bag and one is drawn out, what is the probability that it will be white or black? (Write as a fraction.)
2/7 + 3/7 = 5/7

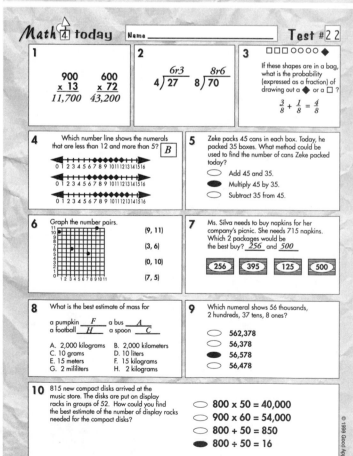

1. 900 × 13 = 11,700   600 × 72 = 43,200

2. 4)27 = 6r3   8)70 = 8r6

3. □□□○○○○◆ If these shapes are in a bag, what is the probability (expressed as a fraction) of drawing out a ◆ or a □?
3/8 + 1/8 = 4/8

4. Which number line shows the numerals that are less than 12 and more than 5? B

5. Zeke packs 45 cans in each box. Today, he packed 35 boxes. What method could be used to find the number of cans Zeke packed today?
○ Add 45 and 35.
● Multiply 45 by 35.
○ Subtract 35 from 45.

6. Graph the number pairs.
(9, 11) (3, 6) (0, 10) (7, 5)

7. Ms. Silva needs to buy napkins for her company's picnic. She needs 715 napkins. Which 2 packages would be the best buy? 256 and 500
256 395 125 500

8. What is the best estimate of mass for
a pumpkin F   a bus A
a football H   a spoon C
A. 2,000 kilograms B. 2,000 kilometers
C. 10 grams D. 10 liters
E. 15 meters F. 15 kilograms
G. 2 milliliters H. 2 kilograms

9. Which numeral shows 56 thousands, 2 hundreds, 37 tens, 8 ones?
○ 562,378
○ 56,378
● 56,578
○ 56,478

10. 815 new compact disks arrived at the music store. The disks are put on display racks in groups of 52. How could you find the best estimate of the number of display racks needed for the compact disks?
○ 800 x 50 = 40,000
○ 900 x 60 = 54,000
○ 800 + 50 = 850
● 800 ÷ 50 = 16

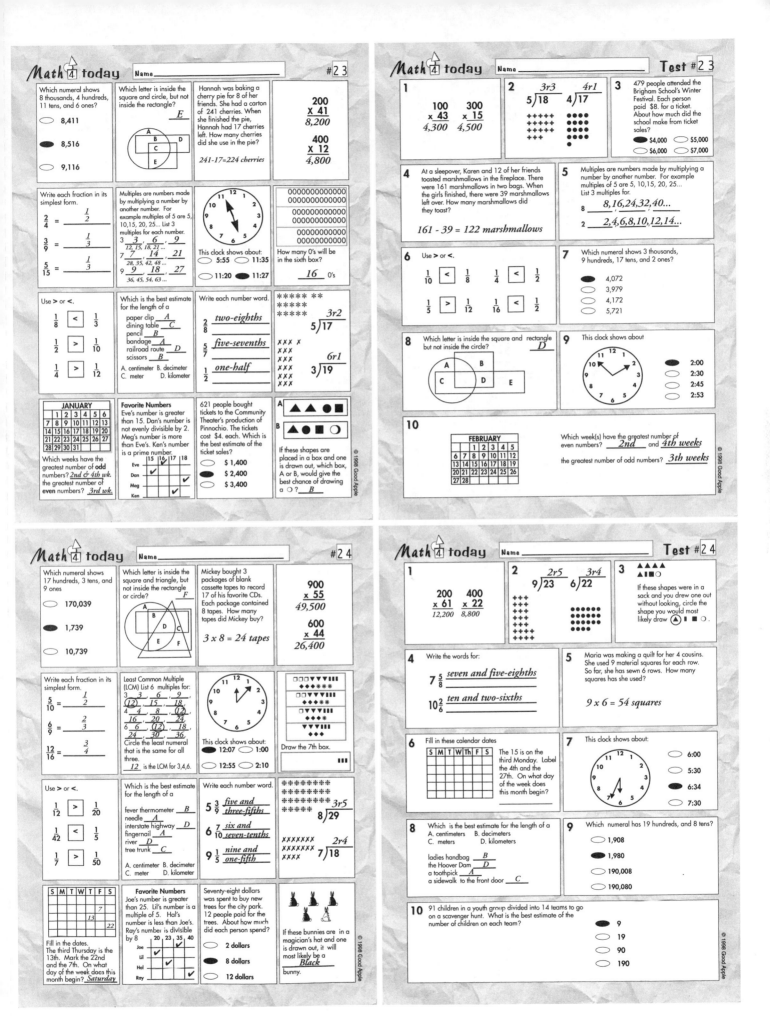

Math 4 today — #23

Which numeral shows 8 thousands, 4 hundreds, 11 tens, and 6 ones?
- ○ 8,411
- ● 8,516
- ○ 9,116

Which letter is inside the square and circle, but not inside the rectangle? *E*

Hannah was baking a cherry pie for 8 of her friends. She had a carton of 241 cherries. When she finished the pie, Hannah had 17 cherries left. How many cherries did she use in the pie?
241-17=224 cherries

200
x 41
8,200

400
x 12
4,800

Write each fraction in its simplest form.
$\frac{2}{4} = \frac{1}{2}$
$\frac{3}{9} = \frac{1}{3}$
$\frac{5}{15} = \frac{1}{3}$

Multiples are numbers made by multiplying a number by another number. For example multiples of 5 are 5, 10,15, 20, 25... List 3 multiples for each number.
3 _3_ , _6_ , _9_ *12, 15, 18, 21...*
7 _7_ , _14_ , _21_ *28, 35, 42, 48...*
9 _9_ , _18_ , _27_ *36, 45, 54, 63...*

This clock shows about:
- ○ 5:55
- ○ 11:35
- ○ 11:20
- ● 11:27

0000000000000
0000000000000
0000000000000
0000000000000
0000000000000
How many 0's will be in the sixth box? _16_ 0's

Use > or <.
$\frac{1}{8} < \frac{1}{3}$
$\frac{1}{2} > \frac{1}{10}$
$\frac{1}{4} > \frac{1}{12}$

Which is the best estimate for the length of a
paper clip _A_
dining table _C_
pencil _B_
bandage _A_
railroad route _D_
scissors _B_
A. centimeter B. decimeter
C. meter D. kilometer

Write each number word.
$\frac{2}{8}$ *two-eighths*
$\frac{5}{7}$ *five-sevenths*
$\frac{1}{2}$ *one-half*

***** **
*****
*****
5)17 = 3r2

XXX X
XXX
XXX
XXX
XXX
XXX
3)19 = 6r1

JANUARY

1	2	3	4	5	6
7	8	9	10	11	12	13
14	15	16	17	18	19	20
21	22	23	24	25	26	27
28	29	30	31

Which weeks have the greatest number of odd numbers? *2nd & 4th wk.*
the greatest number of **even** numbers? *3rd wk.*

Favorite Numbers
Eve's number is greater than 15. Dan's number is not evenly divisible by 2. Meg's number is more than Eve's. Ken's number is a prime number.

	15	16	17	18
Eve				✓
Dan	✓			
Meg				✓
Ken			✓	

621 people bought tickets to the Community Theater's production of Pinnochio. The tickets cost $4. each. Which is the best estimate of the ticket sales?
- ○ $ 1,400
- ● $ 2,400
- ○ $ 3,400

A ▲▲●■
B ▲●■○
If these shapes are placed in a box and one is drawn out, which box, A or B, would give the best chance of drawing a ○? _B_

© 1998 Good Apple

Math 4 today — Test #23

1.
100
x 43
4,300

300
x 15
4,500

2.
5)18 = 3r3
4)17 = 4r1

++++
++++
++++
+++

● ● ● ●
● ● ● ●
● ● ● ●
● ●

3. 479 people attended the Brigham School's Winter Festival. Each person paid $8. for a ticket. About how much did the school make from ticket sales?
- ● $4,000
- ○ $5,000
- ○ $6,000
- ○ $7,000

4. At a sleepover, Karen and 12 of her friends toasted marshmallows in the fireplace. There were 161 marshmallows in two bags. When the girls finished, there were 39 marshmallows left over. How many marshmallows did they toast?
161 - 39 = 122 marshmallows

5. Multiples are numbers made by multiplying a number by another number. For example multiples of 5 are 5, 10,15, 20, 25... List 3 multiples for.
8 *8, 16,24,32,40...*
2 *2,4,6,8,10,12,14...*

6. Use > or <.
$\frac{1}{10} < \frac{1}{8}$
$\frac{1}{4} < \frac{1}{2}$
$\frac{1}{5} > \frac{1}{12}$
$\frac{1}{16} < \frac{1}{2}$

7. Which numeral shows 3 thousands, 9 hundreds, 17 tens, and 2 ones?
- ● 4,072
- ○ 3,979
- ○ 4,172
- ○ 5,721

8. Which letter is inside the square and rectangle but not inside the circle? _D_

9. This clock shows about
- ● 2:00
- ○ 2:30
- ○ 2:45
- ○ 2:53

10.
FEBRUARY

1	2	3	4	5
6	7	8	9	10	11	12
13	14	15	16	17	18	19
20	21	22	23	24	25	26
27	28

Which week(s) have the greatest number of even numbers? *2nd* and *4th weeks*
the greatest number of odd numbers? *3th weeks*

© 1998 Good Apple

Math 4 today — #24

Which numeral shows 17 hundreds, 3 tens, and 9 ones?
- ○ 170,039
- ● 1,739
- ○ 10,739

Which letter is inside the square and triangle, but not inside the rectangle or circle? _F_

Mickey bought 3 packages of blank cassette tapes to record 17 of his favorite CDs. Each package contained 8 tapes. How many tapes did Mickey buy?
3 x 8 = 24 tapes

900
x 55
49,500

600
x 44
26,400

Write each fraction in its simplest form.
$\frac{5}{10} = \frac{1}{2}$
$\frac{6}{9} = \frac{2}{3}$
$\frac{12}{16} = \frac{3}{4}$

Least Common Multiple (LCM) List 6 multiples for:
3 _3_ , _6_ , _9_ , _(12)_ , _15_ , _18_
4 _4_ , _8_ , _(12)_ , _16_ , _20_ , _24_
6 _6_ , _(12)_ , _18_ , _24_ , _30_ , _36_
Circle the least numeral that is the same for all three.
_12_ is the LCM for 3,4,6.

This clock shows about:
- ● 12:07
- ○ 1:00
- ○ 12:55
- ○ 2:10

□□□▼▼▼IIIII
◆◆◆◆◆◆
□□▼▼▼IIIII
◆◆◆◆◆
□▼▼▼IIIII
◆◆◆◆
▼▼▼IIIII
◆◆◆
Draw the 7th box. ▼▼III

Use > or <.
$\frac{1}{12} > \frac{1}{20}$
$\frac{1}{42} < \frac{1}{5}$
$\frac{1}{7} > \frac{1}{50}$

Which is the best estimate for the length of a
fever thermometer _B_
needle _A_
interstate highway _D_
fingernail _A_
river _D_
tree trunk _C_
A. centimeter B. decimeter
C. meter D. kilometer

Write each number word.
$5\frac{3}{9}$ *five and three-fifths*
$6\frac{7}{10}$ *six and seven-tenths*
$9\frac{1}{5}$ *nine and one-fifth*

****
****
*****
8)29 = 3r5

XXXXXXX
XXXXXXX
XXXX
7)18 = 2r4

S	M	T	W	T	F	S
						7
		13				
				22		

Fill in the dates. The third Thursday is the 13th. Mark the 22nd and the 7th. On what day of the week does this month begin? *Saturday*

Favorite Numbers
Joe's number is greater than 25. Lil's number is a multiple of 5. Hal's number is less than Joe's. Ray's number is divisible by 8

	20	23	35	40
Joe				✓
Lil			✓	
Hal	✓			
Ray				✓

Seventy-eight dollars was spent to buy new trees for the city park. 12 people paid for the trees. About how much did each person spend?
- ○ 2 dollars
- ● 8 dollars
- ○ 12 dollars

If these bunnies are in a magician's hat and one is drawn out, it will most likely be a _Black_ bunny.

© 1998 Good Apple

Math 4 today — Test #24

1.
200
x 61
12,200

400
x 22
8,800

2.
9)23 = 2r5
6)22 = 3r4

+++
+++
+++
+++
+++

● ● ● ● ● ● ●
● ● ● ● ● ●
● ●

3. ▲▲▲▲
▲■●
If these shapes were in a sack and you drew one out without looking, circle the shape you would most likely draw ▲ ■ ● .

4. Write the words for:
$7\frac{5}{8}$ *seven and five-eighths*
$10\frac{2}{6}$ *ten and two-sixths*

5. Maria was making a quilt for her 4 cousins. She used 9 material squares for each row. So far, she has sewn 6 rows. How many squares has she used?
9 x 6 = 54 squares

6. Fill in these calendar dates

S	M	T	W	Th	F	S

The 15 is on the third Monday. Label the 4th and the 27th. On what day of the week does this month begin?
_____

7. This clock shows about:
- ○ 6:00
- ○ 5:30
- ● 6:34
- ○ 7:30

8. Which is the best estimate for the length of a
A. centimeters B. decimeters
C. meters D. kilometers
ladies handbag _B_
the Hoover Dam _D_
a toothpick _A_
a sidewalk to the front door _C_

9. Which numeral has 19 hundreds, and 8 tens?
- ○ 1,908
- ● 1,980
- ○ 190,008
- ○ 190,080

10. 91 children in a youth group divided into 14 teams to go on a scavenger hunt. What is the best estimate of the number of children on each team?
- ● 9
- ○ 19
- ○ 90
- ○ 190

© 1998 Good Apple

129

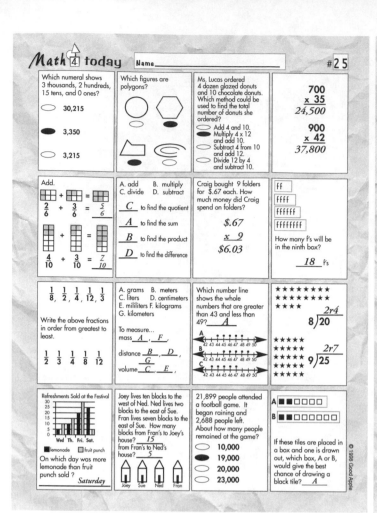
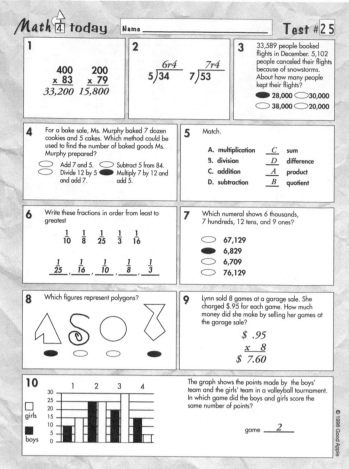
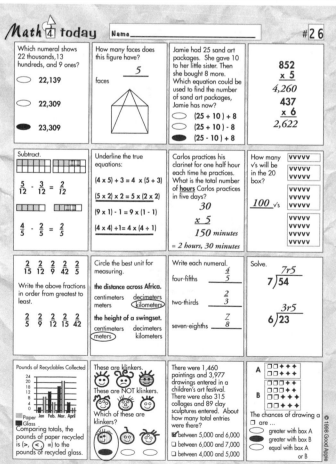
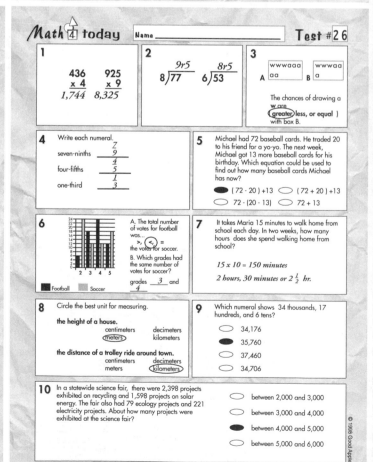

Math 4 today — #25

Which numeral shows 3 thousands, 2 hundreds, 15 tens, and 0 ones?
- ⬭ 30,215
- ⬤ 3,350
- ⬭ 3,215

Which figures are polygons?

Ms. Lucas ordered 4 dozen glazed donuts and 10 chocolate donuts. Which method could be used to find the total number of donuts she ordered?
- ⬭ Add 4 and 10.
- ⬤ Multiply 4 x 12 and add 10.
- ⬭ Subtract 4 from 10 and add 12.
- ⬭ Divide 12 by 4 and subtract 10.

700
x 35
24,500

900
x 42
37,800

Add.

$\frac{2}{6} + \frac{3}{6} = \frac{5}{6}$

$\frac{4}{10} + \frac{3}{10} = \frac{7}{10}$

A. add B. multiply C. divide D. subtract

_C_ to find the quotient
_A_ to find the sum
_B_ to find the product
_D_ to find the difference

Craig bought 9 folders for $.67 each. How much money did Craig spend on folders?

$.67
x 9
$6.03

ff
ffff
ffffff
ffffffff

How many f's will be in the ninth box?

_18_ f's

$\frac{1}{8}, \frac{1}{2}, \frac{1}{4}, \frac{1}{12}, \frac{1}{3}$

Write the above fractions in order from greatest to least.

$\frac{1}{2}, \frac{1}{3}, \frac{1}{4}, \frac{1}{8}, \frac{1}{12}$

A. grams B. meters C. liters D. centimeters E. mililiters F. kilograms G. kilometers

To measure…
mass _A_, _F_,
distance _B_, _D_, _G_
volume _C_, _E_,

Which number line shows the whole numbers that are greater than 43 and less than 49? _A_

$8\overline{)20}$ 2r4
$9\overline{)25}$ 2r7

Refreshments Sold at the Festival

On which day was more lemonade than fruit punch sold?
Saturday

Joey lives ten blocks to the west of Ned. Ned lives two blocks to the east of Sue. Fran lives seven blocks to the east of Sue. How many blocks from Fran's to Joey's house? _15_
from Fran's to Ned's house? _5_

21,899 people attended a football game. It began raining and 2,688 people left. About how many people remained at the game?
- ⬭ 10,000
- ⬤ 19,000
- ⬭ 20,000
- ⬭ 23,000

A ■■□□□□
B ■■■□□□□

If these tiles are placed in a box and one is drawn out, which box, A or B, would give the best chance of drawing a black tile? _A_

Math 4 today — Test #25

1.
400
x 83
33,200

200
x 79
15,800

2.
$5\overline{)34}$ 6r4
$7\overline{)53}$ 7r4

3. 33,589 people booked flights in December. 5,102 people canceled their flights because of snowstorms. About how many people kept their flights?
- ⬤ 28,000 ⬭ 30,000
- ⬭ 38,000 ⬭ 20,000

4. For a bake sale, Ms. Murphy baked 7 dozen cookies and 5 cakes. Which method could be used to find the number of baked goods Ms. Murphy prepared?
- ⬭ Add 7 and 5.
- ⬭ Divide 12 by 5
- ⬭ Subtract 5 from 84.
- ⬤ Multiply 7 by 12 and add 5.

5. Match.
- A. multiplication _C_ sum
- B. division _D_ difference
- C. addition _A_ product
- D. subtraction _B_ quotient

6. Write these fractions in order from least to greatest
$\frac{1}{10}, \frac{1}{8}, \frac{1}{25}, \frac{1}{3}, \frac{1}{16}$

$\frac{1}{25}, \frac{1}{16}, \frac{1}{10}, \frac{1}{8}, \frac{1}{3}$

7. Which numeral shows 6 thousands, 7 hundreds, 12 tens, and 9 ones?
- ⬭ 67,129
- ⬤ 6,829
- ⬭ 6,709
- ⬭ 76,129

8. Which figures represent polygons?

9. Lynn sold 8 games at a garage sale. She charged $.95 for each game. How much money did she make by selling her games at the garage sale?
$ .95
x 8
$ 7.60

10.

The graph shows the points made by the boys' team and the girls' team in a volleyball tournament. In which game did the boys and girls score the same number of points?

game _2_

Math 4 today — #26

Which numeral shows 22 thousands, 13 hundreds, and 9 ones?
- ⬭ 22,139
- ⬭ 22,309
- ⬤ 23,309

How many faces does this figure have?
faces _5_

Jamie had 25 sand art packages. She gave 10 to her little sister. Then she bought 8 more. Which equation could be used to find the number of sand art packages Jamie has now?
- ⬭ (25 + 10) + 8
- ⬭ (25 + 10) - 8
- ⬤ (25 - 10) + 8

852
x 5
4,260

437
x 6
2,622

Subtract.

$\frac{5}{12} - \frac{3}{12} = \frac{2}{12}$

$\frac{4}{5} - \frac{2}{5} = \frac{2}{5}$

Underline the true equations:
(4 x 5) + 3 = 4 x (5 + 3)
(5 x 2) x 2 = 5 x (2 x 2)
(9 x 1) - 1 = 9 x (1 - 1)
(4 x 4) + 1 = 4 x (4 ÷ 1)

Carlos practices his clarinet for one half hour each time he practices. What is the total number of hours Carlos practices in five days?
30
x 5
150 minutes
= 2 hours, 30 minutes

How many v's will be in the 20 box?
_100_ v's

vvvvv vvvvv
vvvvv vvvvv
vvvvv vvvvv
vvvvv vvvvv

$\frac{2}{15}, \frac{2}{12}, \frac{2}{9}, \frac{2}{42}, \frac{2}{5}$

Write the above fractions in order from greatest to least.

$\frac{2}{5}, \frac{2}{9}, \frac{2}{12}, \frac{2}{15}, \frac{2}{42}$

Circle the best unit for measuring.
the distance across Africa.
centimeters decimeters
meters (kilometers)

the height of a swingset.
centimeters decimeters
(meters) kilometers

Write each numeral.
four-fifths $\frac{4}{5}$
two-thirds $\frac{2}{3}$
seven-eighths $\frac{7}{8}$

Solve.
$7\overline{)54}$ 7r5
$6\overline{)23}$ 3r5

Pounds of Recyclables Collected

Comparing totals, the pounds of paper recycled is (>, <) = to the pounds of recycled glass.

These are klinkers.
These are NOT klinkers.
Which of these are klinkers?

There were 1,460 paintings and 3,977 drawings entered in a children's art festival. There were also 315 collages and 89 clay sculptures entered. About how many total entries were there?
- ☑ between 5,000 and 6,000
- ⬭ between 6,000 and 7,000
- ⬭ between 4,000 and 5,000

A
The chances of drawing a ◆ are …
- ⬭ greater with box A
- ⬤ greater with box B
- ⬭ equal with box A or B

Math 4 today — Test #26

1.
436
x 4
1,744

925
x 9
8,325

2.
$8\overline{)77}$ 9r5
$6\overline{)53}$ 8r5

3.
A wwwaaaaa
B wwwaaa a

The chances of drawing a w are (greater) less, or equal) with box B.

4. Write each numeral.
seven-ninths $\frac{7}{9}$
four-fifths $\frac{4}{5}$
one-third $\frac{1}{3}$

5. Michael had 72 baseball cards. He traded 20 to his friend for a yo-yo. The next week, Michael got 13 more baseball cards for his birthday. Which equation could be used to find out how many baseball cards Michael has now?
- ⬤ (72 - 20) + 13
- ⬭ (72 + 20) + 13
- ⬭ 72 - (20 - 13)
- ⬭ 72 + 13

6.
A. The total number of votes for football was…
> , (<) =
the votes for soccer.
B. Which grades had the same number of votes for soccer?
grades _3_ and _4_

■ Football ▨ Soccer

7. It takes Maria 15 minutes to walk home from school each day. In two weeks, how many hours does she spend walking home from school?
15 x 10 = 150 minutes
2 hours, 30 minutes or $2\frac{1}{2}$ hr.

8. Circle the best unit for measuring.
the height of a house.
centimeters decimeters
(meters) kilometers

the distance of a trolley ride around town.
centimeters decimeters
meters (kilometers)

9. Which numeral shows 34 thousands, 17 hundreds, and 6 tens?
- ⬭ 34,176
- ⬤ 35,760
- ⬭ 37,460
- ⬭ 34,706

10. In a statewide science fair, there were 2,398 projects exhibited on recycling and 1,598 projects on solar energy. The fair also had 79 ecology projects and 221 electricity projects. About how many projects were exhibited at the science fair?
- ⬭ between 2,000 and 3,000
- ⬭ between 3,000 and 4,000
- ⬤ between 4,000 and 5,000
- ⬭ between 5,000 and 6,000

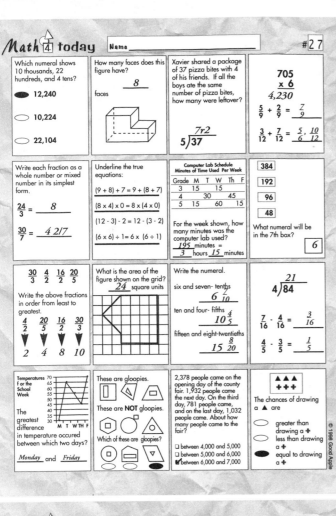

Math 4 today — #27

Which numeral shows 10 thousands, 22 hundreds, and 4 tens?
- ● 12,240
- ○ 10,224
- ○ 22,104

How many faces does this figure have?
8 faces

Xavier shared a package of 37 pizza bites with 4 of his friends. If all the boys ate the same number of pizza bites, how many were leftover?
7r2
5)37

$705 \times 6 = 4,230$

$\frac{5}{9} + \frac{2}{9} = \frac{7}{9}$

$\frac{3}{12} + \frac{7}{12} = \frac{5}{6}, \frac{10}{12}$

Write each fraction as a whole number or mixed number in its simplest form.
$\frac{24}{3} = 8$
$\frac{30}{7} = 4\frac{2}{7}$

Underline the true equations:
$(9 + 8) + 7 = 9 + (8 + 7)$
$(8 \times 4) \times 0 = 8 \times (4 \times 0)$
$(12 - 3) - 2 = 12 - (3 - 2)$
$(6 \times 6) \div 1 = 6 \times (6 \div 1)$

Computer Lab Schedule — Minutes of Time Used Per Week

Grade	M	T	W	Th	F
3	15		15		
4		30		45	
5	15		60		15

For the week shown, how many minutes was the computer lab used? 195 minutes = 3 hours 15 minutes

384
192
96
48
What numeral will be in the 7th box? 6

$\frac{30}{3}\ \frac{4}{2}\ \frac{16}{2}\ \frac{20}{5}$
Write the above fractions in order from least to greatest.
$\frac{4}{2}\ \frac{20}{5}\ \frac{16}{2}\ \frac{30}{3}$
2 4 8 10

What is the area of the figure shown on the grid? 24 square units

Write the numeral.
six and seven-tenths $6\frac{7}{10}$
ten and four-fifths $10\frac{4}{5}$
fifteen and eight-twentieths $15\frac{8}{20}$

21
4)84
$\frac{7}{16} - \frac{4}{16} = \frac{3}{16}$
$\frac{4}{5} - \frac{3}{5} = \frac{1}{5}$

Temperatures for the School Week — The greatest difference in temperature occured between which two days? Monday and Friday

These are gloopies. / These are NOT gloopies. Which of these are gloopies?

2,378 people came on the opening day of the county fair. 1,932 people came the next day. On the third day, 781 people came, and on the last day, 1,032 people came. About how many people came to the fair?
- ☐ between 4,000 and 5,000
- ☑ between 5,000 and 6,000
- ☑ between 6,000 and 7,000

The chances of drawing a ▲ are
- ○ greater than drawing a ✛
- ○ less than drawing a ✛
- ● equal to drawing a ✛

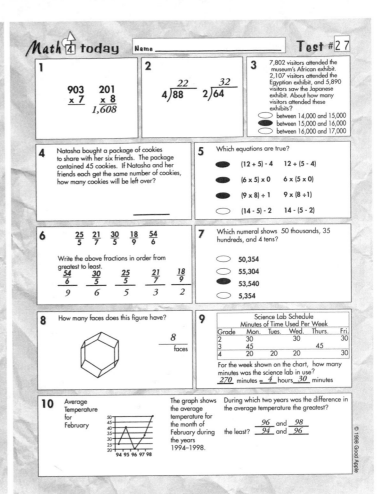

Math 4 today — Test #27

1. $903 \times 7 = ?$ $201 \times 8 = 1,608$

2. $4)\overline{88} = 22$ $2)\overline{64} = 32$

3. 7,802 visitors attended the museum's African exhibit. 2,107 visitors attended the Egyptian exhibit, and 5,890 visitors saw the Japanese exhibit. About how many visitors attended these exhibits?
- ○ between 14,000 and 15,000
- ● between 15,000 and 16,000
- ○ between 16,000 and 17,000

4. Natasha bought a package of cookies to share with her six friends. The package contained 45 cookies. If Natasha and her friends each get the same number of cookies, how many cookies will be left over? _____

5. Which equations are true?
- ● $(12 + 5) - 4 \quad 12 + (5 - 4)$
- ● $(6 \times 5) \times 0 \quad 6 \times (5 \times 0)$
- ● $(9 \times 8) \div 1 \quad 9 \times (8 \div 1)$
- ○ $(14 - 5) - 2 \quad 14 - (5 - 2)$

6. $\frac{25}{5}\ \frac{21}{7}\ \frac{30}{5}\ \frac{18}{9}\ \frac{54}{6}$
Write the above fractions in order from greatest to least.
$\frac{54}{6}\ \frac{30}{5}\ \frac{25}{5}\ \frac{21}{7}\ \frac{18}{9}$
9 6 5 3 2

7. Which numeral shows 50 thousands, 35 hundreds, and 4 tens?
- ○ 50,354
- ○ 55,304
- ● 53,540
- ○ 5,354

8. How many faces does this figure have? 8 faces

9. Science Lab Schedule — Minutes of Time Used Per Week

Grade	Mon.	Tues.	Wed.	Thurs.	Fri.
2	30		30		30
3	45			45	
4	20	20		20	30

For the week shown on the chart, how many minutes was the science lab in use? 270 minutes = 4 hours 30 minutes

10. Average Temperature for February — The graph shows the average temperature for the month of February during the years 1994–1998. During which two years was the difference in the average temperature the greatest? 96 and 98 the least? 94 and 96

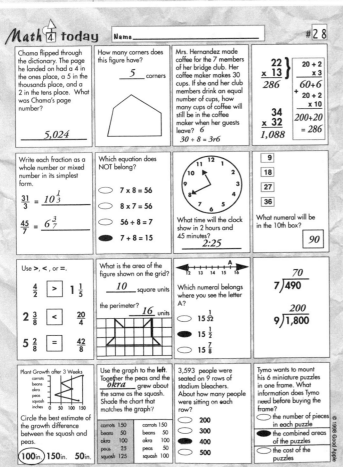

Math 4 today — #28

Chama flipped through the dictionary. The page he landed on had a 4 in the ones place, a 5 in the thousands place, and a 2 in the tens place. What was Chama's page number? 5,024

How many corners does this figure have? 5 corners

Mrs. Hernandez made coffee for the 7 members of her bridge club. Her coffee maker makes 30 cups. If she and her club members drink an equal number of cups, how many cups of coffee will still be in the coffee maker when her guests leave? 6
$30 \div 8 = 3r6$

$22 \times 13 = 286$
$34 \times 32 = 1,088$
$20 + 2 \times 3$
$60+6$
$+ 20 + 2 \times 10$
$200+20 = 286$

Write each fraction as a whole number or mixed number in its simplest form.
$\frac{31}{3} = 10\frac{1}{3}$
$\frac{45}{7} = 6\frac{3}{7}$

Which equation does NOT belong?
- ○ $7 \times 8 = 56$
- ○ $8 \times 7 = 56$
- ○ $56 \div 8 = 7$
- ● $7 + 8 = 15$

What time will the clock show in 2 hours and 45 minutes? 2:25

9
18
27
36
What numeral will be in the 10th box? 90

Use >, <, or =.
$\frac{4}{2} > 1\frac{1}{5}$
$2\frac{3}{8} < \frac{20}{4}$
$5\frac{2}{8} = \frac{42}{8}$

What is the area of the figure shown on the grid? 10 square units the perimeter? 16 units

Which numeral belongs where you see the letter A?
- ○ $15\frac{1}{32}$
- ● $15\frac{1}{2}$
- ○ $15\frac{7}{8}$

70
7)490
200
9)1,800

Plant Growth after 3 Weeks — Circle the best estimate of the growth difference between the squash and peas. (100 in.) 150 in. 50 in.

Use the graph to the left. Together the peas and the okra grew about the same as the squash. Shade the chart that matches the graph.

carrots	150	carrots	150
beans	50	beans	50
okra	100	okra	100
peas	25	peas	50
squash	125	squash	125

3,593 people were seated on 9 rows of stadium bleachers. About how many people were sitting on each row?
- ○ 200
- ○ 300
- ● 400
- ○ 500

Tymo wants to mount his 6 miniature puzzles in one frame. What information does Tymo need before buying the frame?
- ● the number of pieces in each puzzle
- ☐ the combined areas of the puzzles
- ☐ the cost of the puzzles

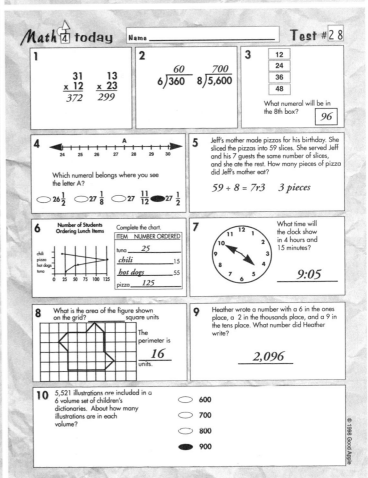

Math 4 today — Test #28

1. $31 \times 12 = 372$ $13 \times 23 = 299$

2. $6)\overline{360} = 60$ $8)\overline{5,600} = 700$

3. 12 / 24 / 36 / 48
What numeral will be in the 8th box? 96

4. Which numeral belongs where you see the letter A?
- ○ $26\frac{1}{2}$
- ○ $27\frac{1}{8}$
- ○ $27\frac{11}{12}$
- ● $27\frac{1}{2}$

5. Jeff's mother made pizzas for his birthday. She sliced the pizzas into 59 slices. She served Jeff and his 7 guests the same number of slices, and she ate the rest. How many pieces of pizza did Jeff's mother eat?
$59 \div 8 = 7r3 \quad 3 \text{ pieces}$

6. Number of Students Ordering Lunch Items — Complete the chart.

ITEM	NUMBER ORDERED
tuna	25
chili	15
hot dogs	55
pizza	125

7. What time will the clock show in 4 hours and 15 minutes? 9:05

8. What is the area of the figure shown on the grid? ___ square units The perimeter is 16 units.

9. Heather wrote a number with a 6 in the ones place, a 2 in the thousands place, and a 9 in the tens place. What number did Heather write? 2,096

10. 5,521 illustrations are included in a 6 volume set of children's dictionaries. About how many illustrations are in each volume?
- ○ 600
- ○ 700
- ○ 800
- ● 900

Leslie was writing the populations of several cities. The population of Nawton had a 9 in the thousands place, a 5 in the ones place, and a 6 in the ten thousands place. What number did Leslie write for Nawton's population?

69,005

How many corners does this figure have?

8 corners

Adam is studying for a six week's spelling test. There are 6 word lists that have 15 words each. Adam studies for his spelling test by writing the words three times. How many words will Adam write?

$15 \times 6 = 90$
$90 \times 3 = 270$ words

$45 \atop \times 25$ } $1,125$

$40 + 5$
$\times 5$
$200 + 25$
$+$
$40 + 5$
$\times 20$
$800 + 100$
$= 1,125$

$62 \atop \times 43$
$2,666$

Add or subtract. Simplify if needed.

$\frac{5}{8} + \frac{2}{8} = \frac{7}{8}$

$\frac{2}{10} + \frac{1}{10} = \frac{3}{10}$

$\frac{4}{6} - \frac{2}{6} = 2\frac{1}{6} \cdot \frac{1}{3}$

To find the average of a group of numbers, add the numbers together, then divide the total by the number of addends.
Example:
5, 7, 9, 3
$5 + 7 + 9 + 3 = 24$
$24 \div 4 = 6$
6 is the average for this group of numbers.
Find the average for:
8, 7, 2, 3, 15
$8 + 7 + 2 + 3 + 15 = 35$
$35 \div 5 = 7$

Robert saved $52.00 so he could attend a concert. He paid $23.50 for the tickets. At the concert, he bought a program for $7.25 and a t-shirt for $15.00. How much money did Robert have after the concert?
$23.50 $52.00
7.25   -45.75
15.00   6.25
45.75

88, 81, 74, 67, 60

What is the rule for the above pattern?

subtract 7

Use >, <, or =.

$\frac{9}{3}$ < $3\frac{1}{3}$

$7\frac{1}{4}$ = $\frac{30}{4}$

$2\frac{1}{16}$ < $\frac{20}{4}$

Use >, <, or =.

3 inches < 3 yards
6 feet = 2 yards
12 inches = 1 foot
8 feet > 1 yard

Which numeral belongs where you see the letter A?

◯ $13\frac{1}{2}$
◯ $12\frac{1}{2}$
⬤ $12\frac{3}{4}$

$3\overline{)9,360}$ **3,120**

$4\overline{)8,048}$ **2,012**

James 🌲🌲🌲🌲🌲
Kevin 🌲🌲🌲🌲🌲
Steve 🌲🌲🌲🌲🌲🌲

each tree = 8
Shade in the graph to show Kevin trimmed 36 trees. Steve trimmed 44 trees. James trimmed 20 trees.

Use the graph to the **left**. How many trees were trimmed by all the boys?
100 trees
One half a tree shaded =
4 trees
Steve trimmed about **2** times the number of trees trimmed by James.

1,593 people were waiting to board 8 planes. About how many passengers will get on each plane?
◯ 100
⬤ 200
◯ 300
◯ 400

Mrs. Jordan needs to make lemonade for the school's field day. A can of lemonade serves 30 people. What information does Mrs. Jordan need before she makes the lemonade?
◯ The cost of the lemonade per can.
◯ How many cans it takes to make a gallon.
⬤ The number of people who will drink lemonade.

© 1998 Good Apple

1
$67 \atop \times 26$ $39 \atop \times 47$
$1,742$ $1,833$

2
$7\overline{)4,200}$ 600 $8\overline{)5,600}$ 700

3 During 1 week, 5,598 people booked tours. The tour line has 7 buses. About how many people did each bus carry during the week?
◯ 600
◯ 700
⬤ 800
◯ 900

4 During 25 days at summer camp, Lisbet swam three times a day. She swam 20 meters each time. How many meters did Lisbet swim during summer camp?
$(20 \times 3 = 60) \times 25 = 1500$ meters

5 Find the average for this group of numbers:
17, 3, 12, 8, 5
$17 + 3 + 12 + 8 + 5 = 45$
$45 \div 5 = 9$

6 Use >, <, or =.
4 = $\frac{12}{3}$
$2\frac{4}{5}$ < $2\frac{6}{5}$
$5\frac{7}{3}$ = $7\frac{1}{3}$

7 Weston used his computer's word count on a report he was writing. The computer counted the words in his report and displayed a 9 in the hundreds place, a 2 in the tens place, and a 1 in the thousands place. How many words were in Weston's report?
1,920 words

8 How many corners does the figure below have? **10** corners

9 Javier saved $72.30 to buy some new compact disks for his CD-ROM. He bought Rocket Race for $21.77 and Pro Ball for $19.85. The tax on the two CDs was $5.75. How much did Javier have after buying the CDs?
$21.77 + 19.85 + 5.75 = $47.37
$72.30 - 47.37 = $24.93

10 Add or subtract. Write the answer in simplest form.
$\frac{3}{7} + \frac{1}{7} = \frac{4}{7}$ $\frac{6}{16} - \frac{2}{16} = \frac{4}{16} = \frac{1}{4}$ $\frac{7}{9} - \frac{5}{9} = \frac{2}{9}$

© 1998 Good Apple

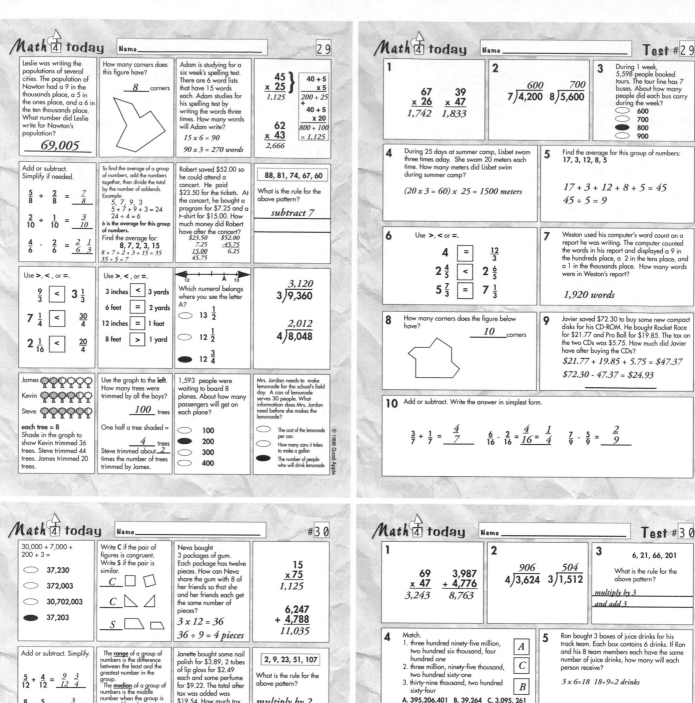

$30,000 + 7,000 + 200 + 3 =$
◯ 37,230
◯ 372,003
◯ 30,702,003
⬤ 37,203

Write **C** if the pair of figures is congruent. Write **S** if the pair is similar.
__C__
__C__
__S__

Neva bought 3 packages of gum. Each package has twelve pieces. How can Neva share the gum with 8 of her friends so that she and her friends each get the same number of pieces?
$3 \times 12 = 36$
$36 \div 9 = 4$ pieces

$15 \atop \times 75$
$1,125$

$6,247 \atop + 4,788$
$11,035$

Add or subtract. Simplify.

$\frac{5}{12} + \frac{4}{12} = \frac{9}{12} \cdot \frac{3}{4}$

$\frac{8}{13} - \frac{5}{13} = \frac{3}{13}$

$\frac{12}{32} + \frac{12}{32} = \frac{24}{32} \cdot \frac{3}{4}$

The **range** of a group of numbers is the difference between the least and the greatest number in the group.
The **median** of a group of numbers is the middle number when the group is arranged from least to greatest. Example:
5,12,15,21,25
range = $25-5=20$; median = 15
For **8,5,3,20,2**
the range = __18__
the median = __5__

Janette bought some nail polish for $3.89, 2 tubes of lip gloss for $2.49 each and some perfume for $9.22. The total after tax was added was $19.54. How much tax did Janette pay on the items she bought?
$3.89 $19.54
2×2.49= 5.80   -18.09
9.22 $1.45
$18.91

2, 9, 23, 51, 107
What is the rule for the above pattern?
multiply by 2 and add 5

Some of the Largest Earth Filled Dams measured in cubic meters.
Tarbela 186,000,000
Oahe 92,000,000
Cornelia 274,026,000
Pati 261,590
Atatürk 110,522
List the names of the dams in order of size from least to greatest.
Atatürk, Pati, Oahe, Tarbela, Cornelia

Use >, <, or =
24 inches < 3 feet
9 feet = 3 yards
36 inches = 1 yard
10 feet > 2 yards

Which numeral is read:
two hundred seventy-five million, nine hundred thousand, forty-six?
⬤ 275, 900,046
◯ 275,946
◯ 200,759,460

$5\overline{)4,525}$ **905**

$9\overline{)7,245}$ **805**

Margie's Gift Wrapping
Sept. ☐☐☐☐▨
Oct. ☐☐☐
Nov. ☐☐☐☐☐☐▨
Dec. ☐☐☐☐☐☐☐▨
each ☐ = 50 gifts wrapped
How many gifts were wrapped in October? **150**
How many gifts were wrapped in September? **225**

Use the graph to the **left**.
How many gifts were wrapped during all four months? **1,125**
How many more gifts were wrapped in November and December than in September? **525**
How many more ☐ would be needed to show 250 gifts wrapped in October? **2**

What is 675,789 rounded to the nearest thousand?
◯ 700,000
⬤ 676,000
◯ 680,000
◯ 674,000

Shane spent $25.00 on vacation souvenirs. His mother spent $40.00, and his dad spent $30.00. Judy, Shane's sister, spent more than Shane and Dad but less than Mother. Which could be true?
◯ Judy spent $45.00
⬤ Judy spent $32.00
◯ Judy spent $29.00

1
$69 \atop \times 47$ $3,987 \atop + 4,776$
$3,243$ $8,763$

2
$4\overline{)3,624}$ 906 $3\overline{)1,512}$ 504

3 6, 21, 66, 201
What is the rule for the above pattern?
multiply by 3 and add 3

4 Match.
1. three hundred ninety-five million, two hundred six thousand, four hundred one   **A**
2. three hundred ninety-five thousand, two hundred sixty-one   **C**
3. thirty-nine thousand, two hundred sixty-four   **B**
A. 395,206,401   B. 39,264   C. 3,095, 261

5 Ron bought 3 boxes of juice drinks for his track team. Each box contains 6 drinks. If Ron and his 8 team members each have the same number of juice drinks, how many will each person receive?
$3 \times 6=18$ $18 \div 9=2$ drinks

6 Operator Assisted Phone Calls From Hotel Farrington
May 📞📞📞📞📞📞   Each 📞 = 80
June 📞📞📞📞📞⌐
July 📞📞📞📞📞📞📞
Aug. 📞📞📞📞📞📞📞
How many operator assisted calls were made in June? **440** in August? **560**
How many more calls were made in August than in May? **280**
In all, how many calls were made? **2,000**

7 Emil earned $57.00 doing odd jobs. Mark earned more than Emil, but less than Jake. Jake earned $72.00. Which could be true?
◯ Mark earned $55.00
◯ Mark earned $75.00
⬤ Mark earned $67.00

8 Use >, <, or =.
36 inches > 2 feet
3 yards = 9 feet
24 inches > 1 foot
1 yard > 24 inches

9
$60,000 + 3,000 + 500 + 4 =$ __63,504__
$500,000 + 80,000 + 2,000 + 1 =$ __582,001__
$20,000 + 300 + 90 + 7 =$ __20,397__

10 What is 782,432 rounded to the nearest thousand?
◯ 780,000
◯ 790,000
◯ 781,400
⬤ 782,000

What is 816,710 rounded to the nearest thousand?
◯ 810,000
⬤ 817,000
◯ 822,400
◯ 825,000

© 1998 Good Apple

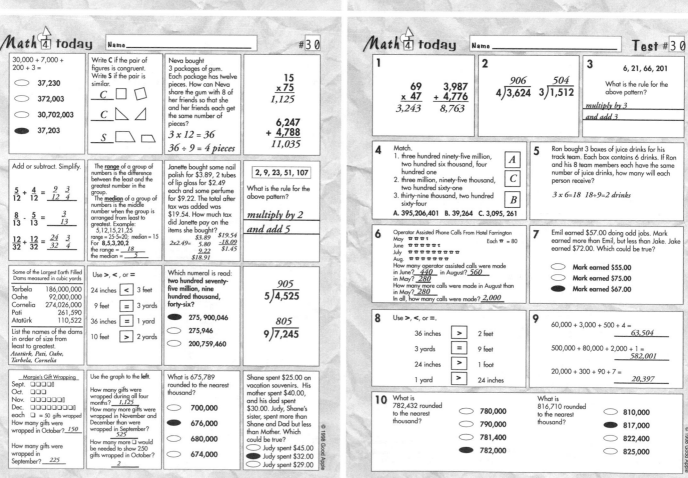

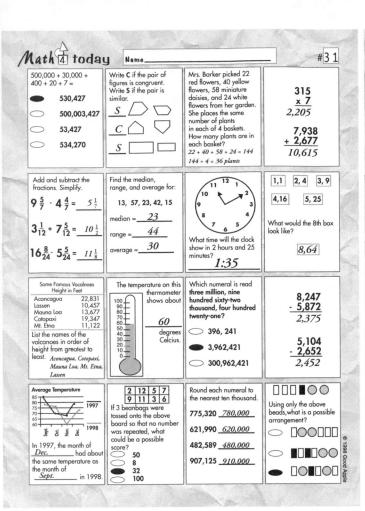

Top-left worksheet (#31):

500,000 + 30,000 + 400 + 20 + 7 =
- ● 530,427
- ○ 500,003,427
- ○ 53,427
- ○ 534,270

Write **C** if the pair of figures is congruent. Write **S** if the pair is similar.
S, C, S

Mrs. Barker picked 22 red flowers, 40 yellow flowers, 58 miniature daisies, and 24 white flowers from her garden. She places the same number of plants in each of 4 baskets. How many plants are in each basket?
22 + 40 + 58 + 24 = 144
144 ÷ 4 = 36 plants

$$315 \times 7 = 2,205$$
$$7,938 + 2,677 = 10,615$$

Add and subtract the fractions. Simplify.
$9\frac{5}{7} - 4\frac{4}{7} = 5\frac{1}{7}$
$3\frac{1}{12} + 7\frac{5}{12} = 10\frac{1}{2}$
$16\frac{8}{24} - 5\frac{5}{24} = 11\frac{1}{8}$

Find the median, range, and average for:
13, 57, 23, 42, 15
median = 23
range = 44
average = 30

What time will the clock show in 2 hours and 25 minutes?
1:35

1,1   2,4   3,9
4,16   5,25
What would the 8th box look like?
8,64

Some Famous Volcanoes Height in Feet
Aconcagua	22,831
Lassen	10,457
Mauna Loa	13,677
Cotopaxi	19,347
Mt. Etna	11,122

List the names of the volcanoes in order of height from greatest to least.
Aconcagua, Cotopaxi, Mauna Loa, Mt. Etna, Lassen

The temperature on this thermometer shows about 60 degrees Celcius.

Which numeral is read three million, nine hundred sixty-two thousand, four hundred twenty-one?
- ○ 396, 241
- ● 3,962,421
- ○ 300,962,421

$$8,247 - 5,872 = 2,375$$
$$5,104 - 2,652 = 2,452$$

Average Temperature (graph: 1997, 1998)
In 1997, the month of Dec. had about the same temperature as the month of Sept. in 1998.

2 12 5 7 / 9 11 3 6
If 3 beanbags were tossed onto the above board so that no number was repeated, what could be a possible score?
- ○ 50
- ● 8
- ● 32
- ○ 100

Round each numeral to the nearest ten thousand.
775,320 __780,000__
621,990 __620,000__
482,589 __480,000__
907,125 __910,000__

Using only the above beads, what is a possible arrangement?

© 1998 Good Apple

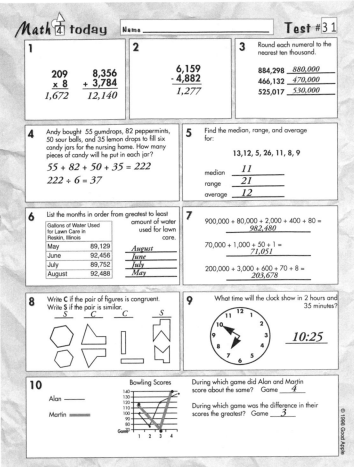

Top-right worksheet (Test #31):

1
$$209 \times 8 = 1,672$$
$$8,356 + 3,784 = 12,140$$

2
$$6,159 - 4,882 = 1,277$$

3 Round each numeral to the nearest ten thousand.
884,298 __880,000__
466,132 __470,000__
525,017 __530,000__

4 Andy bought 55 gumdrops, 82 peppermints, 50 sour balls, and 35 lemon drops to fill six candy jars for the nursing home. How many pieces of candy will he put in each jar?
55 + 82 + 50 + 35 = 222
222 ÷ 6 = 37

5 Find the median, range, and average for:
13, 12, 5, 26, 11, 8, 9
median __11__
range __21__
average __12__

6 List the months in order from greatest to least amount of water used for lawn care.

Gallons of Water Used for Lawn Care in Reskin, Illinois
May	89,129
June	92,456
July	89,752
August	92,488

August
June
July
May

7
900,000 + 80,000 + 2,000 + 400 + 80 = 982,480
70,000 + 1,000 + 50 + 1 = 71,051
200,000 + 3,000 + 600 + 70 + 8 = 203,678

8 Write **C** if the pair of figures is congruent. Write **S** if the pair is similar.
S, C, C, S

9 What time will the clock show in 2 hours and 35 minutes?
10:25

10 Bowling Scores
Alan ——
Martin ━━━
During which game did Alan and Martin score about the same? Game 4
During which game was the difference in their scores the greatest? Game 3

© 1998 Good Apple

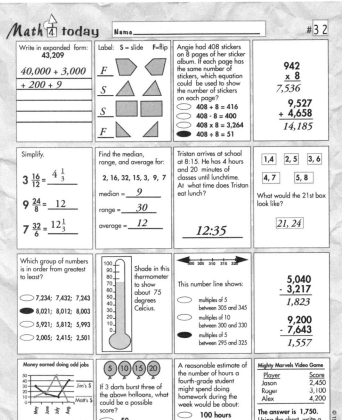

Bottom-left worksheet (#32):

Write in expanded form: 43,209
40,000 + 3,000 + 200 + 9

Label: S = slide   F = flip
F, S, S, F

Angie had 408 stickers on 8 pages of her sticker album. If each page has the same number of stickers, which equation could be used to show the number of stickers on each page?
- ○ 408 + 8 = 416
- ○ 408 - 8 = 400
- ○ 408 x 8 = 3,264
- ● 408 ÷ 8 = 51

$$942 \times 8 = 7,536$$
$$9,527 + 4,658 = 14,185$$

Simplify.
$3\frac{16}{12} = 4\frac{1}{3}$
$9\frac{24}{8} = 12$
$7\frac{32}{6} = 12\frac{1}{3}$

Find the median, range, and average for:
2, 16, 32, 15, 3, 9, 7
median = 9
range = 30
average = 12

Tristan arrives at school at 8:15. He has 4 hours and 20 minutes of classes until lunchtime. At what time does Tristan eat lunch?
12:35

1,4   2,5   3,6
4,7   5,8
What would the 21st box look like?
21, 24

Which group of numbers is in order from greatest to least?
- ○ 7,234; 7,432; 7,243
- ● 8,021; 8,012; 8,003
- ○ 5,921; 5,812; 5,993
- ○ 2,005; 2,415; 2,501

Shade in this thermometer to show about 75 degrees Celcius.

This number line shows:
- ○ multiples of 5 between 305 and 345
- ○ multiples of 10 between 300 and 330
- ● multiples of 5 between 295 and 325

$$5,040 - 3,217 = 1,823$$
$$9,200 - 7,643 = 1,557$$

Money earned doing odd jobs (graph: Jim's $, Matt's $)
During which month did Jim and Matt earn about the same amount of money? June

5 10 15 20
If 3 darts burst three of the above balloons, what could be a possible score?
- ○ 50
- ● 45
- ○ 15
- ○ 38

A reasonable estimate of the number of hours a fourth-grade student might spend doing homework during the week would be about:
- ○ 100 hours
- ○ 45 hours
- ● 5 hours
- ○ 1 hour

Mighty Marvels Video Game
Player	Score
Jason	2,450
Roger	3,100
Alex	4,200

The answer is 1,750. Using the chart, write a question for this answer.
How many more points did Alex score than Jason?

© 1998 Good Apple

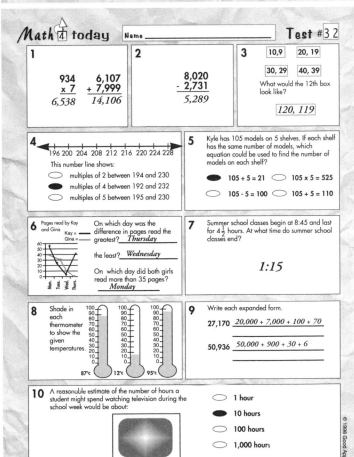

Bottom-right worksheet (Test #32):

1
$$934 \times 7 = 6,538$$
$$6,107 + 7,999 = 14,106$$

2
$$8,020 - 2,731 = 5,289$$

3
10,9   20,19
30,29   40,39
What would the 12th box look like?
120, 119

4 196 200 204 208 212 216 220 224 228
This number line shows:
- ○ multiples of 2 between 194 and 230
- ● multiples of 4 between 192 and 232
- ○ multiples of 5 between 195 and 230

5 Kyle has 105 models on 5 shelves. If each shelf has the same number of models, which equation could be used to find the number of models on each shelf?
- ● 105 ÷ 5 = 21
- ○ 105 x 5 = 525
- ○ 105 - 5 = 100
- ○ 105 + 5 = 110

6 Pages read by Kay and Gino
Kay = ——   Gina = ----
On which day was the difference in pages read the greatest? Thursday
the least? Wednesday
On which day did both girls read more than 35 pages? Monday

7 Summer school classes begin at 8:45 and last for $4\frac{1}{2}$ hours. At what time do summer school classes end?
1:15

8 Shade in each thermometer to show the given temperatures.
87°c   12°c   95°c

9 Write each expanded form.
27,170 __20,000 + 7,000 + 100 + 70__
50,936 __50,000 + 900 + 30 + 6__

10 A reasonable estimate of the number of hours a student might spend watching television during the school week would be about:
- ○ 1 hour
- ● 10 hours
- ○ 100 hours
- ○ 1,000 hours

© 1998 Good Apple

Worksheet #33

Write in expanded form.
390,682

300,000 +
90,000 + 600 +
80 + 2

Label: S = slide; F = flip

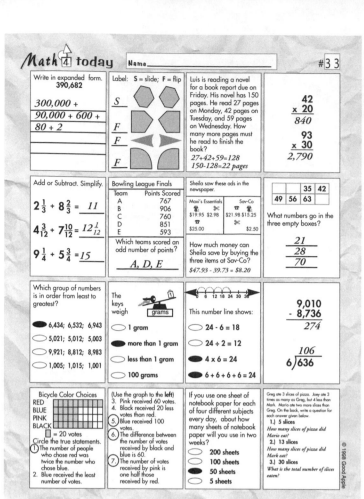

S
F
F
F

Luis is reading a novel for a book report due on Friday. His novel has 150 pages. He read 27 pages on Monday, 42 pages on Tuesday, and 59 pages on Wednesday. How many more pages must he read to finish the book?
27+42+59=128
150-128=22 pages

42
x 20
840

93
x 30
2,790

Add or Subtract. Simplify.

$2\frac{1}{3} + 8\frac{2}{3} = 11$

$4\frac{3}{12} + 7\frac{10}{12} = 12\frac{1}{12}$

$9\frac{1}{4} + 5\frac{3}{4} = 15$

Bowling League Finals

Team	Points Scored
A	767
B	906
C	760
D	851
E	593

Which teams scored an odd number of points?
A, D, E

Sheila saw these ads in the newspaper.

Maxi's Essentials
$19.95 $2.98
$25.00

Sav-Co
$21.98 $15.25
$2.50

How much money can Sheila save by buying the three items at Sav-Co?
$47.93 - 39.73 = $8.20

		35	42
49	56	63	

What numbers go in the three empty boxes?
21
28
70

Which group of numbers is in order from least to greatest?

● 6,434; 6,532; 6,943
○ 5,021; 5,012; 5,003
○ 9,921; 8,812; 8,983
○ 1,005; 1,015; 1,001

The keys weigh
grams

○ 1 gram
● more than 1 gram
○ less than 1 gram
○ 100 grams

This number line shows:

○ 24 - 6 = 18
○ 24 ÷ 2 = 12
● 4 x 6 = 24
○ 6 + 6 + 6 + 6 = 24

9,010
- 8,736
274

106
6)636

Bicycle Color Choices
RED
BLUE
PINK
BLACK
□ = 20 votes
Circle the true statements.
1. The number of people who chose red was twice the number who chose blue.
2. Blue received the least number of votes.

(Use the graph to the left.)
3. Pink received 60 votes.
4. Black received 20 less votes than red.
5. Blue received 100 votes.
6. The difference between the number of votes received by black and blue is 60.
7. The number of votes received by pink is one half those received by red.

If you use one sheet of notebook paper for each of four different subjects every day, about how many sheets of notebook paper will you use in two weeks?
○ 200 sheets
○ 100 sheets
● 50 sheets
○ 5 sheets

Greg ate 3 slices of pizza. Joey ate 3 times as many as Greg, but 4 less than Mark. Mario ate two more slices than Greg. On the back, write a question for each answer given below.
1.) 5 slices
How many slices of pizza did Mario eat?
2.) 13 slices
How many slices of pizza did Mark eat?
3.) 30 slices
What is the total number of slices eaten?

© 1998 Good Apple

Test #33

1
64
x 20
1,280

4,070
- 2,398
1,672

2
81
8)648

3 Billy reads an average of 7 pages a night during the **school week**. About how many pages will he read in 3 weeks?
○ 35   ○ 50
● 100   ○ 135

4 Jay's baseball team set a goal of getting 5 more runs this season than in the last 3 seasons combined. In 1996, the team had 23 runs, in 1997 the team had 19 runs, and in 1998, they had 14 runs. So far this year, they have 17 runs. How many more runs does Jay's team need in order to meet their goal?
5 + 23 + 19 + 14 + = 61 - 17= 44 runs

5
Number of Baby-sitting Jobs Last Year

Milly	72
Jean	24
Susan	12
Andrea	41
Carla	58

Which girls had an even number of baby-sitting jobs last year?
Milly, Jean, Carla

6 Which group of numbers is in order from least to greatest?
○ 7,892; 7,880; 7,782
○ 5,208; 5,590; 5,579
○ 6,890; 6,895; 6,080
● 3,207; 3,227; 3,303

7 Write the expanded forms.
801,267 800,000+1,000+200+60+7
420,198 400,000+20,000+100+90+8

8 Label: S = slide; F = flip

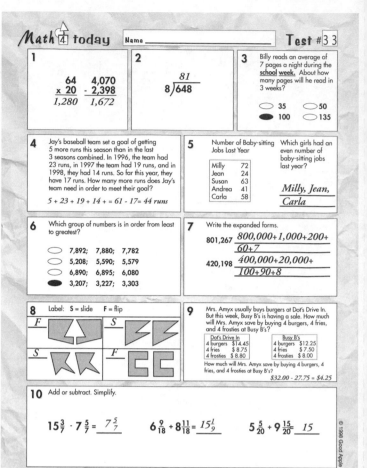

F   S
S   F

9 Mrs. Amyx usually buys burgers at Dot's Drive In. But this week, Busy B's is having a sale. How much will Mrs. Amyx save by buying 4 burgers, 4 fries, and 4 frosties at Busy B's?

Dot's Drive In	Busy B's
4 burgers $14.45	4 burgers $12.25
4 fries $8.75	4 fries $7.50
4 frosties $8.80	4 frosties $8.00

How much will Mrs. Amyx save by buying 4 burgers, 4 fries, and 4 frosties at Busy B's?
$32.00 - 27.75 = $4.25

10 Add or subtract. Simplify.

$15\frac{3}{7} - 7\frac{5}{7} = 7\frac{5}{7}$

$6\frac{9}{18} + 8\frac{11}{18} = 15\frac{1}{9}$

$5\frac{5}{20} + 9\frac{15}{20} = 15$

© 1998 Good Apple

Worksheet #34

Which numeral shows 7 hundred thousands, 12 ten thousands, 4 hundreds, 2 tens?
○ 701,242
○ 712,042
● 820,420
○ 802,452

Name the vertex of each angle.

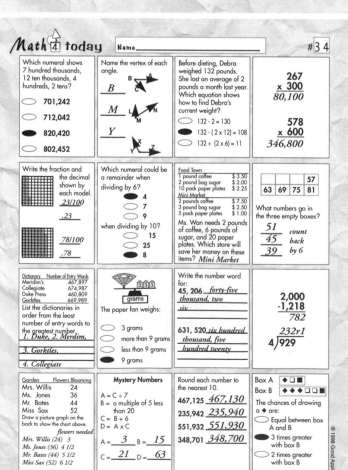

B ___
M ___
Y ___

Before dieting, Debra weighed 132 pounds. She lost an average of 2 pounds a month last year. Which equation shows how to find Debra's current weight?
○ 132 - 2 = 130
● 132 - (2 x 12) = 108
○ 132 ÷ (2 x 6) = 11

267
x 300
80,100

578
x 600
346,800

Write the fraction and the decimal shown by each model.
23/100
.23

78/100
.78

Which numeral could be a remainder when dividing by 6?
● 4
○ 7
○ 9
when dividing by 10?
○ 15
○ 25
● 8

Food Town
1 pound coffee	$ 3.50
2 pound bag sugar	$ 2.00
10 pack paper plates	$ 2.25

Mini Market
2 pounds coffee	$ 7.50
3 pound bag sugar	$ 2.50
5 pack paper plates	$ 1.00

Ms. Wan needs 2 pounds of coffee, 6 pounds of sugar, and 20 paper plates. Which store will save her money on these items? Mini Market

| | | | 57 |
| 63 | 69 | 75 | 81 |

What numbers go in the three empty boxes?
51
45 count
39 back by 6

Dictionary   Number of Entry Words
Meridim's	467,897
Collegiate	674,987
Duke Press	460,809
Gorktles	669,989

List the dictionaries in order from the least number of entry words to the greatest number.
1. Duke, 2. Meridim,
3. Gorktles,
4. Collegiate

The paper fan weighs
grams
○ 3 grams
○ more than 9 grams
○ less than 9 grams
● 9 grams

Write the number word for:
45, 206 forty-five thousand, two six

631, 520 six hundred thousand, five hundred twenty

2,000
-1,218
782

232r1
4)929

Garden   Flowers Blooming
Mrs. Willis	24
Ms. Jones	36
Mr. Bates	44
Miss Sax	52

Draw a picture graph on the back to show the chart above.
flowers needed
Mrs. Willis (24) 3
Ms. Jones (36) 4 1/2
Mr. Bates (44) 5 1/2
Miss Sax (52) 6 1/2

Mystery Numbers
A = C ÷ 7
B = a multiple of 5 less than 20
C = B + 6
D = A x C

A = 3   B = 15
C = 21   D = 63

Round each number to the nearest 10.
467,125 467,130
235,942 235,940
551,932 551,930
348,701 348,700

Box A ◆□■
Box B ■■■
The chances of drawing a ◆ are:
○ Equal between box A and B
● 3 times greater with box B
○ 2 times greater with box B

© 1998 Good Apple

Test #34

1
398
x 600
238,800

5,000
- 4,231
769

2
57r3
5)288

3
| | | | 65 |
| 74 | 83 | 92 | 101 |

What numbers go in the three empty boxes?
56   47   38
(count by 9)

4 Write the number word for:
503,291 five hundred three thousand, two hundred ninety-one
48,603 forty-eight thousand, six hundred three

5 Eight months ago Tad weighed 98 pounds. He has gained an average of 3 pounds a month. Which equation could be used to find Tad's current weight?
○ 98 - 8=
○ 98 - (3 x 8)=
○ 98 x 3 =
● 98 + (3 x 8)=

6
Snow Cones Sold
| Blueberry Ice | 33 | Coconut Freeze | 27 |
| Mocha Cream | 18 | Cherry Blizzard | 42 |
💡 = 6

Shade the graph to match the chart data.
Blueberry Ice
Coconut Freeze
Mocha Cream
Cherry Blizzard

7
Apple School Supply	ABC School Supply
10 pencils $5.00	5 pencils $2.00
Notebook $12.50	2 Notebook $26.00
Writing Tablets	Writing Tablets
3 for $3.75	2 for $3.50

Raul needs to buy 10 pencils, 2 notebooks, and 6 writing tablets for school. Which store will save him the most money on these items?
Apple School Supply

8
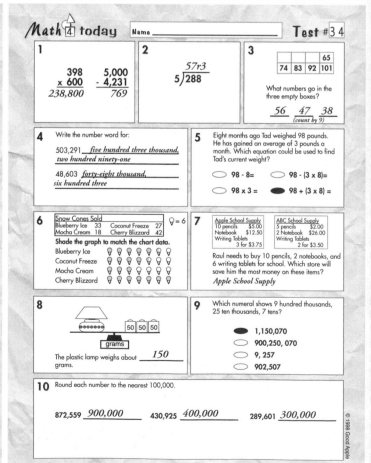
50 50 50
grams
The plastic lamp weighs about ___ grams.
150

9 Which numeral shows 9 hundred thousands, 25 ten thousands, 7 tens?
● 1,150,070
○ 900,250, 070
○ 9, 257
○ 902,507

10 Round each number to the nearest 100,000.
872,559 900,000
430,925 400,000
289,601 300,000

© 1998 Good Apple

Which numeral shows 2 million, 17 hundred thousands, 8 ten thousands, 4 tens, 3 ones?
- ● 3,780,043
- ○ 2,170,843
- ○ 3,878,403
- ○ 2,170,800,443

How many vertices are in the figures below?

_8_

_5_

Luigi sold a total of 1,321 raffle tickets in three weeks. He sold 467 tickets the first week and 299 tickets the second week. How many tickets did Luigi sell in the third week?

467   1321
+299 - 766
766   555 tickets

Solve.
52
x 33
1,716

28
x 56
1,568

Write the fraction and the decimal shown by each model.

30/100
.30

49/100
.49

Which numeral could be a remainder when dividing by 9?
- ○ 12
- ● 7
- ○ 9

when dividing by 3?
- ○ 10
- ● 5
- ○ 1

Floyd and Kyle have 17 Super NES™ video games, 13 Nintendo™ video games, and 20 Sega™ video games. If they played each game for thirty minutes, could they play all the games in one day? _no_

17 + 13 + 20 = 50
50 x 30 = 1,500
÷ 60 = 25 hours

○○○****✗✗**
✓***✓✗**○○✓
Which series below would continue the pattern? _3_

1. *****✓✗**
2. **✗✗*✓*✓**
3. ****✗✗✓✓**

Write the numeral that is 100 more than:

234,967 _235,067_
529,920 _530,020_
862,425 _862,525_
999,901 _1,000,001_

1 cup = 8 ounces
1 pint = 2 cups
1 quart = 2 pints
1 gallon = 4 quarts

3 gallons = _12_ quarts
5 pints = _10_ cups
8 quarts = _16_ pints
1 quart = _32_ ounces

Write the number word for:

2,450,137 _two million, four hundred fifty thousand, one hundred thirty-seven_

5,320,664 _five million, three hundred twenty thousand, six hundred sixty-four_

121r1
6)727

209r2
4)838

Red = 36   Green = 48
Blue = 24   Black = 12
To correctly color the pie graph so that it matches the above data, each section must stand for the same number. Determine **that** number, then color the graph. Each part = _12_

Mystery Numbers
A = 18 - (D x D)
B = C ÷ 4
C= D + A
D = the remainder of 47 ÷ 9

A = _14_   B = _4_
C = _16_   D = _2_

On Tuesday, Jet Air sold 45,951 airline tickets. Concourse Flights sold 31,764 tickets, and Miami Intrastate sold 18,752 tickets. What is the best estimate of the number of tickets sold by all 3 airlines?
- ● 100,000 tickets
- ○ 125,000 tickets
- ○ 150,000 tickets

Box A LLBBB
Box B LLLLB
The chances of drawing an **L** are:
- ○ Equal between box A and B
- ○ Less with box B
- ● 2 times greater with box B

1
98   44
x 52 x 61
5,096 2,684

2
83r1
9)748

3
CompuCom made 55,210 computer chips in March, 71,560 chips in April and 66,102 chips in May. What is the best estimate of the number of computer chips made in all three months?
- ○ 250,000
- ● 200,000
- ○ 150,000
- ○ 100,000

4 Megan's Girl Scout troop collected 1,072 pounds of aluminum cans last summer. In June, they collected 397 pounds and in July they collected 289 pounds. How many pounds of aluminum cans did they collect in August?

397 + 289 = 686
1,072 - 686 = 386 pounds

5 Which numeral could be a remainder when dividing by 4?
- ○ 7
- ● 2
- ○ 8
- ○ 10

when dividing by 8?
- ● 7
- ○ 16
- ○ 9
- ○ 10

6 Write the numeral that is 100 less than:

782,945 _782,845_
541,099 _540,999_
610,056 _609,956_

7 Which numeral shows 6 million, 29 hundred thousands, 6 ten thousands, 1 ten, 5 ones?
- ○ 6,296,150
- ● 8,960,015
- ○ 6,290,615
- ○ 82,900,105

8 How many vertices are in the space figures below?

_8_   _6_

9 Elliot has a playoff game on Saturday at 4:00. This week, he has offered to do 3 chores for his grandmother, 5 chores for his mom, and 2 chores for his dad. Each chore takes about thirty minutes. Will he have time to do all the chores and still make it to the game on time if he gets up at 10:00? _yes_

3 + 5 + 2 = 10x30 = 300 ÷ 60 = 5 hours
10:00 - 4:00 = 6 hours

10 Write the fraction and the decimal for each model.

60/100   93/100
.60   .93

Which numeral has a larger digit in the hundreds place than in the ten thousands place?
- ● 3,928,743
- ○ 5,190,812
- ○ 6,278,421
- ○ 2,593,928

A square has 4 lines of symmetry.

How many lines of symmetry does a hexagon have?

_6_

Kalyn is baking 7 batches of cookies for the church social. Each batch uses the same amount of sugar. If she uses a total of 28 cups of sugar, which equation would tell the cups of sugar needed for each batch?
- ○ 7 x 28 = □
- ● 28 ÷ 7 = □
- ○ 28 + 7 = □
- ○ 28 - 7 = □

8,679
4,527
+ 6,382
19,588

622
x 52
32,344

Write the decimal shown by each model.

_1.35_

_1.90_

Which equation below best expresses the quotient for a number fact that equals 5?
- ○ 1 + 4 = 5
- ○ 25 - 20 = 5
- ○ 5 X 1 = 5
- ● 25 ÷ 5 = 5

Mrs. Ganzer spends an hour doing laundry, 45 minutes vacuuming, a half hour dusting, and 25 minutes mopping when she cleans house. How long does it take her to complete her housework?

60 + 45 + 30 + 25 = min./60
2 hr. 40 min.

...✂✚✚✖✗✛✚
✚✚✖✗✛✖✛○...
Which series continues the pattern? _2_
1. ✂✖✚✚✖○✚○
2. ★✖✛✖✚✂✖✛
3. ✂★✚★✛✖✚✛
(Can you draw the series that begins this pattern?)
✖✂✚✖✂○✖

Continue counting.
739,995
739,996
739,997
_739,998_
_739,999_
_740,000_
_740,001_
_740,002_
_740,003_
_740,004_

Find the volume for each solid figure below:

_8_ cubic units

_7_ cubic units

The star best represents what number?
- ○ 12.5
- ○ 12.7
- ● 13.5
- ○ 13.7

Solve.
75
8)600

65
6)390

Orange = 40   Green = 24
White = 16   Purple = 48
To correctly color the pie graph so that it matches the above data, each section must stand for the same number. Determine that number, then color the graph. Each part = _8_

Tam's age is an even number less than 14. He is one half his sister's age. His sister's age is a number between 16 and 24.

How old is Tam? _10_

How old is his sister? _20_

Casey's bead art set has 372 beads for each of 12 colors. She saw 23 more sets like hers in the craft store. Which is the best estimate for the number of beads in all the art sets?
- ● 80,000
- ○ 70,000
- ○ 60,000
- ○ 50,000

1 5 9 1 5
If these cards are shuffled and placed face down, the chances of drawing a _1_ are _equal_ to the chances of drawing a 5, and _2_ times greater than the chances of drawing a 9.

1
345   4,254
x 47   9,897
16,215 + 6,579
20,730

2
75
4)300

3
✓ ✗ ✗ ✗ ▲
▲ ▲ ○
If these cards are shuffled and placed face down, the chances of drawing a ✗ are **equal** to the chances of drawing a ▲ and _3_ times greater than drawing a ✓.

4

The letter **A** best represents what number?
- ○ 11.9
- ○ 10.5
- ● 11.5
- ○ 10.7

5 Wayne is boxing fireworks for sale at his uncle's stand. Each box contains the same number. So far he has boxed 210 fireworks in 7 boxes. Which equation would tell how many fireworks are in each box?
- ○ 210 + 7 = □
- ○ 210 - 7 = □
- ○ 210 x 7 = □
- ● 210 ÷ 7 = □

6 Artworks exhibited at the Children's Art Fairs
1995= 25   color white
1996= 20   color green
1997= 40   color blue
1998= 35   color red
Color the pie graph to match the above data by determining the value of each section. Each part = _5_

7 Mindy and her friends went to the county fair. They spent 1 hour and twenty minutes riding the rides. They played games at the booths for 45 minutes, visited the exhibits for a half hour, then went into the Fun House for fifteen minutes before going home. How long did Mindy and her friends stay at the fair?

80 + 45 + 30 + 15 = 170 min.
= 2 hr. 50 min.

8 Find the volume for the solid figures below.

_24_ cubic units   _14_ cubic units

9 Which numeral has a lesser digit in the hundred thousands place than in the tens place?
- ○ 5,836,170
- ● 8,208,957
- ○ 6,530,659
- ○ 2,970,885

10 At the candy factory, the workers pack 47 chocolate delights in each box. They can pack about 53 boxes each hour. What is the best estimate of the number of chocolate delights packed in 8 hours?
- ● 20,000
- ○ 21,000
- ○ 22,000
- ○ 23,000

Math 4 today — #37

Which numeral has a lesser digit in the thousands place than in the ten millions place? ◯ 347,928,743 ◯ 562,147,812 ◯ 620,213,401 ● 754,563,928	A square has 4 lines of symmetry. How many lines of symmetry does a pentagon have? _1_	What is the difference in length between a hiking trail 20,402 meters long and a trail 13,857 meters long? 20,402 - 13,857 6,545 meters	321 x 52 16,692 $12\frac{15}{30}$ $+ 6\frac{25}{30}$ $19\frac{1}{3}$
Add the decimals shown by each model. + = 3.52	Tony's math grades are: 85, 92, 95, 81, 92 What is his average in math? 89	How can you make $1.27 using a minimal collection of these coins? _1_ nickels _12_ dimes _2_ pennies using a minimal collection of these coins? _5_ quarters _2_ pennies	Shade in the next two squares to continue the pattern.
Continue counting. 995,985 995,990 995,995 _996,000_ _996,005_ _996,010_ _996,015_ _996,020_ _996,025_ _996,030_	Find the volume for each solid figure below: _16_ cubic units _27_ cubic units	The star best represents what number? ◯ 13.25 ◯ 13.50 ● 13.75 ◯ 14.10	Solve. $\frac{90}{50)4500}$ $25\frac{2}{12}$ $- 14\frac{10}{12}$ $10\frac{1}{3}$
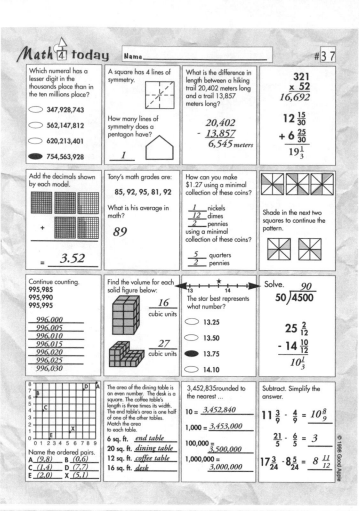Name the ordered pairs. A _(9,8)_ B _(0,6)_ C _(1,4)_ D _(7,7)_ E _(2,0)_ X _(5,1)_	The area of the dining table is an even number. The desk is a square. The coffee table's length is three times its width. The end table's area is one half of one of the other tables. Match the area to each table. 6 sq. ft. _end table_ 20 sq. ft. _dining table_ 12 sq. ft. _coffee table_ 16 sq. ft. _desk_	3,452,835 rounded to the nearest ... 10 = _3,452,840_ 1,000 = _3,453,000_ 100,000 = _3,500,000_ 1,000,000 = _3,000,000_	Subtract. Simplify the answer. $11\frac{3}{9} - \frac{4}{9} = 10\frac{8}{9}$ $\frac{21}{5} - \frac{6}{5} = 3$ $17\frac{3}{24} - 8\frac{5}{24} = 8\frac{11}{12}$

© 1998 Good Apple

Math 4 today — Test #37

1	2	3
345 x 32 11,040	$\frac{70}{40)2800}$	6,251,481 rounded to the nearest ... 100 = _6,251,500_ 10,000 = _6,250,000_ 100,000 = _6,300,000_

Subtract and simplify.
$12\frac{3}{14} - 7\frac{10}{14} = 4\frac{1}{2}$
$\frac{24}{8} - \frac{20}{8} = \frac{1}{2}$

4	5
What is the difference in length between a highway 147,895 meters long and a highway 601,234 meters long? 601,234 - 147,895 453,339 meters	What is Ray's average score in bowling? **Ray's Bowling Scores** Game / Points Per Game 1 / 102 2 / 98 3 / 129 4 / 201 5 / 80 122

6	7
Continue counting. 895,680 _896,080_ 895,780 _896,180_ 895,880 _896,280_ 895,980 _896,380_ _896,480_ _896,580_ _896,680_	Which numeral has a digit of greater value in the hundred thousands place than in the ten millions place? ● 875,836,170 ◯ 861,508,957 ◯ 651,530,659 ◯ 280,190,885

8	9
How many lines of symmetry for each figure? Draw in the lines of symmetry. _4_ _4_ _3_	How can you make $2.38 using a minimal collection of these coins? quarters _9_ nickles _2_ pennies _3_ using a minimal collection of these coins? half-dollars _4_ quarters _1_ dimes _1_ pennies _3_

10 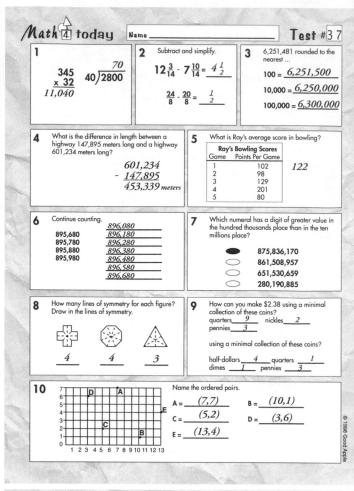Name the ordered pairs.
A = _(7,7)_   B = _(10,1)_
C = _(5,2)_   D = _(3,6)_
E = _(13,4)_

© 1998 Good Apple

Math 4 today — #38

In 1978, the most expensive coin was a $20.00 gold piece. Hal read that the gold piece sold for an approximate dollar amount that had an 8 in the tens place, a 4 in the thousands place, a 5 in the ones place, a 9 in the hundred thousands place. What was the price of the coin? $ _904,085_ .00	Label the lines; I = intersecting PA = parallel P = perpendicular _PA_ _I_ _P_	The greatest oil gusher was at Spindletop, Texas in 1901. It yeilded about 810,459 barrels of oil in 9 days. About how many barrels of oil did this oil gusher produce each day? 810,459 ÷ 9 = 90,051 barrels	605 x 85 51,425 $\frac{22r13}{20)453}$
Subtract the decimals shown by each model. - = 1.56	Circle the common factors for each number pair. 4, 16 ②④ 8, 10, 16, 20, 10, 20 ② 3, 4, ⑤ ⑩ 20, 18, 36 ② ③ 4, ⑥ ⑨ 12, ⑱	Oscar earns $5.25 per hour working part time at the grocery store. Last week he worked 4 hours a day for 6 days. How much did Oscar earn last week? $5.25 x 24 = $126.00	9, 11, 15, 23, 39, 71 What is the rule for the above pattern? (hint: use 2 operations) multiply by 2 subtract 7
Japanese Cities Populations Tokyo 8,112,000 Osaka 2,601,000 Yokohama 3,276,000 Sapporo 1,719,000 Nagoya 2,162,000 List the cities in order from least to greatest populations. _Sapporo, Nagoya, Osaka, Yokohama, Tokyo_	Using the lines of symmetry, find the perimeter of this hexagon. 2 cm 5 cm perimeter = _28_ cm	The continent of Asia has a land mass of forty-three million, nine hundred seventy-five thousand square kilometers. This number is written as: ● 43,975,000 ◯ 430,975 ◯ 439,750,000 ◯ 43,975	4.37 9.82 6.22 3.41 +4.50 +7.25 15.09 20.48 9.82 8.12 -3.25 -6.78 6.57 1.34
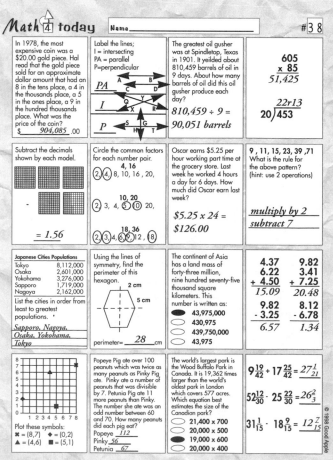Plot these symbols: ✖ = (8,7) ● = (0,2) ▲ = (4,6) ■ = (5,1)	Popeye Pig ate over 100 peanuts which was twice as many peanuts as Pinky Pig ate. Pinky ate a number of peanuts that was divisible by 7. Petunia Pig ate 11 more peanuts than Pinky. The number she ate was an odd number between 60 and 70. How many peanuts did each pig eat? Popeye _112_ Pinky _56_ Petunia _67_	The world's largest park is the Wood Buffalo Park in Canada. It is 19,362 times larger than the world's oldest park in London which covers 577 acres. Which equation best estimates the size of the Canadian park? ◯ 21,400 x 700 ◯ 20,000 x 500 ● 19,000 x 600 ◯ 20,000 x 400	$9\frac{19}{42} + 17\frac{25}{42} = 27\frac{1}{21}$ $52\frac{12}{30} - 25\frac{22}{30} = 26\frac{2}{3}$ $31\frac{1}{15} - 18\frac{9}{15} = 12\frac{7}{15}$

© 1998 Good Apple

Math 4 today — Test #38

1	2	3
403 x 75 30,225	$\frac{6r25}{60)385}$ 3.05 12.21 2.61 -9.85 +9.85 2.36 15.51	4, 17, 56, 173, 524 What is the rule for the pattern? (x 3) + 5

4	5
In square miles, the country of India has an area of one million, two hundred twenty-nine thousand, seven hundred thirty-seven. This number is written: ◯ 12,297,037 ● 1,229,737 ◯ 122,973,007	During one week in August, the Icey Freeze Shop used 140,210 ice cubes to make snow cones. If the Icey Freeze Shop used the same number of ice cubes each day, how many ice cubes were used daily? 140,210 ÷ 7 = 20,030 ice cubes

6	7
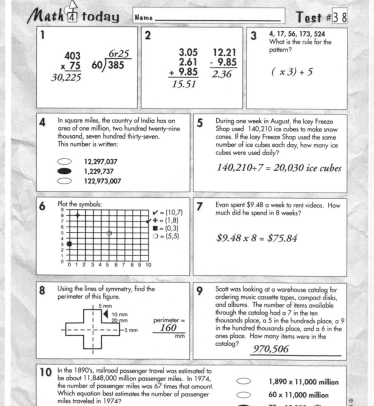Plot the symbols: ✔ = (10,7) ✚ = (1,8) ■ = (0,3) ◯ = (5,5)	Evan spent $9.48 a week to rent videos. How much did he spend in 8 weeks? $9.48 x 8 = $75.84

8	9
Using the lines of symmetry, find the perimeter of this figure. 5 mm 10 mm 20 mm 5 mm perimeter = _160_ mm	Scott was looking at a warehouse catalog for ordering music cassette tapes, compact disks, and albums. The number of items available through the catalog had a 7 in the ten thousands place, a 5 in the hundreds place, a 9 in the hundred thousands place, and a 6 in the ones place. How many items were in the catalog? 970,506

10 In the 1890's, railroad passenger travel was estimated to be about 11,848,000 million passenger miles. In 1974, the number of passenger miles was 67 times that amount. Which equation best estimates the number of passenger miles traveled in 1974?
◯ 1,890 x 11,000 million
◯ 60 x 11,000 million
● 70 x 12,000 million
◯ 60 x 10,000 million

© 1998 Good Apple

Susan read that one of the longest toy balloon flights achieved a record length in miles. The balloon traveled an approximate distance that had an 1 in the hundreds place, a 5 in the tens place, a 9 in the thousands place and a 7 in the hundredths place and a 5 in the tenths place. How far did the balloon travel?
9,150.57 miles

Number each plane figure.
1. a pentagon with 2 right angles
2. a quadrilateral with 1 right angle
3. an equilateral triangle
4. a right triangle

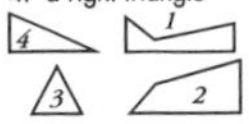

One of the largest living trees, the General Sherman tree is a sequoia tree in California. It is about 272.3 feet tall. The tallest redwood tree is about 367.8 feet tall. What is the difference in height between the two trees?
367.8 − 272.3 = 95.5 feet

923 × 381 = 351,663

30r32
50)1,532

Solve.
☐ + ☐
☐ + ☐
= 3 × .23 = .69

What is the greatest common factor for:
12 and 16 — 4
20 and 30 — 10
36 and 45 — 9

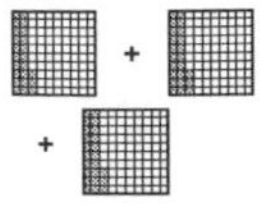

How many?
8 hours = 480 minutes
3 days = 72 hours
1 hour = 3,600 seconds
one quarter hour = 15 minutes
1 year = 8,760 hours

Create your own pattern.
answers vary

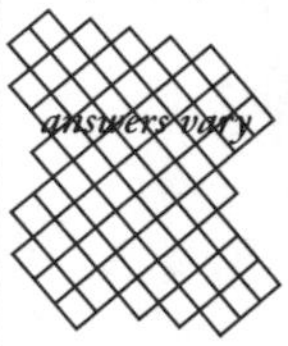

Write the decimals in order from least to greatest.
3.45 3.5 3.82 3.02 3.1 3.67
1. 3.02 2. 3.1 3. 3.45 4. 3.5 5. 3.67 6. 3.82

Use the grid to enlarge the top figure 2 times its size.

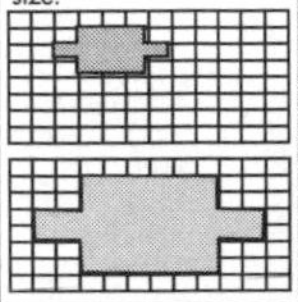

In 1970, a car, The Blue Flame achieved an average speed of six hundred twenty-seven and twenty-nine hundredths miles per hour. This number is written:
62,729.0029
● 627.29
627.029

34.97 16.2 +54.03 = 105.20
30.02 −16.18 = 13.84
42.12 −29.9 = 12.22
73.69 −13.5 = 106.21
19.02

Number of Girls & Boys Enrolled at Burns Elementary School 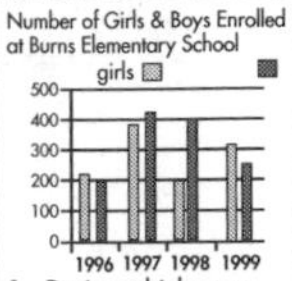
(girls/boys bar graph 1996 1997 1998 1999)
1. During which year was the enrollment for the girls and boys about the same? 1996

Use the graph at the left.
2. In which years was the enrollment less for the girls than the boys? 1997 1998
3. In which year was the enrollment for the boys about 390? 1998
4. In which years was the enrollment for the girls about 200? 1996 1998

Adrian has 4 collections, rocks, shells, stamps, and marbles. Each collection has between 20 and 50 items. What is a reasonable total for all the items in his collections?
75
520
● 150

In a meter race, Alan ran 3 times as far as Cathy. Cathy ran one-half as far as David. David's total meters run was a multiple of 7 less than 50. Becky ran 21 times less than the number of meters run by Alan. How many meters did each child run?
Alan 42
Becky 2
Cathy 14
David 28

---

1 726 × 438 = 317,988

2 70r25 80)5,625
71.90 36.7 +19.09 = 127.69
31.04 −17.18 = 13.86

3 Emil played hoops 5 times. Each time he made between 10 and 40 baskets. What is a reasonable total for the baskets made by Emil?
205   ● 185
50   20

4 In 1965, an American aviator flew his plane at speeds of about 333.5 kilometers per hour. In 1962, a Russian aviator flew his plane at about 2,680.99 kilometers per hour. What is the difference in speed between the two flights?
650.51 kph

5 Circle the common factors for the pairs of numerals.
10, 15   2, (5), 3,
24, 40   (2), 3, 5, 6, (8), 10

6 Write the decimals in order from greatest to least.
7.28; 7.02; 7.82; 7.08; 7.8; 8.1
1. 8.1 2. 7.82 3. 7.8 4. 7.28 5. 7.08 6. 7.02

7 Manuel was reading that one of the tallest structures in the world was a radio tower in Poland. The tower's height in feet had a 1 in the hundreds place, a 2 in the tens place, a 2 in the thousands place and a eight in the tenths place. Write the height of the building.
2,120 ft. 8 in.

8 Number each plane figure.
1. a pentagon with 2 right angles
2. a quadrilateral with 2 right angles
3. a right triangle 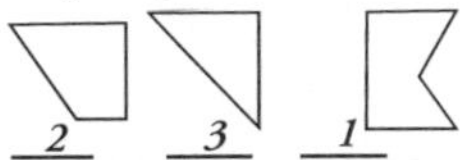
2   3   1

9 How many?
6 hours = 360 minutes
5 days = 120 hours
one quarter hour = 15 minutes
1 hour = 3,600 seconds

10 Use the models to multiply the decimals.
× 2 = .80   × 5 = .40

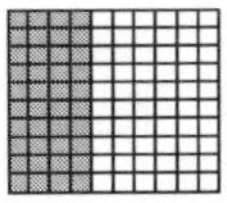

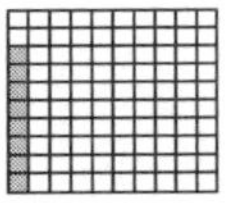

Which numeral has a 5 in the ten thousands place, an 8 in the hundreds place an 8 in the millions place and a 6 in the hundredths place?
850,308.60
8,005,308.30
● 8,057,308.06
85,360,016.6

Number each triangle.
1. right triangle
2. scalene
3. acute 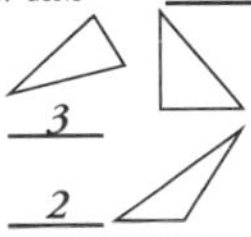
1   3   2

Each student in Mr. Hernandez's class brought $3.25 pizza for the end of the year pizza party. The party cost $78.00. What information is needed to determine whether there would be enough money?
The number of students. (24)
(Can you find the number for the missing information?)

145 × 20 = 2,900
51 50)2,550

☐ + ☐
☐ + ☐
.13 × 4 = .52

If 30 is 4 times less than a number, which equation could be used to find the number?
● 30 × 4 = n
30 ÷ 4 = n
30 + 4 = n
30 − 4 = n

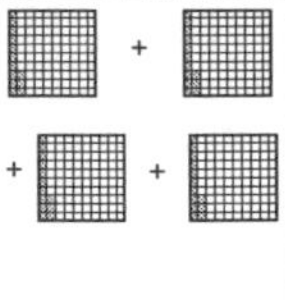

Ikito spends 4 and one half hours practicing his violin each week. He has practiced for 1 and three quarters hours this week. How many more minutes does he need to practice?
4½ = 270 min.
−1¾ = 105 min.
165 minutes

10 13 19 22
7 10 16 19
What two numbers are missing in this pattern?
16
13

Write the decimals in order from greatest to least.
12.85 13.2 12.08 13.02 13.50 12.6
1. 13.50 2. 13.2 3. 13.02 4. 12.85 5. 12.6 6. 12.08

Use the grid to enlarge the top figure 3 times its size.

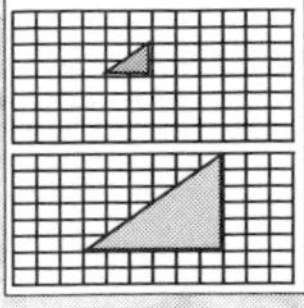

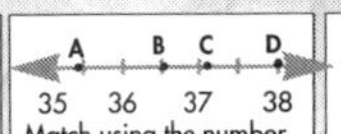

A B C D
35 36 37 38
Match using the number line.
C 37.21
A 35.4
D 37.89
B 36.5

5,340 − 1,638 = 3,702
9,846 + 4,926 = 14,772

Average Minutes to Complete 1 K Race (Jim/Ted bar graph 1996 1997 1998)
Which chart to the right best matches the data on the above graph? chart A

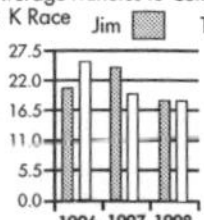

		Jim	Ted
A	1996	20.2	25.5
	1997	24.7	20.5
	1998	19.21	18.85
B	1996	16.5	27.5
	1997	20.7	20.5
	1998	11.21	12.85
C	1996	22.0	25.5
	1997	28.7	20.5
	1998	19.21	5.85

Each year Rita had between 21 and 45 classmates. What is a reasonable total for the number of classmates she had in grades one through six?
● 150
250
350

For a community food drive, Mrs. Witt needed to pack 438 cans of vegetables. She can pack 40 cans in each box. What is the least number of boxes she can use to pack all the cans?
498 ÷ 40 = 10.95
11 boxes

---

1 225 × 50 = 11,250   30 70)2,100

2 7,109 − 2,272 = 4,387   8,298 + 4,807 = 13,105

3
11 18 25 39
2 9 14 30
Which two numbers are missing from this pattern?
32
23

4 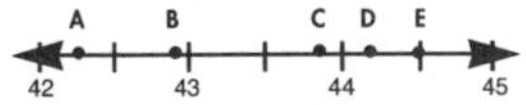
(number line A B C D E, 42 43 44 45)
Match using the number line.
D 44.10   B 42.92
E 44.5   C 43.75
A 42.25

5 Several friends went to Six Flags Amusement Park. Their total entrance fee was $264.00. What information do you need to find out the entrance fee for each person?
(Can you find a reasonable number for the missing information?)
number of friends going (8)
other possible answers 264+any other even numbers

6 Average Miles On Road Race Video Game (Sam/Joe bar graph)
Circle the chart that best matches the graph?

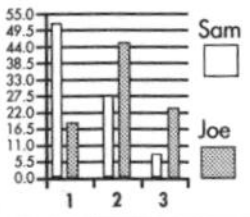

Game:	1	2	3
Sam	53.5	22.1	8.79
Joe	12.3	38.2	17.5
Game:	1	2	3
Sam	52.2	27.9	8.79
Joe	19.3	45.2	22.3

7 Paula's goal is to jog for 2 hours and 45 minutes a week. So far this week, she has jogged for three quarters of an hour. How many more minutes does she need to jog to meet her weekly goal?
120 + 45 = 165 min.
45 min.
120 minutes

8 Use the empty grid to enlarge this shape 2 times.

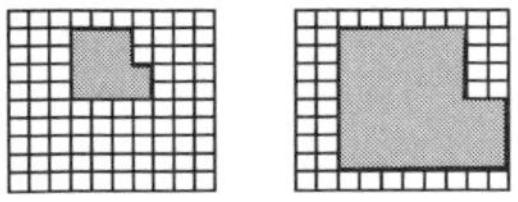

9 Which numeral has a 5 in the tens place, a 7 in the ten thousands place, a 6 in the millions place, and a 4 in the hundredths place?
5,760,401
● 6,270,052.04
5,670,219.4
6,870,059.40

10 Erin goes swimming between 52 and 105 times each summer. What would be a reasonable total of the times she has gone swimming over the last 6 years?
● 525
725
825
225

Name the place and the value of the 4 in each number.

34,127 *4,000*
value
thousands
place name

41,980 *40,000*
value
ten thousands
place name

Iso means *bend*. Equi means *same*. Ska means *uneven*. Use the clues to number each triangle.
1. isosceles
2. equilateral
3. scalene

1   *3*

2

Soccer camp costs $125.00 per team. The team washed 50 cars to earn money for camp. What information is needed to determine whether they earned enough money?
How much money charged per car ($2.50)
(Can you find the number for the missing information?)

$$86\frac{25}{27}$$
$$+ 48\frac{11}{27}$$
$$135\frac{1}{3}$$

$$73\frac{7}{49}$$
$$- 29\frac{14}{49}$$
$$43\frac{6}{7}$$

Write the decimal for each model.

.38   *.70*

.2   *.7*

If 120 is 3 times more than a number, which equation could be used to find the number?
○ 120 x 3 = n
● 120 ÷ 3 = n
○ 120 + 3 = n
○ 120 - 3 = n

Fernando worked after school to save money for a video game that cost $63.00. At the end of 3 months, he had enough money to buy the game. How much money did he save each month?
$63. ÷ 3 = $21.00 each month

| 144 | 121 | 100 | 64 |
| 12 | 11 | 10 | 8 |

What two numbers are missing in this pattern?

| 81 |
| 9 |

Math Average
List the students in order from highest to lowest math average.

Cathy	81.55
Paul	97.2
Roberto	88.25
Hakeem	96.7
Leslie	92.5

1. *Paul*
2. *Hakeem*
3. *Leslie*
4. *Roberto*
5. *Cathy*

Enlarge the top figure 2 times.

A B C D
73 74 75 76
Match using the number line.
B _73.92_
D _75.75_
A _73.08_
C _74.42_

4,681
- 3,238
1,443

876
+ 986
1,862

VALUE OF MINERALS PRODUCED BILLIONS IN DOLLARS

USA	62.27
China	16.7
S. Africa	8.51
Saudia Arabia	19.42

Which chart to the right best matches the data on the above graph?
chart *A*

A
USA	62.27
China	16.7
S. Africa	8.51
Saudia Arabia	19.42

B
USA	8.51
China	16.7
S. Africa	62.27
Saudia Arabia	19.42

C
USA	19.42
China	8.51
S. Africa	16.7
Saudia Arabia	62.27

Movie Opening	$ Gross
Dino Island	$ 37,539.
Tidal Terror	$ 9,210.
Star Invasion	$ 69,510.

What is the best estimate of the money grossed by all three movies?
○ $120,000.
● $155,000.
○ $250,000.

The cooks at the Grand Hotel are preparing a special shrimp dish for their menu. They will need 729 shrimp. The shrimp comes in bulk packages of 80. What is the least number of packages the cooks can buy?
729 ÷ 80 = 9r9 = 10 packages

© 1998 Good Apple

1
$$62\frac{31}{60}$$
$$+ 38\frac{29}{60}$$
101

$$73\frac{3}{64}$$
$$- 28\frac{35}{64}$$
44 1/2

2
5,802
- 4,453
1,349

4,307
+ 7,157
11,464

3 What is the best estimate of the money grossed in ticket sales for all three concerts?

Ponytails Concert	$ Gross Ticket Sales
Houston	$21,135.
Chicago	$59,421.
Seattle	$77,982.

● $160,000   ○ $150,000
○ $140,000   ○ $130,000

4 Ms. Alipour needed $236.00 to buy an air conditioner for the kennels at her pet grooming shop. She groomed 12 dogs. What information is needed to find out if this would be enough money to buy the air conditioner?
$ charged per dog

5 If 450 is 3 times more than a number, which equation could be used to find the number?
○ 450 x 3 = n
○ 450 + 3 = n
● 450 ÷ 3 = n
○ 450 - 3 = n

6
Average Scores on Diving Competition
Rudi	72.3
Brook	88.21
Lindsay	88.57
Milly	71.9
Cecily	72.71

List the competitors' names in order from the highest to lowest average score.
Lindsay
Brook
Cecily
Rudi
Milly

7 Name the place and the value for the 7 in each numeral below.
72,509 _70,000_
value
ten thousands
place name

29,709 _700_
value
hundreds
place name

8 Match.
A. equilateral B. isosceles C. scalene
B   *C*   *A*

9 Tiffany worked at her father's florist shop after school to save money for a summer gymnastic camp. Tuition for the camp was $108.00. She was paid the same amount for each week she worked and at the end of nine weeks she had enough money to pay the tuition. How much did she earn each week?
$108.00 ÷ 9 = $12.00 each week

10 Write the decimal for each model.
_.90_   _.9_   _.30_   _.3_

© 1998 Good Apple

Name the place and the value of the 5 in each numeral.

520,347 _500,000_
value
hundred thousands
place name

5,201,968 _5,000,000_
value
millions
place name

A
C   B
D
E
F

Name each line segment.
radius *AD*
chord *EF*
diameter *CB*

Alleha weighs 89 pounds. To find the weight of her baby brother, she held him as she weighed again. This time the scale showed 102 pounds. How much does Alleha's baby brother weigh?
102 - 89 = 13 lb.

31,094
- 867
30,227

20,532
- 785
19,747

Shade in and write an equivalent decimal for each model.

.7 = *.70*

.3 = *.30*

---

240 drivers competed in the 8 day road rally. On the average, how many drivers raced each day?
240 ÷ 8 = 30

The spirit club sold banners to earn money for a party. They sold 108 banners at $3.00 each. How much money did the spirit club earn?
$3.00 x 108 = $324.00

Tim and his friends designed paper airplanes. Their best model could fly 103 inches. The next day, they improved the model so it could fly 112 inches. If the improvement continues in this pattern, how far will the plane fly on the 5th day?
139 inches

Use >, <, or =.
52.13 *<* 52.3
10.10 *=* 10.1
75.42 *<* 75.49
23.08 *<* 23.8

Each □ = 3 foot.
What is the perimeter of the shape? *72*
the area? _315_ sq. ft.

Match.
A. 74.2 B. 72.04 C. 72.4 D. 70.42
B seventy-two and four hundredths
D seventy and forty-two hundredths
A seventy-four and two tenths
C seventy-two and four tenths

215,743
315,094
+ 867,255
1,398,092

8,200,999
+ 12,836,487
21,037,486

Reforestation Project
Park Number of New Trees
King
Ford
Taft
Bush
each ▒ = 25 trees

The forestry service wishes to plant 850 new trees in these four parks. Shade the graph to show how many more trees are needed in Bush Park to meet this goal.

---

wrapping papers
ribbons

Kalyn is wrapping gifts. Using the above ribbons and paper, how many different combinations can she make?
12 different combinations

Round each numeral to the nearest tenth:
36.42 _36.4_
92.19 _92.2_
77.87 _77.9_
14.64 _14.6_

In the above group of flowers, the odds of picking a ✿ over a ✿ are 3 to 1. What are the odds of picking a ✿ over a ✿?
3 to *2*

© 1998 Good Apple

1
47,084
- 31,267
15,817

2
831,457
217,886
+ 504,108
1,553,451

3 Round each numeral to the nearest tenth.
84.12 _84.1_
15.58 _15.6_
27.07 _27.1_

4 Match.
A. 94.4 B. 94.7 C. 94.07 D. 94.47
C ninety-four and seven hundredths
B ninety-four and seven tenths
D ninety-four and forty-seven hundredths
A ninety-four and four tenths

5 Andy wanted to find the weight of a pumpkin he bought. When he got on the scales alone, he weighed 92 pounds. When he weighed holding the pumpkin the scales read 110 pounds. How much did his pumpkin weigh?
110 - 92 = 18 lb.

6
Park Number of Bears Collared
Yellowstone
Yosemite
Smokey Mt.
Glacier
Each ▒ = 20
2 more

To study the habitats of bears, the park service plans to radio collar 620 bears in these 4 parks. Shade the graph to show how many more bears need to be collared in Yosemite to meet their total.

7 Papers
Designs

Pavet was designing covers for his journals. Using the above papers and designs, how many different combinations of covers can he make?
_16_ different combinations

8 What is the perimeter of the shape? _112_ ft.
the area? _528_ sq. ft.
Each ▒ = 4 feet

9 Name the place and the value for the 2 in each numeral below.
2,631,980 value _2,000,000_
place name *millions*

8,219,443 value _200,000,000_
place name *hundred thousands*

10
★★★★★○○○
The odds of drawing a ★ over a ○ are 4 to 3 with the above group of shapes.

▼▼▼▼▼▼□□
With the above group of shapes, the odds of drawing a ▼ over a □ are
_6_ to _2_

© 1998 Good Apple

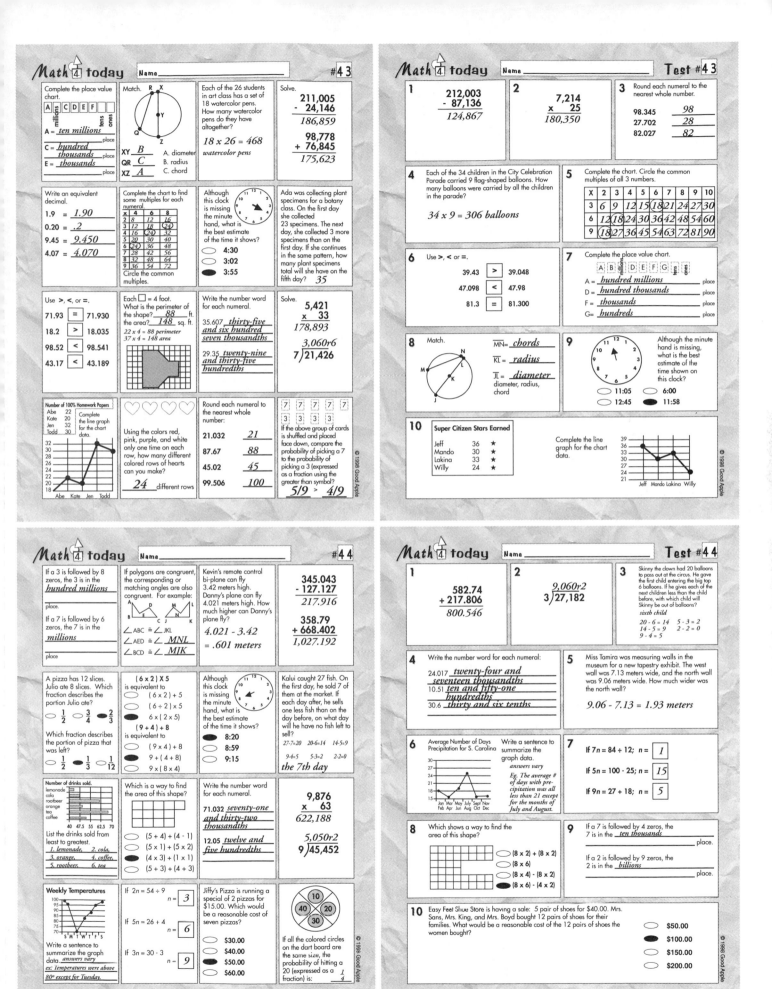

Math 4 today — #43

Complete the place value chart.

A	B	C	D	E	F		

millions / ten / ones

A = *ten millions* place
C = *hundred thousands* place
E = *thousands* place

Match.

XY *B*
QR *C*
XZ *A*

A. diameter
B. radius
C. chord

Each of the 26 students in art class has a set of 18 watercolor pens. How many watercolor pens do they have altogether?

18 x 26 = 468
watercolor pens

Solve.

211,005
- 24,146
186,859

98,778
+ 76,845
175,623

Write an equivalent decimal.

1.9 = *1.90*
0.20 = *.2*
9.45 = *9.450*
4.07 = *4.070*

Complete the chart to find some multiples for each numeral.

x	4	6	8
2	8	12	16
3	12	18	(24)
4	16	(24)	32
5	20	30	40
6	(24)	36	48
7	28	42	56
8	32	48	64
9	36	54	72

Circle the common multiples.

Although this clock is missing the minute hand, what is the best estimate of the time it shows?

○ 4:30
○ 3:02
● 3:55

Ada was collecting plant specimens for a botany class. On the first day she collected 23 specimens. The next day, she collected 3 more specimens than on the first day. If she continues in the same pattern, how many plant specimens total will she have on the fifth day? *35*

Use >, <, or =.

71.93 = 71.930
18.2 > 18.035
98.52 < 98.541
43.17 < 43.189

Each □ = 4 foot. What is the perimeter of the shape? *88*
the area? *148* sq. ft.

22 x 4 = 88 perimeter
37 x 4 = 148 area

Write the number word for each numeral.

35.607 *thirty-five and six hundred seven thousandths*
29.35 *twenty-nine and thirty-five hundredths*

Solve.

5,421
x 33
178,893

3,060r6
7)21,426

Number of 100% Homework Papers

Abe	22
Kate	20
Jen	32
Todd	30

Complete the line graph for the chart data.

Using the colors red, pink, purple, and white only one time each on each row, how many different colored rows of hearts can you make? *24* different rows

Round each numeral to the nearest whole number:

21.032 *21*
87.67 *88*
45.02 *45*
99.506 *100*

If the above group of cards is shuffled and placed face down, compare the probability of picking a 7 to the probability of picking a 3 (expressed as a fraction) using the greater than symbol?
5/9 > 4/9

© 1998 Good Apple

Math 4 today — Test #43

1
212,003
- 87,136
124,867

2
7,214
x 25
180,350

3 Round each numeral to the nearest whole number.
98.345 *98*
27.702 *28*
82.027 *82*

4 Each of the 34 children in the City Celebration Parade carried 9 flag-shaped balloons. How many balloons were carried by all the children in the parade?
34 x 9 = 306 balloons

5 Complete the chart. Circle the common multiples of all 3 numbers.

X	2	3	4	5	6	7	8	9	10
3	6	9	12	15	(18)	21	24	27	30
6	12	(18)	24	30	36	42	48	54	60
9	(18)	27	36	45	54	63	72	81	90

6 Use >, < or =.
39.43 > 39.048
47.098 < 47.98
81.3 = 81.300

7 Complete the place value chart.

A	B	C	D	E	F	G		

A = *hundred millions* place
D = *hundred thousands* place
F = *thousands* place
G = *hundreds* place

8 Match.
MN = *chords*
KL = *radius*
JL = *diameter*
diameter, radius, chord

9 Although the minute hand is missing, what is the best estimate of the time shown on this clock?
○ 11:05 ○ 6:00
○ 12:45 ● 11:58

10

Super Citizen Stars Earned

Jeff	36	★
Mando	30	★
Lakina	33	★
Willy	24	★

Complete the line graph for the chart data.

© 1998 Good Apple

Math 4 today — #44

If a 3 is followed by 8 zeros, the 3 is in the *hundred millions* place.

If a 7 is followed by 6 zeros, the 7 is in the *millions* place.

If polygons are congruent, the corresponding or matching angles are also congruent. For example:

∠ABC ≅ ∠JKL
∠AED ≅ ∠ *MNL*
∠BCD ≅ ∠ *MJK*

Kevin's remote control bi-plane can fly 3.42 meters high. Danny's plane can fly 4.021 meters high. How much higher can Danny's plane fly?

4.021 - 3.42 = .601 meters

345.043
- 127.127
217.916

358.79
+ 668.402
1,027.192

A pizza has 12 slices. Julio ate 8 slices. Which fraction describes the portion Julio ate?
○ 1/2 ○ 3/4 ● 2/3

Which fraction describes the portion of pizza that was left?
○ 1/2 ● 1/3 ○ 1/12

(6 x 2) X 5 is equivalent to
○ (6 x 2) + 5
○ (6 ÷ 2) x 5
● 6 x (2 x 5)

(9 + 4) + 8 is equivalent to
● (9 x 4) + 8
○ 9 + (4 + 8)
○ 9 x (8 x 4)

Although this clock is missing the minute hand, what is the best estimate of the time it shows?
● 8:20
○ 8:59
○ 9:15

Kalui caught 27 fish. On the first day, he sold 7 of them at the market. If each day after, he sells one less fish than on the day before, on what day will he have no fish left to sell?
27-7=20 20-6=14 14-5=9
9-4=5 5-3=2 2-2=0
the 7th day

Number of drinks sold.

lemonade, cola, rootbeer, orange, tea, coffee

40 47.5 55 62.5 70

List the drinks sold from least to greatest.
1. lemonade, 2. cola, 3. orange, 4. coffee, 5. rootbeer, 6. tea

Which is a way to find the area of this shape?
○ (5 + 4) + (4 - 1)
○ (5 x 1) + (5 x 2)
● (4 x 3) + (1 x 1)
○ (5 + 3) + (4 + 3)

Write the number word for each numeral.
71.032 *seventy-one and thirty-two thousandths*
12.05 *twelve and five hundredths*

9,876
x 63
622,188

5,050r2
9)45,452

Weekly Temperatures

100
95
90
85
80
75
70
S M T W T F S

Write a sentence to summarize the graph data. *answers vary*
ex: *temperatures were all 80° except for Tuesday.*

If 2n = 54 ÷ 9; n = 3
If 5n = 26 + 4; n = 6
If 3n = 30 - 3; n = 9

Jiffy's Pizza is running a special of 2 pizzas for $15.00. Which would be a reasonable cost of seven pizzas?
○ $30.00
○ $40.00
● $50.00
○ $60.00

If all the colored circles on the dart board are the same size, the probability of hitting a 20 (expressed as a fraction) is: 1/4

© 1998 Good Apple

Math 4 today — Test #44

1
582.74
+ 217.806
800.546

2
9,060r2
3)27,182

3 Skinny the clown had 20 balloons to pass out at the circus. He gave the first child entering the big top 6 balloons. If he gives each of the next children one less than the child before, with which child will Skinny be out of balloons?
sixth child
20 - 6 = 14   5 - 3 = 2
14 - 5 = 9   2 - 2 = 0
9 - 4 = 5

4 Write the number word for each numeral:
24.017 *twenty-four and seventeen thousandths*
10.51 *ten and fifty-one hundredths*
30.6 *thirty and six tenths*

5 Miss Tamira was measuring walls in the museum for a new tapestry exhibit. The west wall was 7.13 meters wide, and the north wall was 9.06 meters wide. How much wider was the north wall?
9.06 - 7.13 = 1.93 meters

6 Average Number of Days Precipitation for S. Carolina

30
27
24
21
18
15
Jan Mar May July Sept Nov
Feb Apr June Aug Oct Dec

Write a sentence to summarize the graph data. *answers vary*
Eg. *The average # of days with precipitation was all less than 21 except for July and August.*

7
If 7n = 84 ÷ 12; n = 1
If 5n = 100 - 25; n = 15
If 9n = 27 + 18; n = 5

8 Which shows a way to find the area of this shape?
○ (8 x 2) + (8 x 2)
○ (8 x 6)
○ (8 x 4) - (8 x 2)
● (8 x 6) - (4 x 2)

9 If a 7 is followed by 4 zeros, the 7 is in the *ten thousands* place.

If a 2 is followed by 9 zeros, the 2 is in the *billions* place.

10 Easy Feet Shoe Store is having a sale: 5 pair of shoes for $40.00. Mrs. Sans, Mrs. King, and Mrs. Boyd bought 12 pairs of shoes for their families. What would be a reasonable cost of the 12 pairs of shoes the women bought?
○ $50.00
● $100.00
○ $150.00
○ $200.00

© 1998 Good Apple

© 1998 Good Apple

139

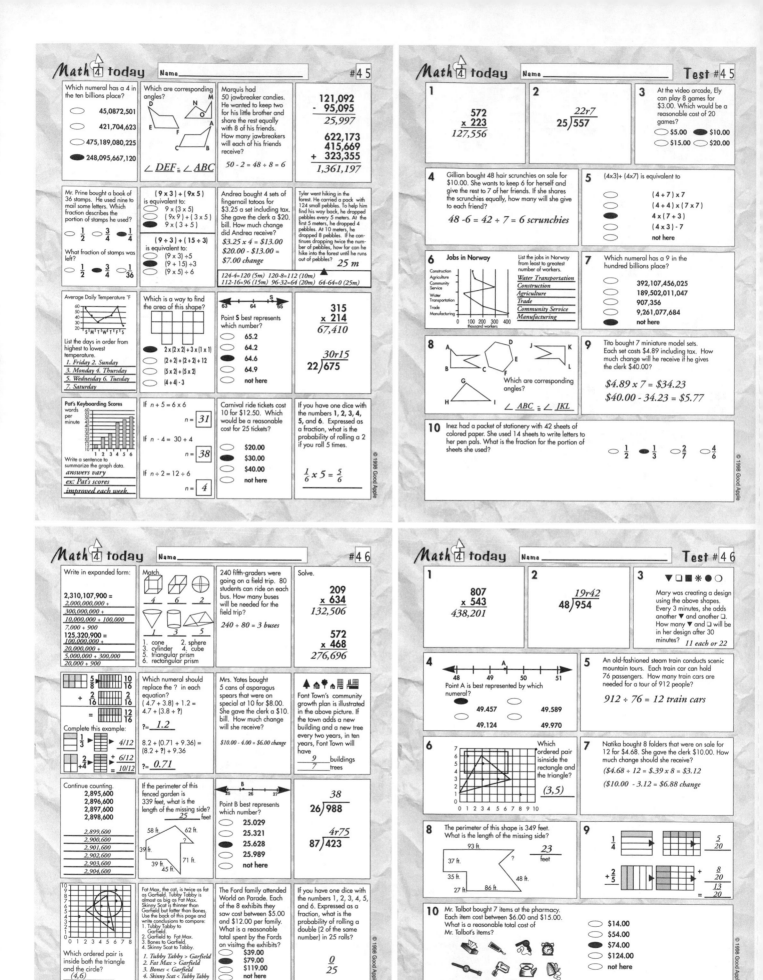

Math 4 today — #45

Which numeral has a 4 in the ten billions place?
- ⭕ 45,0872,501
- ⭕ 421,704,623
- ⭕ 475,189,080,225
- ⬤ 248,095,667,120

Which are corresponding angles?

∠ _DEF_ ≅ ∠ _ABC_

Marquis had 50 jawbreaker candies. He wanted to keep two for his little brother and share the rest equally with 8 of his friends. How many jawbreakers will each of his friends receive?

50 - 2 = 48 ÷ 8 = 6

121,092
- 95,095
25,997

622,173
415,669
+ 323,355
1,361,197

Mr. Prine bought a book of 36 stamps. He used nine to mail some letters. Which fraction describes the portion of stamps he used?
- ⭕ 1/2 ⭕ 3/4 ⬤ 1/4

What fraction of stamps was left?
- ⭕ 1/2 ⬤ 3/4 ⭕ 1/36

(9 x 3) + (9 x 5) is equivalent to:
- ⭕ 9 x (3 x 5)
- ⭕ (9 x 9) + (3 x 5)
- ⬤ 9 x (3 + 5)

(9 ÷ 3) + (15 ÷ 3) is equivalent to:
- ⭕ (9 x 3) ÷ 3
- ⬤ (9 + 15) ÷ 3
- ⭕ (9 x 5) ÷ 6

Andrea bought 4 sets of fingernail tatoos for $3.25 a set including tax. She gave the clerk a $20. bill. How much change did Andrea receive?

$3.25 x 4 = $13.00
$20.00 - $13.00 =
$7.00 change

Tyler went hiking in the forest. He carried a pack with 124 small pebbles. To help him find his way back, he dropped pebbles every 5 meters. At the first 5 meters, he dropped 4 pebbles. At 10 meters, he dropped 8 pebbles. If he continues dropping twice the number of pebbles, how far can he hike into the forest until he runs out of pebbles?   ▲ 25 m

124-4=120 (5m) 120-8=112 (10m)
112-16=96 (15m) 96-32=64 (20m) 64-64=0 (25m)

Average Daily Temperature °F

List the days in order from highest to lowest temperature.
1. Friday 2. Sunday
3. Monday 4. Thursday
5. Wednesday 6. Tuesday
7. Saturday

Which is a way to find the area of this shape?
- ⬤ 2 x (2 x 2) + 3 x (1 x 1)
- ⭕ (2 + 2) + (2 + 2) + 12
- ⭕ (5 x 2) + (5 x 2)
- ⭕ (4 + 4) - 3

Point S best represents which number?
- ⭕ 65.2
- ⭕ 64.2
- ⬤ 64.6
- ⭕ 64.9
- ⭕ not here

315
x 214
67,410

30r15
22)675

Pat's Keyboarding Scores

Write a sentence to summarize the graph data.
answers vary
ex: Pat's scores
improved each week

If n + 5 = 6 x 6
n = 31

If n - 4 = 30 + 4
n = 38

If n ÷ 2 = 12 ÷ 6
n = 4

Carnival ride tickets cost 10 for $12.50. Which would be a reasonable cost for 25 tickets?
- ⭕ $20.00
- ⬤ $30.00
- ⭕ $40.00
- ⭕ not here

If you have one dice with the numbers 1, 2, 3, 4, 5, and 6. Expressed as a fraction, what is the probability of rolling a 2 if you roll 5 times.

1/6 x 5 = 5/6

© 1998 Good Apple

Math 4 today — Test #45

1
572
x 223
127,556

2
22r7
25)557

3 At the video arcade, Ely can play 8 games for $3.00. Which would be a reasonable cost of 20 games?
- ⭕ $5.00 ⬤ $10.00
- ⭕ $15.00 ⭕ $20.00

4 Gillian bought 48 hair scrunchies on sale for $10.00. She wants to keep 6 for herself and give the rest to 7 of her friends. If she shares the scrunchies equally, how many will she give to each friend?

48 - 6 = 42 ÷ 7 = 6 scrunchies

5 (4x3)+ (4x7) is equivalent to
- ⭕ (4 + 7) x 7
- ⭕ (4 + 4) x (7 x 7)
- ⬤ 4 x (7 + 3)
- ⭕ (4 x 3) - 7
- ⭕ not here

6 Jobs in Norway

List the jobs in Norway from least to greatest number of workers.
Water Transportation
Construction
Agriculture
Trade
Community Service
Manufacturing

7 Which numeral has a 9 in the hundred billions place?
- ⭕ 392,107,456,025
- ⭕ 189,502,011,047
- ⭕ 907,356
- ⬤ 9,261,077,684
- ⭕ not here

8 Which are corresponding angles?

∠ _ABC_ ≅ ∠ _JKL_

9 Tito bought 7 miniature model sets. Each set costs $4.89 including tax. How much change will he receive if he gives the clerk $40.00?

$4.89 x 7 = $34.23
$40.00 - 34.23 = $5.77

10 Inez had a packet of stationery with 42 sheets of colored paper. She used 14 sheets to write letters to her pen pals. What is the fraction for the portion of sheets she used?
- ⭕ 1/2 ⬤ 1/3 ⭕ 2/7 ⭕ 4/6

© 1998 Good Apple

Math 4 today — #46

Write in expanded form:

2,310,107,900 =
2,000,000,000 +
300,000,000 +
10,000,000 + 100,000
7,000 + 900

125,320,900 =
100,000,000 +
20,000,000 +
5,000,000 + 300,000
20,000 + 900

Match.

4   6   2

1   3   5

1. cone 2. sphere
3. cylinder 4. cube
5. triangular prism
6. rectangular prism

240 fifth-graders were going on a field trip. 80 students can ride on each bus. How many buses will be needed for the field trip?

240 ÷ 80 = 3 buses

Solve.
209
x 634
132,506

572
x 468
276,696

5/8 + 10/16
2/16 + 2/16
= 12/16

Complete this example:
1/3 ▶ 4/12
+ 2/4 ▶ + 6/12
= 10/12

Which numeral should replace the ? in each equation?
(4.7 + 3.8) + 1.2 =
4.7 + (3.8 + ?)
?= 1.2

8.2 + (0.71 + 9.36) =
(8.2 + ?) + 9.36
= 0.71

Mrs. Yates bought 5 cans of asparagus spears that were on special at 10 for $8.00. She gave the clerk a $10. bill. How much change will she receive?

$10.00 - 4.00 = $6.00 change

Font Town's community growth plan is illustrated in the above picture. If the town adds a new building and a new tree every two years, in ten years, Font Town will have
9 buildings
7 trees

Continue counting.
2,895,600
2,896,600
2,897,600
2,898,600
2,899,600
2,900,600
2,901,600
2,902,600
2,903,600
2,904,600

If the perimeter of this fenced garden is 339 feet, what is the length of the missing side?
25 feet

58 ft. 62 ft.
39 ft. 71 ft.
39 ft. 45 ft.

Point B best represents which number?
- ⭕ 25.029
- ⭕ 25.321
- ⬤ 25.628
- ⭕ 25.989
- ⭕ not here

38
26)988

4r75
87)423

Which ordered pair is inside both the triangle and the circle?
(4,6)

Fat Max, the cat, is twice as fat as Garfield. Tubby Tabby is almost as big as Garfield. Skinny Scat is thinner than Garfield but fatter than Bones. Use the back of this page and write conclusions to compare:
1. Tubby Tabby to Garfield.
2. Garfield to Fat Max.
3. Bones to Garfield.
4. Skinny Scat to Tubby Tabby.

1. Tubby Tabby > Garfield
2. Fat Max > Garfield
3. Bones < Garfield
4. Skinny Scat < Tubby Tabby

The Ford family attended World on Parade. If each of the 8 exhibits they saw cost between $5.00 and $12.00 per family. What is a reasonable total spent by the Fords on visiting the exhibits?
- ⭕ $39.00
- ⬤ $79.00
- ⭕ $119.00
- ⭕ not here

If you have one dice with the numbers 1, 2, 3, 4, 5, and 6. Expressed as a fraction, what is the probability of rolling a double (2 of the same number) in 25 rolls?

0/25

© 1998 Good Apple

Math 4 today — Test #46

1
807
x 543
438,201

2
19r42
48)954

3 ▼ □ ■ ✳ ● ○

Mary was creating a design using the above shapes. Every 3 minutes, she adds another ▼ and another □. How many ▼ and □ will be in her design after 30 minutes?   11 each or 22

4
Point A is best represented by which numeral?
- ⬤ 49.457
- ⭕ 49.124
- ⭕ 49.589
- ⭕ 49.970

5 An old-fashioned steam train conducts scenic mountain tours. Each train car can hold 76 passengers. How many train cars are needed for a tour of 912 people?

912 ÷ 76 = 12 train cars

6 Which ordered pair is inside the rectangle and the triangle?

(3,5)

7 Natika bought 8 folders that were on sale for 12 for $4.68. She gave the clerk $10.00. How much change should she receive?

($4.68 ÷ 12 = $.39 x 8 = $3.12
($10.00 - 3.12 = $6.88 change

8 The perimeter of this shape is 349 feet. What is the length of the missing side?
23 feet
93 ft.
37 ft.
35 ft.
48 ft.
27 ft. 86 ft.

9
1/4 ▶
+ 2/5 ▶
5/20
+ 8/20
= 13/20

10 Mr. Talbot bought 7 items at the pharmacy. Each item cost between $6.00 and $15.00. What is a reasonable total cost of Mr. Talbot's items?
- ⭕ $14.00
- ⭕ $54.00
- ⬤ $74.00
- ⭕ $124.00
- ⭕ not here

© 1998 Good Apple

© 1998 Good Apple

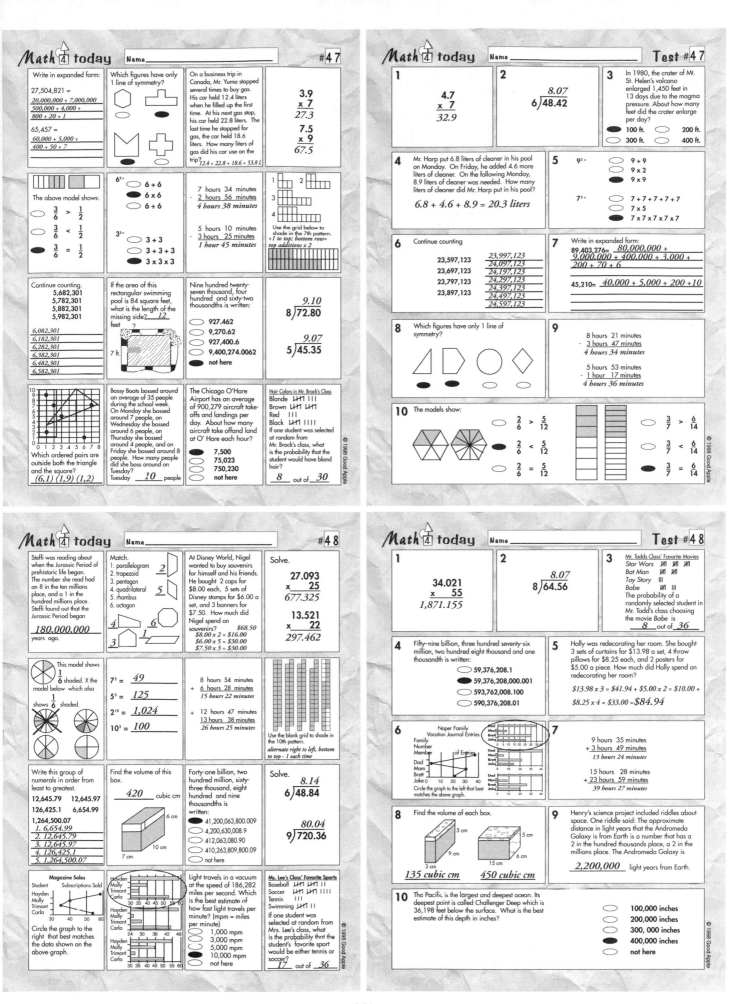

Math 4 today — Name _____ #47

Write in expanded form:
27,504,821 =
20,000,000 + 7,000,000
500,000 + 4,000 +
800 + 20 + 1

65,457 =
60,000 + 5,000 +
400 + 50 + 7

Which figures have only 1 line of symmetry?

On a business trip in Canada, Mr. Yuma stopped several times to buy gas. His car held 12.4 liters when he filled up the first time. At his next gas stop, his car held 22.8 liters. The last time he stopped for gas, the car held 18.6 liters. How many liters of gas did his car use on the trip? 12.4 + 22.8 + 18.6 = 53.8 L

3.9
× 7
27.3

7.5
× 9
67.5

The above model shows:
3/6 > 1/2
3/6 < 1/2
3/6 = 1/2

6² =   6 + 6 / **6 × 6** / 6 ÷ 6
3³ =   3 + 3 / 3 + 3 + 3 / **3 × 3 × 3**

7 hours 34 minutes
− 2 hours 56 minutes
4 hours 38 minutes

5 hours 10 minutes
− 3 hours 25 minutes
1 hour 45 minutes

Use the grid below to shade in the 7th pattern. +1 to top; bottom row= top additions x 2

Continue counting.
5,682,301
5,782,301
5,882,301
5,982,301
6,082,301
6,182,301
6,282,301
6,382,301
6,482,301
6,582,301

If the area of this rectangular swimming pool is 84 square feet, what is the length of the missing side? 12 feet 7 ft.

Nine hundred twenty-seven thousand, four hundred and sixty-two thousandths is written:
927.462
9,270.62
927,400.6
9,400,274.0062
not here

9.10
8)72.80

9.07
5)45.35

Which ordered pairs are outside both the triangle and the square?
(6,1) (1,9) (1,2)

Bossy Boots bossed around an average of 35 people during the school week. On Monday she bossed around 7 people, on Wednesday she bossed around 6 people, on Thursday she bossed around 4 people, and on Friday she bossed around 8 people. How many people did she boss around on Tuesday? 10 people

The Chicago O'Hare Airport has an average of 900,279 aircraft take-offs and landings per day. About how many aircraft take off and land at O'Hare each hour?
7,500
75,023
750,230
not here

Hair Colors in Mr. Brock's Class
Blonde |||| ||||
Brown |||| ||||
Red ||||
Black |||| ||||
If one student was selected at random from Mr. Brock's class, what is the probability that the student would have blond hair? 8 out of 30

Math 4 today — Name _____ Test #47

1.
4.7
× 7
32.9

2.
8.07
6)48.42

3. In 1980, the crater of Mt. St. Helen's volcano enlarged 1,450 feet in 13 days due to the magma pressure. About how many feet did the crater enlarge per day?
● 100 ft.   ○ 200 ft.
○ 300 ft.   ○ 400 ft.

4. Mr. Harp put 6.8 liters of cleaner in his pool on Monday. On Friday, he added 4.6 more liters of cleaner. On the following Monday, 8.9 liters of cleaner was needed. How many liters of cleaner did Mr. Harp put in his pool?
6.8 + 4.6 + 8.9 = 20.3 liters

5. 9² =
○ 9 + 9
○ 9 × 2
● 9 × 9
7⁵ =
○ 7 + 7 + 7 + 7 + 7
○ 7 × 5
● 7 × 7 × 7 × 7 × 7

6. Continue counting
23,597,123 → 23,997,123
23,697,123 → 24,097,123
23,797,123 → 24,197,123
23,897,123 → 24,297,123
24,397,123
24,497,123
24,597,123

7. Write in expanded form:
89,403,276 = 80,000,000 + 9,000,000 + 400,000 + 3,000 + 200 + 70 + 6
45,210 = 40,000 + 5,000 + 200 + 10

8. Which figures have only 1 line of symmetry?

9.
8 hours 21 minutes
− 3 hours 47 minutes
4 hours 34 minutes

5 hours 53 minutes
− 1 hour 17 minutes
4 hours 36 minutes

10. The models show:
○ 2/6 > 5/12   ● 2/6 < 5/12   ○ 2/6 = 5/12
○ 3/7 > 6/14   ○ 3/7 < 6/14   ● 3/7 = 6/14

Math 4 today — Name _____ #48

Steffi was reading about when the Jurassic Period of prehistoric life began. The number she read had an 8 in the ten millions place, and a 1 in the hundred millions place. Steffi found out that the Jurassic Period began 180,000,000 years ago.

Match.
1. parallelogram — 2
2. trapezoid
3. pentagon — 5
4. quadrilateral — 4, 6
5. rhombus — 1
6. octagon — 3

At Disney World, Nigel wanted to buy souvenirs for himself and his friends. He bought 2 caps for $8.00 each, 5 sets of Disney stamps for $6.00 a set, and 3 banners for $7.50. How much did Nigel spend on souvenirs? $68.50
$8.00 × 2 = $16.00
$6.00 × 5 = $30.00
$7.50 × 3 = $30.00

Solve.
27.093
× 25
677.325

13.521
× 22
297.462

This model shows 1/6 shaded. X the model below which also shows 1/6 shaded.

7² = 49
5³ = 125
2¹⁰ = 1,024
10² = 100

8 hours 54 minutes
+ 6 hours 28 minutes
15 hours 22 minutes

+ 12 hours 47 minutes
13 hours 38 minutes
26 hours 25 minutes

Use the blank grid to shade in the 10th pattern. alternate right to left, bottom to top - 1 each time

Write this group of numerals in order from least to greatest.
12,645.79   12,645.97
126,425.1   6,654.99
1,264,500.07
1. 6,654.99
2. 12,645.79
3. 12,645.97
4. 126,425.1
5. 1,264,500.07

Find the volume of this box.
420 cubic cm
6 cm, 10 cm, 7 cm

Forty-one billion, two hundred million, sixty-three thousand, eight hundred and nine thousandths is written:
● 41,200,063,800.009
○ 4,200,630,008.9
○ 412,063,080.90
○ 410,263,809,800.09
○ not here

Solve.
8.14
6)48.84

80.04
9)720.36

Magazine Sales — Subscriptions Sold
Student: Hayden, Molly, Trimont, Carla
Circle the graph to the right that best matches the data shown on the above graph.

Light travels in a vacuum at the speed of 186,282 miles per second. Which is the best estimate of how fast light travels per minute? (mpm = miles per minute)
○ 1,000 mpm
○ 3,000 mpm
○ 5,000 mpm
● 10,000 mpm
○ not here

Ms. Lee's Class' Favorite Sports
Baseball |||| |||| ||
Soccer |||| |||| ||||
Tennis |||
Swimming |||| ||
If one student was selected at random from Mrs. Lee's class, what is the probability that the student's favorite sport would be either tennis or soccer? 17 out of 36

Math 4 today — Name _____ Test #48

1.
34.021
× 55
1,871.155

2.
8.07
8)64.56

3. Mr. Todds Class' Favorite Movies
Star Wars |||| ||||
Bat Man |||| ||||
Toy Story |||
Babe |||| |||
The probability of a randomly selected student in Mr. Todd's class choosing the movie Babe is 8 out of 36

4. Fifty-nine billion, three hundred seventy-six million, two hundred eight thousand and one thousandth is written:
○ 59,376,208.1
● 59,376,208,000.001
○ 593,762,008.100
○ 590,376,208.01

5. Holly was redecorating her room. She bought 3 sets of curtains for $13.98 a set, 4 throw pillows for $8.25 each, and 2 posters for $5.00 a piece. How much did Holly spend on redecorating her room?
$13.98 × 3 = $41.94 + $5.00 × 2 = $10.00 + $8.25 × 4 = $33.00 = $84.94

6. Naper Family Vacation Journal Entries — Family Number of Entries — Dad, Mom, Brett, Jake. Circle the graph to the left that best matches the above graph.

7.
9 hours 35 minutes
+ 3 hours 49 minutes
13 hours 24 minutes

15 hours 28 minutes
+ 23 hours 59 minutes
39 hours 27 minutes

8. Find the volume of each box.
135 cubic cm   450 cubic cm

9. Henry's science project included riddles about space. One riddle said: The approximate distance in light years that the Andromeda Galaxy is from Earth is a number that has a 2 in the hundred thousands place, and a 2 in the millions place. The Andromeda Galaxy is 2,200,000 light years from Earth.

10. The Pacific is the largest and deepest ocean. Its deepest point is called Challenger Deep which is 36,198 feet below the surface. What is the best estimate of this depth in inches?
○ 100,000 inches
○ 200,000 inches
○ 300,000 inches
● 400,000 inches
○ not here

© 1998 Good Apple

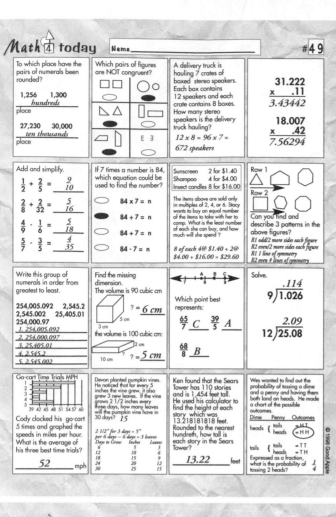

To which place have the pairs of numerals been rounded?
1,256   1,300 — *hundreds* place
27,230   30,000 — *ten thousands* place

Which pairs of figures are NOT congruent?

A delivery truck is hauling 7 crates of boxed stereo speakers. Each box contains 12 speakers and each crate contains 8 boxes. How many stereo speakers is the delivery truck hauling?
12 x 8 = 96 x 7 = 672 speakers

31.222 x .11 = 3.43442
18.007 x .42 = 7.56294

Add and simplify.
$\frac{1}{2} + \frac{2}{5} = \frac{9}{10}$
$\frac{2}{8} + \frac{2}{32} = \frac{5}{16}$
$\frac{4}{9} - \frac{1}{6} = \frac{5}{18}$
$\frac{5}{7} - \frac{3}{5} = \frac{4}{35}$

If 7 times a number is 84, which equation could be used to find the number?
84 x 7 = n
84 ÷ 7 = n
84 + 7 = n
84 - 7 = n

Sunscreen 2 for $1.40
Shampoo 9 for $2.00
Insect candles 8 for $16.00
The items above are sold only in multiples of 2, 4, or 6. Stacy wants to buy an equal number of the items to take with her to camp. What is the least number of each she can buy, and how much will she spend?
8 of each 4@ $1.40 + 2@ $4.00 + $16.00 = $29.60

Row 1 / Row 2 — Can you find and describe 3 patterns in the above figures?
R1 odd/2 more sides each figure
R2 even/2 more sides each figure
R1 1 line of symmetry
R2 even # lines of symmetry

Write this group of numerals in order from greatest to least.
254,005.092   2,545.2   2,545.002   25,405.01   254,000.97
1. 254,005.092
2. 254,000.097
3. 25,405.01
4. 2,545.2
5. 2,545.002

Find the missing dimension. The volume is 90 cubic cm. ? = 6 cm
the volume is 100 cubic cm: ? = 5 cm

Which point best represents: $\frac{65}{7}$ C $\frac{39}{5}$ A $\frac{68}{8}$ B

Solve.
$9\overline{)1.026} = .114$
$12\overline{)25.08} = 2.09$

Go-cart Time Trials MPH — Cody clocked his go-cart 5 times and graphed the speeds in miles per hour. What is the average of his three best time trials? 52 mph

Devon planted pumpkin vines. He noticed that for every 5 inches the vine grew, it also grew 3 new leaves. If the vine grows 2 1/2 inches every three days, how many leaves will the pumpkin vine have in 30 days? 15
2 1/2" for 3 days = 5" per 6 days – 6 days = 3 leaves

Days to Grow	Inches	Leaves
6	5	3
12	10	6
18	15	9
24	20	12
30	25	15

Ken found that the Sears Tower has 110 stories and is 1,454 feet tall. He used his calculator to find the height of each story which was 13.218181818 feet. Rounded to the nearest hundreth, how tall is each story in the Sears Tower? 13.22 feet

Wes wanted to find out the probability of tossing a dime and a penny and having them both land on heads. He made a chart of the possible outcomes.
Dime Penny Outcomes
heads { tails = HT, heads = HH
tails { tails = TT, heads = TH
Expressed as a fraction, what is the probability of tossing 2 heads? $\frac{1}{4}$

© 1998 Good Apple

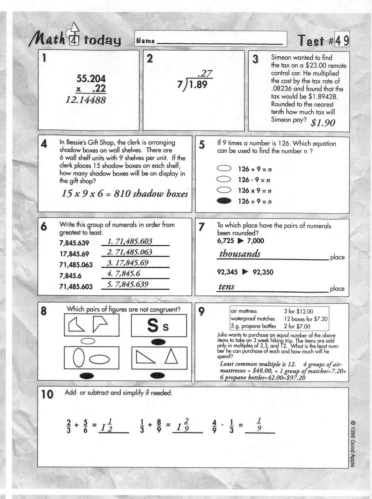

1. 55.204 x .22 = 12.14488

2. $7\overline{)1.89} = .27$

3. Simeon wanted to find the tax on a $23.00 remote control car. He multiplied the cost by the tax rate of .08236 and found that the tax would be $1.89428. Rounded to the nearest tenth how much tax will Simeon pay? $1.90

4. In Bessie's Gift Shop, the clerk is arranging shadow boxes on wall shelves. There are 6 wall shelf units with 9 shelves per unit. If the clerk places 15 shadow boxes on each shelf, how many shadow boxes will be on display in the gift shop? 15 x 9 x 6 = 810 shadow boxes

5. If 9 times a number is 126. Which equation can be used to find the number n?
126 ÷ 9 = n
126 - 9 = n
126 x 9 = n
● 126 ÷ 9 = n

6. Write this group of numerals in order from greatest to least.
7,845.639   17,845.69   71,485.063   7,845.6   71,485.603
1. 71,485.603
2. 71,485.063
3. 17,845.69
4. 7,845.6
5. 7,845.639

7. To which place have the pairs of numerals been rounded?
6,725 ▶ 7,000 — *thousands* place
92,345 ▶ 92,350 — *tens* place

8. Which pairs of figures are not congruent?

9. air mattress 3 for $12.00
waterproof matches 12 boxes for $7.20
5 g. propane bottles 2 for $7.00
Julio wants to purchase an equal number of the above items to take on 3 week hiking trip. The items are sold only in multiples of 2,3, and 12. What is the least number he can purchase of each and how much will he spend?
Least common multiple is 12. 4 groups of air-mattresses = $48.00, + 1 group of matches=7.20+ 6 propane bottles=42.00=$97.20

10. Add or subtract and simplify if needed.
$\frac{2}{3} + \frac{5}{6} = 1\frac{1}{2}$ $\frac{1}{3} + \frac{8}{9} = 1\frac{2}{9}$ $\frac{4}{9} - \frac{1}{3} = \frac{1}{9}$

© 1998 Good Apple

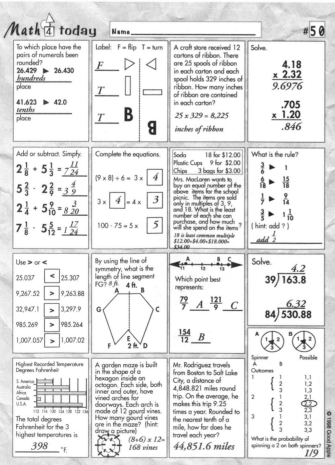

To which place have the pairs of numerals been rounded?
26.429 ▶ 26.430 — *hundreds* place
41.623 ▶ 42.0 — *tenths* place

Label: F = flip T = turn
F, T, T, B

A craft store received 12 cartons of ribbon. There are 25 spools of ribbon in each carton and each spool holds 329 inches of ribbon. How many inches of ribbon are contained in each carton? 25 x 329 = 8,225 inches of ribbon

Solve.
4.18 x 2.32 = 9.6976
.705 x 1.20 = .846

Add or subtract. Simpfy.
$2\frac{1}{8} + 5\frac{1}{8} = 7\frac{11}{24}$
$5\frac{2}{3} - 2\frac{2}{9} = 3\frac{4}{9}$
$2\frac{1}{4} + 5\frac{9}{10} = 8\frac{3}{20}$
$7\frac{1}{8} - 5\frac{5}{12} = 1\frac{17}{24}$

Complete the equations.
(9 x 8) ÷ 6 = 3 x [4]
3 x [4] = 4 x [3]
100 - 75 = 5 x [5]

Soda 18 for $12.00
Plastic Cups 9 for $2.00
Chips 3 bags for $3.00
Mrs. MacLaren wants to buy an equal number of the above items for the school picnic. The items are sold only in multiples of 3, 9, and 18. What is the least number of each she can purchase, and how much will she spend on the items?
18 is least common multiple
$12.00+$4.00+$18.00=$34.00

What is the rule?
$\frac{3}{6}$ ▶ 1
$\frac{6}{18}$ ▶ $\frac{5}{18}$
$\frac{1}{7}$ ▶ $\frac{9}{14}$
$\frac{3}{5}$ ▶ $1\frac{1}{10}$
(hint: add ?)
add $\frac{1}{2}$

Use > or <
25.037 < 25.307
9,267.52 > 9,263.88
32,947.1 > 3,297.9
985.269 > 985.264
1,007.057 > 1,007.02

By using the line of symmetry, what is the length of line segment FG? 8 ft.
4 ft. ... 2 ft.

Which point best represents: $\frac{79}{7}$ A $\frac{121}{9}$ C $\frac{154}{12}$ B

Solve.
$39\overline{)163.8} = 4.2$
$84\overline{)530.88} = 6.32$

Highest Recorded Temperature Degrees Fahrenheit — S. America, Australia, Africa, Canada, U.S.A. — 112 116 120 124 128 132
The total degrees Fahrenheit for the 3 highest temperatures is 398 °F.

A garden maze is built in the shape of a hexagon inside an octagon. Each side, both inner and outer, have vined arches for doorways. Each arch is made of 12 gourd vines. How many gourd vines are in the maze? (hint: draw a picture)
(8+6) x 12= 168 vines

Mr. Rodriguez travels from Boston to Salt Lake City, a distance of 4,848.821 miles round trip. On the average, he makes this trip 9.25 times a year. Rounded to the nearest tenth of a mile, how far does he travel each year? 44,851.6 miles

Spinner A / Spinner B — Possible Outcomes
1,1 1,2 1,3 2,1 2,2 2,3 3,1 3,2 3,3
What is the probability of spinning a 2 on both spinners? $\frac{1}{9}$

© 1998 Good Apple

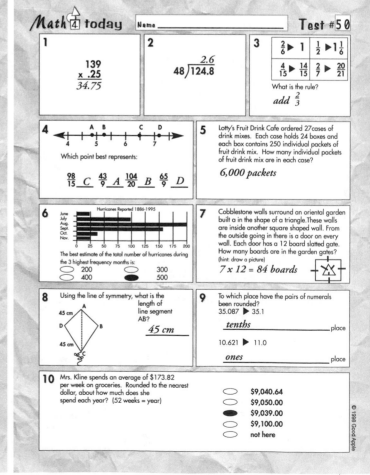

1. 139 x .25 = 34.75

2. $48\overline{)124.8} = 2.6$

3. $\frac{2}{6}$ ▶ 1 $\frac{1}{2}$ ▶ $1\frac{1}{6}$
$\frac{4}{15}$ ▶ $\frac{14}{15}$ $\frac{2}{7}$ ▶ $\frac{20}{21}$
What is the rule? add $\frac{2}{3}$

4. Which point best represents: $\frac{98}{15}$ C $\frac{43}{9}$ A $\frac{104}{20}$ B $\frac{65}{9}$ D

5. Lotty's Fruit Drink Cafe ordered 27 cases of drink mixes. Each case holds 24 boxes and each box contains 250 individual packets of fruit drink mix. How many individual packets of fruit drink mix are in each case? 6,000 packets

6. Hurricanes Reported 1886-1995 (June, July, Aug., Sept., Oct., Nov.) 0 25 50 75 100 125 150 175 200
The best estimate of the total number of hurricanes during the 3 highest frequency months is:
200
● 400
300
500

7. Cobblestone walls surround an oriental garden built in the shape of a triangle. These walls are inside another square shaped wall. From the outside going in there is a door on every wall. Each door has a 12 board slatted gate. How many boards are in the garden gates? (hint: draw a picture) 7 x 12 = 84 boards

8. Using the line of symmetry, what is the length of line segment AB? 45 cm, 45 cm, 45 cm

9. To which place have the pairs of numerals been rounded?
35.087 ▶ 35.1 — *tenths* place
10.621 ▶ 11.0 — *ones* place

10. Mrs. Kline spends an average of $173.82 per week on groceries. Rounded to the nearest dollar, about how much does she spend each year? (52 weeks = year)
$9,040.64
$9,050.00
● $9,039.00
$9,100.00
not here

© 1998 Good Apple

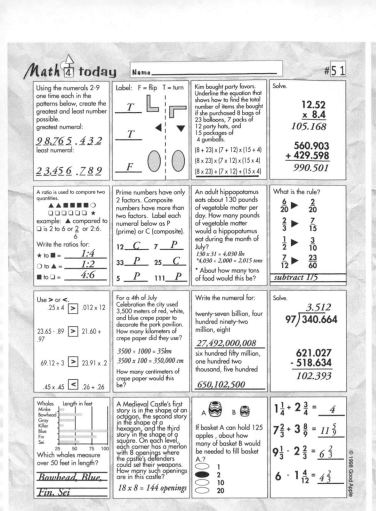

Using the numerals 2-9 one time each in the patterns below, create the greatest and least number possible.
greatest numeral: 98,765.432
least numeral: 23,456.789

Label: F = flip T = turn
T, T, F

Kim bought party favors. Underline the equation that shows how to find the total number of items she bought if she purchased 8 bags of 23 balloons, 7 packs of 12 party hats, and 15 packages of 4 gumballs.
(8 + 23) + (7 + 12) x (15 + 4)
(8 x 23) x (7 x 12) x (15 x 4)
(8 x 23) + (7 x 12) + (15 x 4)

Solve.
12.52 x 8.4 = 105.168
560.903 + 429.598 = 990.501

A ratio is used to compare two quantities.
▲▲■■■■□○
example: ▲ compared to □ is 2 to 6 or 2/6 or 2:6.
Write the ratios for:
★ to ■ = 1:4
○ to ▲ = 1:2
■ to □ = 4:6

Prime numbers have only 2 factors. Composite numbers have more than two factors. Label each numeral below as P (prime) or C (composite).
12 C   7 P
33 P   25 C
5 P   111 P

An adult hippopotamus eats about 130 pounds of vegetable matter per day. How many pounds of vegetable matter would a hippopotamus eat during the month of July?
130 x 31 = 4,030 lbs
*4,030 ÷ 2,000 = 2,015 tons
*So about how many tons of food would this be?

What is the rule?
6/20 ▶ 2/20
2/3 ▶ 7/15
1/2 ▶ 3/10
7/12 ▶ 23/60
subtract 1/5

Use > or <.
.25 x 4 > .012 x 12
23.65 - .89 > 21.60 + .97
69.12 ÷ 3 > 23.91 x .2
.45 x .45 < .26 + .26

For a 4th of July Celebration the city used 3,500 meters of red, white, and blue crepe paper to decorate the park pavilion. How many kilometers of crepe paper did they use?
3500 ÷ 1000 = 35km
3500 x 100 = 350,000 cm
How many centimeters of crepe paper would this be?

Write the numeral for:
twenty-seven billion, four hundred ninety-two million, eight
27,492,000,008
six hundred fifty million, one hundred two thousand, five hundred
650,102,500

Solve.
3.512 / 97)340.664
621.027 - 518.634 = 102.393

Whales / Length in feet
Minke, Bowhead, Gray, Killer, Blue, Fin, Sei
25 50 75 100
Which whales measure over 50 feet in length?
Bowhead, Blue, Fin, Sei

A Medieval Castle's first story is in the shape of an octagon, the second story in the shape of a hexagon, and the third story in the shape of a square. On each level, each corner has a merlon with 8 openings where the castle's defenders could set their weapons. How many such openings are in this castle?
18 x 8 = 144 openings

If basket A can hold 125 apples, about how many of basket B would be needed to fill basket A?
1, 2, 10, 20

1 1/4 + 2 3/4 = 4
7 2/5 + 3 8/9 = 11 5/9
9 1/3 - 2 2/3 = 6 2/3
6 - 1 4/12 = 4 2/3

© 1998 Good Apple

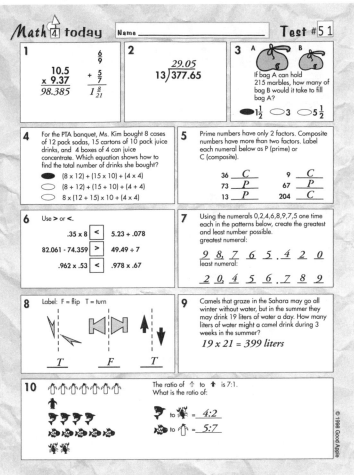

1. 10.5 x 9.37 = 98.385 ; 6/9 + 5/7 = 1 8/21

2. 13)377.65 = 29.05

3. If bag A can hold 215 marbles, how many of bag B would it take to fill bag A? 1 1/2, 3, 5 1/2

4. For the PTA banquet, Ms. Kim bought 8 cases of 12 pack sodas, 15 cartons of 10 pack juice drinks, and 4 boxes of 4 can juice concentrate. Which equation shows how to find the total number of drinks she bought?
(8 x 12) + (15 x 10) + (4 x 4)
(8 + 12) + (15 + 10) + (4 + 4)
8 x (12 + 15) x 10 + (4 x 4)

5. Prime numbers have only 2 factors. Composite numbers have more than two factors. Label each numeral below as P (prime) or C (composite).
36 C   9 C
73 P   67 C
13 P   204 C

6. Use > or <.
.35 x 8 < 5.23 + .078
82.061 - 74.359 > 49.49 ÷ 7
.962 x .53 < .978 x .67

7. Using the numerals 0,2,4,6,8,9,7,5 one time each in the patterns below, create the greatest and least number possible.
greatest numeral: 98,765.420
least numeral: 20,456.789

8. Label: F = flip T = turn
T, F, T

9. Camels that graze in the Sahara may go all winter without water, but in the summer they may drink 19 liters of water a day. How many liters of water might a camel drink during 3 weeks in the summer?
19 x 21 = 399 liters

10. The ratio of ⇑ to ↑ is 7:1. What is the ratio of:
[penguin] to [crab] = 4:2
[fish] to ↑ = 5:7

© 1998 Good Apple

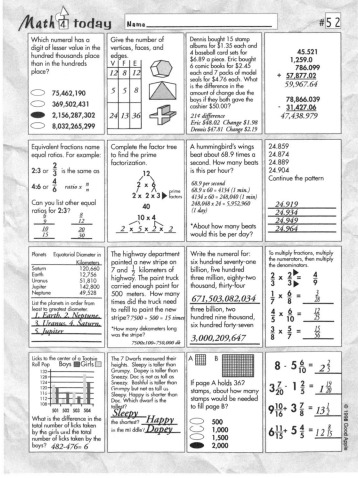

Which numeral has a digit of lesser value in the hundred thousands place than in the hundreds place?
75,462,190
369,502,431
2,156,287,302
8,032,265,299

Give the number of vertices, faces, and edges.

V	F	E
12	8	18
5	5	8
24	13	36

Dennis bought 15 stamp albums for $1.35 each and 4 baseball card sets for $6.89 a piece. Eric bought 6 comic books for $2.45 each and 7 packs of model seals for $4.76 each. What is the difference in the amount of change due the boys if they both gave the cashier $50.00?
21¢ difference
Eric $48.02 Change $1.98
Dennis $47.81 Change $2.19

45.521 + 1,259.0 + 786.099 + 57,877.02 = 59,967.64
78,866.039 - 31,427.06 = 47,438.979

Equivalent fractions name equal ratios. For example:
2:3 or 2/3 is the same as
4:6 or 4/6 ratio x n/n
Can you list other equal ratios for 2:3?
6/9, 8/12, 10/15, 20/30

Complete the factor tree to find the prime factorization.
12 = 2 x 6 = 2 x 2 x 3 prime factors
40 = 10 x 4 = 2 x 5 x 2 x 2

A hummingbird's wings beat about 68.9 times a second. How many beats is this per hour?
68.9 per second
68.9 x 60 = 4134 (1 min.)
4134 x 60 = 248,040 (1 min)
248,048 x 24 = 5,952,960 (1 day)
*About how many beats would this be per day?

24.859, 24.874, 24.889, 24.904
Continue the pattern
24.919, 24.934, 24.949, 24.964

Planets	Equatorial Diameter in Kilometers
Saturn	120,660
Earth	12,756
Uranus	51,810
Jupiter	142,800
Neptune	49,528

List the planets in order from least to greatest diameter:
1. Earth, 2. Neptune, 3. Uranus, 4. Saturn, 5. Jupiter

The highway department painted a new stripe on 7 and 1/2 kilometers of highway. The paint truck carried enough paint for 500 meters. How many times did the truck need to refill to paint the new stripe?
7500 ÷ 500 = 15 times
*How many dekameters long was the stripe?
7500÷100=750,000 dk

Write the numeral for:
six hundred seventy-one billion, five hundred three million, eighty-two thousand, thirty-four
671,503,082,034
three billion, two hundred nine thousand, six hundred forty-seven
3,000,209,647

To multiply fractions, multiply the numerators, then multiply the denominators.
2/3 x 2/3 = 4/9
1/7 x 6/8 = 3/28
4/5 x 6/10 = 12/25
3/4 x 5/9 = 15/36

Licks to the center of a Tootsie Roll Pop
Boys ■ Girls □
501 502 503 504
What is the difference in the total number of licks taken by the girls and the total number of licks taken by the boys?
482-476= 6

The 7 Dwarfs measured their heights. Sleepy is taller than Grumpy. Dopey is taller than Sneezy. Doc is not as tall as Sneezy. Bashful is taller than Grumpy but not as tall as Sleepy. Happy is shorter than Doc. Which dwarf is the tallest?
Sleepy
Who's the shortest? Happy
in the middle? Dopey

If page A holds 362 stamps, about how many stamps would be needed to fill page B?
500, 1,000, 1,500, 2,000

8 - 5 6/10 = 2 2/5
3 7/20 - 1 2/5 = 1 19/20
9 10/16 + 3 7/8 = 13 1/2
6 11/15 + 5 4/5 = 12 8/15

© 1998 Good Apple

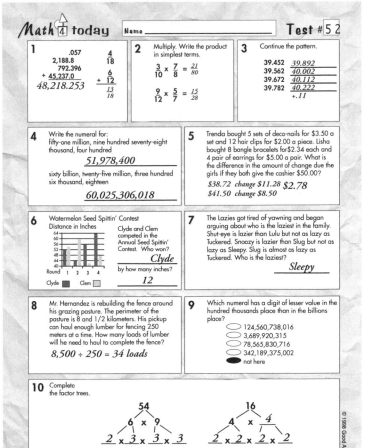

1. .057 + 2,188.8 + 792.396 + 45,237.0 = 48,218.253 ; 4/18 + 6/12 + 13/18

2. Multiply. Write the product in simplest terms.
3/10 x 7/8 = 21/80
9/12 x 5/7 = 15/28

3. Continue the pattern.
39.452, 39.562, 39.672, 39.782 → 39.892, 40.002, 40.112, 40.222, +.11

4. Write the numeral for:
fifty-one million, nine hundred seventy-eight thousand, four hundred
51,978,400
sixty billion, twenty-five million, three hundred six thousand, eighteen
60,025,306,018

5. Trenda bought 5 sets of deco-nails for $3.50 a set and 12 hair clips for $2.00 a piece. Lisha bought 8 bangle bracelets for $2.34 each and 4 pair of earrings for $5.00 a pair. What is the difference in the amount of change due the girls if they both give the cashier $50.00?
$38.72 change $11.28 $2.78
$41.50 change $8.50

6. Watermelon Seed Spittin' Contest
Distance in Inches
Clyde and Clem competed in the Annual Seed Spittin' Contest. Who won? Clyde
by how many inches? 12
Round 1 2 3 4; Clyde, Clem

7. The Lazies got tired of yawning and began arguing about who is the laziest in the family. Shut-eye is lazier than Lulu but not as lazy as Tuckered. Snoozy is lazier than Slug but not as lazy as Sleepy. Slug is almost as lazy as Tuckered. Who is the laziest?
Sleepy

8. Mr. Hernandez is rebuilding the fence around his grazing pasture. The perimeter of the pasture is 8 and 1/2 kilometers. His pickup can haul enough lumber for fencing 250 meters at a time. How many loads of lumber will he need to haul to complete the fence?
8,500 ÷ 250 = 34 loads

9. Which numeral has a digit of lesser value in the hundred thousands place than in the billions place?
124,560,738,016
3,689,920,315
78,565,830,716
342,189,375,002
not here

10. Complete the factor trees.
54 = 6 x 9 = 2 x 3 x 3 x 3
16 = 4 x 4 = 2 x 2 x 2 x 2

© 1998 Good Apple

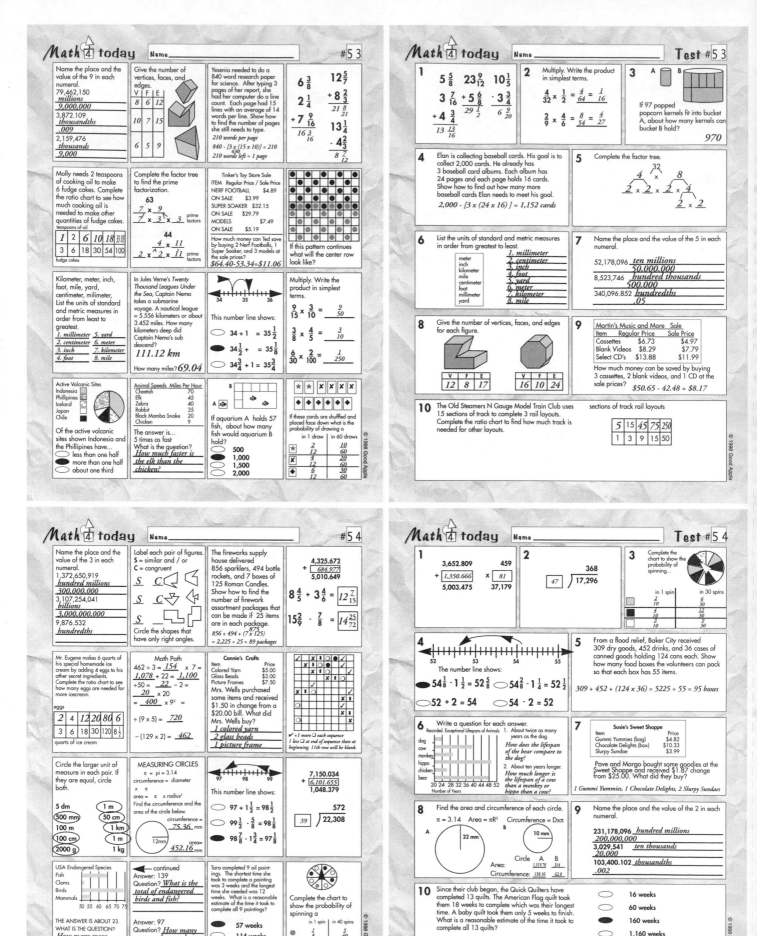